Imperial Messages

Studies in German Literature, Linguistics, and Culture

Imperial Messages

Orientalism as Self-Critique in the Habsburg *Fin de Siècle*

Robert Lemon

CAMDEN HOUSE
Rochester, New York

First published 2011
by Camden House

Camden House is an imprint of Boydell & Brewer Inc.
668 Mt. Hope Avenue, Rochester, NY 14620, USA
www.camden-house.com
and of Boydell & Brewer Limited
PO Box 9, Woodbridge, Suffolk IP12 3DF, UK
www.boydellandbrewer.com

ISBN-13: 978-1-57113-500-1
ISBN-10: 1-57113-500-6

Library of Congress Cataloging-in-Publication Data

Lemon, Robert, 1971–
 Imperial messages: Orientalism as self-critique in the Habsburg fin de siècle /
Robert Lemon.
  p. cm. — (Studies in German literature, linguistics, and culture)
 Includes bibliographical references and index.
 ISBN-13: 978-1-57113-500-1 (alk. paper)
 ISBN-10: 1-57113-500-6 (alk. paper)
 1. Orientalism in literature. 2. Orientalism. 3. East and West in literature.
4. Austrian fiction—19th century—History and criticism. 5. Austrian fiction—
20th century—History and criticism. 6. Hofmannsthal, Hugo von, 1874-1929—
Criticism and interpretation. 7. Musil, Robert, 1880–1942—Criticism and inter-
pretation. 8. Kafka, Franz, 1883–1924—Criticism and interpretation. I. Title.
II. Series.
 PT3822.L46 2011
 833'.7093585—dc22

                                                              2010053203

For Ellen, Ben, and Eliot

Contents

Acknowledgments

IT GIVES ME GREAT PLEASURE to express my gratitude to those individuals and institutions that have helped bring this project, which has been a long time coming, to fruition. I was able to lay the foundation for this study thanks to a Writing Fellowship from the Minda de Gunzburg Center for European Studies, while a Dissertation Completion Fellowship from the Graduate Society at Harvard University enabled me to finish the main structure. Special thanks go to my dissertation advisor, Judith Ryan, whose wit, wisdom, and wiles smoothed the transition from seminar paper to dissertation, and to Joel Westerdale, whose friendship, sagacity, and shortbread made graduate studies not only feasible, but also enjoyable. On joining the University of Oklahoma, I received invaluable support during the revision process in the form of several Junior Faculty Research grants. I am also indebted to my colleagues in the OU Department of Modern Languages, Literatures, and Linguistics, for their steadfast support for this project during what has been a medically eventful time for my family. For his quiet encouragement during this time, I would like to thank Jim Walker at Camden House. I would also like to take this opportunity to express my gratitude to Rolf Goebel and Jim Hardin, whose thoughtful, helpful, and prompt evaluations of this manuscript made the process of revision much easier. For their constant encouragement and love during what was for all of us a sometimes baffling and arduous process, I thank my mother, father, sister, and brother. Finally, I would like to express my unending gratitude to my wife, Ellen, and sons, Ben and Eliot, who are my East, my West, and my whole world, and to whom I dedicate this book.

Sections of the introduction, chapter 2, and the conclusion have already been published in "Imperial Mystique and Empiricist Mysticism: Inner Colonialism and Exoticism in Musil's *Törleß*," *Modern Austrian Literature* 42.1 (2009): 1–22. The section of chapter 3 on "In the Penal Colony" has already appeared in "Cargo Colonies and Penal Cults: Ethnology and Ethnocentrism in Kafka's "In der Strafkolonie," *Colloquia Germanica: Internationale Zeitschrift für Germanistik* 40.3–4 (2007, pub. September 2009): 279–95.

Abbreviations

CS   Franz Kafka, *Franz Kafka: The Complete Stories,* ed. Nahum N. Glatzer (New York: Schocken, 1995).

DL   Franz Kafka, "Schakale und Araber," in *Drucke zu Lebzeiten*, ed. Wolf Kittler, Hans-Gerd Koch, and Gerhard Neumann (Frankfurt am Main: S. Fischer, 1994), 270–75.

MN   Hugo von Hofmannsthal, "Das Märchen der 672. Nacht," in *Sämtliche Werke,* vol. 28, *Erzählungen I,* ed. Ellen Ritter (Frankfurt am Main: S. Fischer Verlag, 1975), 15–30.

NS   Franz Kafka, *Nachgelassene Schriften und Fragmente I,* ed. Malcolm Pasley (Frankfurt am Main: S. Fischer Verlag, 1993).

PR   Hermann Broch, *Pasenow oder die Romantik,* in *Die Schlafwandler: Eine Romantrilogie,* ed. Paul Michael Lützeler (Frankfurt am Main: Suhrkamp Verlag, 1979), 9–181.

Sl   *The Sleepwalkers,* trans. Willa and Edwin Muir (New York: Pantheon, 1964).

T   *Die Verwirrungen des Zöglings Törleß,* in *Prosa und Stücke,* vol. 6 of *Gesammelte Werke in neun Bänden,* ed. Adolf Frisé (Hamburg: Rowohlt Taschenbuch Verlag, 1978), 7–140.

Ta   Franz Kafka, *Tagebücher,* ed. Hans-Gerd Koch, Michael Müller, and Malcolm Pasley (Frankfurt am Main: S. Fischer Verlag, 1990).

TB   Wolf Kittler, *Der Turmbau zu Babel und das Schweigen der Sirenen* (Erlangen: Verlag Palm & Enke, 1985).

TN   Hugo von Hofmannsthal, "The Tale of Night Six Hundred and Seventy-Two," trans. Michael Henry Heim, in *The Whole Difference: Selected Writings of Hugo von Hofmannsthal,* ed. J. D. McClatchy (Princeton, NJ: Princeton UP, 2008), 39–56.

YT   Robert Musil, *Young Törless,* trans. Eithner Wilkins and Ernst Kaiser (New York: Noonday, 1958).

Translations in this book are my own except where otherwise credited.

Introduction

"ORIENTALISM AS SELF-CRITIQUE": the juxtaposition of these terms warrants immediate explanation. In his groundbreaking study *Orientalism* (1978) Edward Said at once defines and denounces orientalism as a hegemonic discourse, "a Western style for dominating, restructuring, and having authority over the Orient."[1] As the ideological cohort to occidental imperialism, orientalism as described by Said appears to be exclusively concerned with European self-aggrandizement rather than self-critique, invariably casting the Orient as the feeble Other dominated by the mighty West (40). However, in recent years, some postcolonial critics have argued against such a monolithic interpretation. Indeed, for Ziauddin Sardar, Said's elision of diversity and heterogeneity within the discourse "amounts to Occidentalism, stereotyping in reverse", since it "ignores all manifestations of counter-hegemonic thought" and creates the illusion of a unified and constant European/Western identity.[2] Other critics, such as Lisa Lowe, have also argued for a conception of orientalism as "heterogeneous and contradictory,"[3] a pluralist discourse that can even encompass critical representations of the West.[4] My purpose here is to advance this line of enquiry by addressing the orientalist fiction produced by a European empire that receives no mention in *Orientalism*: Austria-Hungary. Through close analysis of works by Hugo von Hofmannsthal, Robert Musil, and Franz Kafka, I seek to demonstrate that far from promulgating Western imperialism, these texts subvert received notions of national and cultural identity and thus problematize the very practice of orientalism. Moreover, my readings of these fictions show how all three authors adopt politically or culturally self-critical stances, invoking the oriental "Other" not to bolster Occidental imperialism but rather to express concerns about their own troubled empire. This is not to say, however, that Said's definition of the discourse has no relevance for my study. On the contrary, his analysis of British, French, and American orientalisms represents the standard against which the subversive, anti-imperialist exoticism of the Habsburg authors can be properly judged. Furthermore, in order to identify the transgressive tendencies in these Austrian texts, I adapt strategies developed by postcolonial theorists such as Benedict Anderson, Mary Louise Pratt, and Homi Bhabha, who were in turn inspired by Said's seminal study of orientalism.

To begin, let us address those factors peculiar to Austria-Hungary that gave rise to what I will argue is a type of orientalist fiction marked by self-reflection and self-critique. Firstly, as the name Österreich or "eastern empire" suggests,[5] Austria traditionally had a foot in both the East and the West, occupying a liminal position vis-à-vis the Orient and serving as a gateway to the Ottoman Empire. (As a *porta Orientis*, Vienna also experienced the trauma of reverse traffic in the form of the Turkish sieges of 1529 and 1683, as well as numerous wars.) The eastward sprawl of the Dual Monarchy resulted in a multi-ethnic empire, which in 1910 encompassed, in descending order of population, German Austrians, Hungarians, Czechs, Poles, Ruthenians, Romanians, Croats, Slovaks, Serbs, Slovenes, and Italians.[6] Not surprisingly, this patchwork of peoples produced internal divisions between "East" and "West" that transcended the customary orientalist notion of a global dichotomy between two clearly demarcated hemispheres.[7] At the turn of the century many Viennese German-speakers held that the Orient began not at the border with the Ottoman Empire, but rather at the doors of their Slavic, Jewish, and (following the annexation of Bosnia-Herzogovina in 1908) Muslim compatriots. To unite these increasingly restive minorities, Austria-Hungary offered the Habsburg myth, the notion of a supra-national allegiance to the imperial throne. This unique conception of imperialism marks the most important distinction between the Dual Monarchy and the other European powers. For Britain, France, and, belatedly, Germany, imperialism represented the overseas expansion of nationalist ideology. In contrast, as a contiguous territory devoid of overseas colonies, the Habsburg authorities conceived of imperialism as a matter of domestic, rather than foreign policy, a foundational myth that did not harness, but rather repressed the nationalist energies of its diverse population. In light of Austria-Hungary's easterly orientation and imperial ideology, we can begin to read ostensibly exotic texts such as Hugo von Hofmannsthal's poetic monologue "Der Kaiser von China Spricht" (The Emperor of China Speaks) (1897) and Franz Kafka's Chinese stories "Beim Bau der chinesischen Mauer" ("The Great Wall of China") and "Ein altes Blatt" ("An Old Manuscript," both 1917) as invocations of the authors' own "eastern empire." Thus the location, ethnic composition, and imperial self-mythologizing of the Dual Monarchy all influenced orientalist works that tend towards self-critique and thereby subvert the fundamental dichotomy between East and West found in conventional orientalism.

However, before situating this study in the broader discussion of orientalism in German and Austrian literature, we should consider its relation to current scholarship that addresses the issue of postcoloniality in Gemanophone Central Europe. In claiming that Austrian orientalist fiction harbors anti-hegemonic tendencies, this book seeks to intervene in the ongoing debate among critics and historians on both sides of the Atlantic regarding the application of postcolonial theory to the Austro-Hungarian Empire and its culture.[8] This discussion has generated controversy, and with good reason. Indeed, most critics agree that Austria-Hungary cannot qualify as a colonial power in the strict sense of the term.[9] Several factors distinguish the situation of the Dual Monarchy from the empires of Britain and France. First, as we have already noted, the Habsburg Empire lacked overseas colonies, and indeed, some of its territorial possessions, such as Bohemia, Moravia, and Silesia, had not been conquered or seized by force but instead shared a political union with Austria that stretched back to the Medieval Holy Roman Empire.[10] Further, the Habsburg Monarchy formally granted equal rights to all its multi-ethnic citizenry, in stark contrast to the systematic racist oppression inflicted on indigenous populations under overseas colonialism.[11] Finally, it is difficult to reconcile the notion of colonialist economic exploitation with the fact that just before the First World War the regions of Bohemia and Moravia enjoyed a higher per capita income than all but one of the provinces of Austria proper.[12] No, the argument for the use of postcolonial theory cannot rely on retrospective analogies between the disparate historical and geographical situations of the Dual Monarchy and those European empires with remote colonial possessions. Rather, it draws strength from observing contemporary depictions of the relations between the Germanophone population and its various "subject peoples," which frequently imply assumptions of ethnic and cultural superiority in the manner of a colonial power.[13] Consequently, most critics agree that it is in the realm of cultural expression, in the construction of images of the self and the Other, and in the subsequent establishment of a hierarchical relationship, that postcolonial theories have the most relevance.[14] For this reason I have restricted my consideration of Habsburg orientalism to fiction, since this realm not only offers the semantically richest expressions of cultural identity and alterity but also provides insights into the psychological processes by which protagonists develop their views of the self and Other.

Granted, the idiosyncratic situation of the Austro-Hungarian Empire sometimes does make for an awkward fit with postcolonial theories that draw largely from British and French imperial models. However, the proliferation of colonialist and orientalist scenarios in late Habsburg fiction compels the critic to explain why writers in an empire devoid of colonies should show such a marked interest in such themes. By arguing that the Austrian authors Hugo von Hofmannsthal, Robert Musil, and Franz Kafka deploy oriental motifs and topoi to engage in self-critique rather than advance imperialist hegemony, this study will show how Austrian fiction challenges the conventional post-Saidian view of the orientalist discourse. Thus we will examine not only how postcolonial studies inform readings of Habsburg fiction, but also how Austrian texts question received notions found in postcolonial theory. In this way, the tensions between the generalizing tendencies of the theoretical approach and the particularities of the region emerge not as obstacles to dialogue but as opportunities for reciprocal reevaluation.

The fact that critics on both sides of the Atlantic have started calling for a postcolonial approach to Habsburg texts only in the last decade or so can be attributed to the pervasive influence of German studies on discussions of Austrian literature and culture. Here we must first consider that the belatedness and brevity of the German colonial experience, which consisted of a mere thirty-five years between 1884 and 1919, have led critics to question its cultural significance, particularly compared to the lengthy colonial histories of Britain, France, and other European nations. In their introduction to *The Imperialist Imagination: German Colonialism and Its Legacy* (1998), Sara Friedrichsmeyer, Sara Lennox, and Susanne Zantop explain that it was US scholars who from the mid-eighties played a vanguard role in opening up the fields of colonialism and postcoloniality in German studies.[15] The authors cite several historical factors that "occluded Germans' view of European colonialism and their complicity as Europeans in it": the absence of postcolonial literature, that is "writing by formerly colonized people in the language of their colonizers"; the lack, until very recently, of "a diasporic presence of formerly colonized peoples in Germany"; and the "German focus on the Holocaust and the central and unavoidable fact of German history" (3–4). Clearly, all the historical factors that have obscured German understanding of their imperialist past are also applicable to the Austrian experience and account for the further delay in the introduction of postcolonial theory into Habsburg and Austrian studies. However, Austria-Hungary offers a radical departure from the German model in its utter lack of overseas colonies and in its supranational imperialist ideal. Thus while Friedrichsmeyer, Lennox, and Zantop contend that in pre-1871 Germany "the coincidence of these two desires — for nation and for empire — had [. . .] ramifications for Germans in their attempts to understand themselves as a political entity" (19), I argue that the inherent conflict between nationalist and imperialist impulses in Austria-Hungary, between the restive "subject peoples'" desire for self-determination on the one hand and the Habsburg myth of supranational and dynastic loyalty on the other, gave rise to that empire's self-conception, which was unique among Western European powers.

The introduction by US critics of postcolonial theory into German studies has had a discernible impact on current research in Germany. Axel Dunker's 2008 study of colonialism in nineteenth-century German-language literature is a case in point.[16] Drawing on Edward Said's notion of a contrapuntal reading that takes into account the perspectives of both the colonizer and the colonized, Dunker raises issues regarding German nineteenth-century literature that are of direct relevance to this study. For example, he argues that colonialism was a global phenomenon that influenced German-speaking areas beyond Imperial Germany, such as Austria-Hungary and Switzerland, depite their lack of overseas territories (8–9). He also raises the possibility that canonical works of German fiction may subvert, rather than support, the inequality between European and non-European ethnic groups that is a feature of much colonial literature (12). However, when he cites the works of Franz Kafka, "a Jewish writer from Prague," as an example of the global reach of colonial fantasies, he runs into taxonomical difficulties (8). According to Dunker, the example of Kafka shows that *from a German perspective* the concept of colonial fantasies must not be limited to the establishment of a German colonial empire or the standing of the colonial in Germany's imagined position in the world (8, my italics). While Dunker's central point about the imaginative and geographic scope of colonial fantasies is well taken, his assumption of a *German* perspective with regard to Kafka, a German-speaking Jewish writer born in the largely Czech city of Prague in the Austro-Hungarian Empire, does not do justice to the complexities of that author's ethnic and cultural situation. In this way, Dunker maintains the longstanding quasi-colonial territorial claim of German *Germanistik* over Austrian and Austro-Hungarian literature and culture.

This tendency to subsume Austria under the rubric of its northern neighbor has long been standard practice in discussions of Germanophone orientalist literature. In the pre-Saidian era, scholars often aimed for a transhistorical overview of the topic that tended to ignore national divisions within the field of German-language literature. Thus Otto Spies's 1949 account of the Orient in German literature refers to the Austrian Hugo von Hofmannsthal's early poems as among the most beautiful German ghazals without mentioning his nationality,[17] and Franz Babinger's 1957 contribution on the same topic enfolds references to the Austrian *Türkendrama* into a general account of "the Orient and German literature."[18] This unexamined incorporation of Austrian orientalism continues in the work of Ingrid Schuster, whose investigations into the cultural interrelations between German literature and China and Japan span three decades, from the pre-Saidian era of her initial 1977 study of the topic to her most recent publication in 2007.[19] It is particularly telling that although both these works discuss Hofmannsthal's orientalist texts,[20] neither ascribes any significance to his Austrian nationality. Indeed, in her discussion of the Austrian Hofmannsthal and the German writer and philosopher Rudolf Pannwitz, Schuster refers to the events after "the cultural crisis" of the First World War in Germany, that is, the Weimar Republic and the catastrophe of Nazism, as if they both represented a shared national experience for the two authors.[21]

Schuster's interest in the cultural interrelationships between Europe and China and Japan brings us to another reason why the critical discourse often omits specific discussion of Austrian orientalism: the Janus-faced nature of orientalist literature, which simultaneously looks East and West, and, by extension, of the scholarship surrounding it. For many critics focus not on Western depictions of the East but rather on the oriental influences on occidental literature. Often such studies posit a spiritual affinity between orientalist authors and Eastern philosophy or religion. For example, Joo-Dong Lee argues for a "Taoist world-view" in Kafka's works,[22] while in a more recent article Dennis McCort discerns a shared "mystical insight" between Kafka and the Zen tradition.[23] By conceiving the author's relation to the East in purely spiritual terms, such arguments tend to reinforce the stereotypical notion of the mystical East in opposition to the rational West.[24]

Although the tendencies described above predate Said's 1977 *Orientalism* and persist after it, Said's work nevertheless exerts a pervasive influence over many critics' conception of German orientalism. In *Orientalism* Said offers a relatively benign view of German orientalism as an academic and literary discourse operating outside the bounds of nationalist imperialism. According to Said, Germany, which had no possessions in the first two-thirds of the nineteenth century corresponding to the British and French territories in the East, had no opportunity to develop "a close partnership . . . between Orientalists and a *sustained* national interest in the Orient" (19, Said's italics). He then contrasts the German Orient, which he characterizes as "almost exclusively a scholarly, or at least a Classical, Orient" with the "actual" Orient experienced by nineteenth-century British and French writers through their colonial presence in the region (19). Said finds it significant that "the two most renowned German works on the Orient, Goethe's *Westöstlicher Diwan* [*sic*] and Friedrich Schlegel's Über die Sprache und Weisheit der Inder, were based respectively on a Rhine journey and on hours spent in Paris libraries" and sums up the German contribution to orientalist scholarship as the refinement and elaboration of techniques applied to "texts, myths, ideas and languages almost literally gathered from the Orient by imperial Britain and France" (19). The sedate German theory undertaken on Rhine journeys and in Parisian libraries is of course preferable to the sanguinary British and French practice of actual imperial conquest. Nevertheless, Said does align German orientalism with its British, French, and American equivalents in its assumption of an intellectual authority over the Orient (19), an authority that arises from its textual appropriation of the region. For Said, German orientalism thus emerges as a kind of scholarly subaltern to the British and French discourses.

Said's fairly uncritical portrayal of German orientalism leads subsequent critics to challenge not only the applicability of his definition of orientalism to German literature but also the viability of his definition in general. For example, Andrea Fuchs-Sumiyoshi borrows freely without citation from Said's account of German orientalism to support her claim that his critique of the discourse does not pertain to the German tradition and that a new definition is therefore required. Exaggerating Said's claims, she argues that the relationship of Germany *and* Austria to the East *never* had the actuality of that of the colonial states to their colonies.[25] Further, she asserts that since the German image of the Orient was thoroughly theoretical, classical, and academic, German orientalism can only be said to share an intellectual authority over the Orient with Britain and France if we understand "orientalism" to mean any writing by a Westerner about the East (5). Moreover, Fuchs-Sumiyoshi argues, this "orientalism" is characterized by a generalizing depiction of the Orient that lies beyond human reality and is colored by a centuries-old tradition and Western categories of thought (5). Here the author attempts to transform some of the most insidious aspects of the orientalist discourse into virtues: the casual assumption of intellectual authority over a huge region that encompasses the vast majority of the planet's population, the tendency to generalize about this enormously diverse area, the hermetic discourse that the West has conducted for centuries, which is influenced only by indigenous intellectual categories and bears no relation to human reality, all become signs of a pristine and apolitical intellectual tradition, that is, precisely that image of orientalism that Said's study overturns.

More recently, Andrea Polaschegg has also sought to distinguish and rehabilitate German orientalism. Focusing on texts from the early nineteenth century, she argues persuasively for the need to address the implicit and unquestioned assumption that Britain and France are necessarily representative of all European orientalism.[26] Further, she identifies the self-critical potential in orientalist fiction in that instance when the ethnological gaze of the Western writer turns inward to examine his or her own culture (44). Nevertheless, like Fuchs-Sumiyoshi, Polaschegg asserts that Germany never possessed territories in the Orient[27] and thus ignores the colonial concession of Kiao-Chau in China (1898–1914) as well as several islands in the Pacific. (Although some critics maintain that the German term "der Orient" generally refers to the Middle East and North Africa,[28] Polaschegg herself notes that in the eighteenth and nineteenth centuries the term had come to denote India, Mongolia, China, and even Japan as well (83).) I do not wish to overstate the cultural significance of these "oriental" German possessions, but their existence means that it is Austria-Hungary, rather than Germany, that provides a more compelling challenge to Said's notion that orientalism and overseas colonialism are inseparable.

However, some critics have been successful in using German-language orientalism to challenge some aspects of Said's definition of the discourse. For example, in *German Orientalisms* (2004), Todd Kontje adopts Thomas Mann's term "Das Land der Mitte" (the country of the center) to describe Germany's position within a "symbolic geography"[29] and thus signals an interest in overturning the customary dichotomy between Occident and Orient that Said considers intrinsic to the discourse. Moreover, this study readily acknowledges in both its pluralized title and its methodology the dynamic, historically contingent nature of a discourse that has produced several distinct and even contradictory articulations of orientalism over the centuries. Polaschegg takes this historical specificity a step further, arguing not only that it is illogical to attempt to write the history of German orientalism as a panoramic survey, but also that orientalist forms and topoi only acquire the power to signify *in actu*, that is, in the specific context of their usage (531). In the same spirit of particularity, my study of Austrian orientalism limits itself to three authors, Hofmannsthal, Musil, and Kafka, and to a specific era in Habsburg history: 1890–1919. This time frame encompasses overlapping historical and cultural developments that are crucial to my reading of Austrian orientalism: the heyday of European interest in East Asia from 1890 to 1925,[30] the advent of literary modernism, and the collapse of the Habsburg Empire following the First World War.

To my knowledge, only two other critics, Nina Berman and Rolf Goebel, focus specifically on the Austrian orientalist literature of the *fin de siècle*.[31] In both cases, however, I would argue that the author does not sufficiently connect the topic of orientalist fiction to the specifically Austrian historical, political, and cultural contexts. For example, in her 1996 study of orientalism, colonialism, and modernity, Berman's analysis of Hofmannsthal's "Das Märchen der 672. Nacht" (The Tale of the 672nd Night) offers a generalized discussion of motifs more or less loosely associated with orientalism, such as the harem, melancholia, and the *femme fatale*, and thus subsumes Hofmannsthal's text to the common tropes of European orientalist fiction. Similarly, in her article "K.u.k. Colonialism: Hofmannsthal in North Africa" (1998) Berman looks outside the Austrian context to Susanne Zantop's account of German precolonial fantasies for insights into Hofmannsthal's responses to his journey to North Africa in 1925. Berman supports her claim that "Hofmannsthal's writings take part in the creation of a non-occupational imperialist ideology" (8) by citing Susanne Zantop's assertion that "precisely the lack of actual colonialism . . . created a pervasive desire for colonial possessions and a sense of entitlement to such possessions in the minds of many Germans."[32] However, in describing Hofmannsthal's journey, Berman comes across another form of imperialism, one that is of more immediate relevance to the Austrian author. When Berman recounts how the French General Marshal Lyautey commiserates with Hofmannsthal at the loss of the Habsburg Empire, she observes: "The very structures of colonial rule resemble those of the lost Austrian Empire and of an aristocratic, premodern world that Hofmannsthal continued to believe in."[33] Yet Berman leaves this intriguing analogy between the overseas colonies and the domestic imperialism of the Habsburg Empire unexplored.

In many respects the approach taken by Rolf Goebel in *Constructing China: Kafka's Orientalist Discourse* (1997) closely resembles my own.

Most important, Goebel discerns a self-critical attitude towards Western orientalism in Kafka's references to China, which, Goebel argues, were written not to provide a faithful representation of historical reality but rather "to critique the Western project of representing the Orient" (2). However, our readings differ considerably on the issue of an extra-diegetic referent for Kafka's Chinese stories: while Goebel connects Kafka's texts with specific historical events during the Q'ing dynasty, I argue that Kafka's works invoke China in order to allude to the Habsburg Empire and thus reflect on the nature of national and imperial identity in general. Further, the texts by Hofmannsthal and Musil that I examine here also demonstrate that authors can deploy orientalist tropes not to bolster Western colonial hegemony but rather to critique the authors' own "eastern empire."

Throughout the following pages my main concern has been to trace this double movement of self-critique that encompasses both the Habsburg Empire and the orientalist discourse itself. The first chapter offers an analysis of two early texts by Hugo von Hofmannsthal, the short story "Das Märchen der 672. Nacht" and the poetic monologue "Der Kaiser von China Spricht." Here I argue that Hofmannsthal undermines the basic East/West dichotomy underlying traditional orientalism by endowing the supposedly Arabian protagonist of his tale with the sensibility and attitudes of a Viennese aesthete and by using the figure of the Chinese Emperor to allude to his Austrian counterpart, Franz Josef. Moreover, I show how the two works engage critically with the very practice of orientalism: in the *Märchen* the alternately fearful and fascinated attitude of the protagonist toward his servants mirrors that of the orientalist to his subject; in the monologue the fact that an East Asian speaker expresses ethnocentric and racist sentiments implicitly calls into question the validity of such notions *per se*.

The second chapter focuses on Robert Musil's 1906 novel *Die Verwirrungen des Zöglings Törleß* (translated as *Young Törless*) and considers how this text, set in an Austro-German boarding school in the Czech province of Moravia, depicts a quasi-colonial relationship between the schoolboys and the local villagers that suggests the orientalization of the eastern "Other." This section also examines how the novel explicitly addresses orientalism as a cultural phenomenon through the figure of Beineberg, one of the hero's classmates, who expresses and enacts his mania for Eastern philosophy.

In contrast to Beineberg's textual appreciation for the Orient, chapter three tackles actual, physical encounters between Western protagonists and Eastern interlocutors in Franz Kafka's stories "Beschreibung eines Kampfes" (Description of a Struggle, 1904–8), "Schakale und Araber" (Jackals and Arabs, 1917), and "In der Strafkolonie" (In the Penal Colony, 1919). Here I claim that Kafka's fiction repeatedly explores ethnological encounters between East and West to subvert not only the assumption of Occidental superiority, but also the fundamental orientalist claim to know and understand the Eastern Other. The supposedly unknowable nature of the Oriental receives ironic expression in Kafka's stories "Beim Bau der chinesischen Mauer" and "Ein altes Blatt," which are the subject of the fourth and final chapter. This section considers how these texts parody the stereotype of oriental inscrutability by depicting Chinese narrators who are themselves baffled by their country and its institutions. Moreover, they do so while raising issues of national and imperial identity of great moment to a domestic audience in the throes of the First World War.

My discussion of these texts shows how they not only deconstruct national and cultural identity but also pose a more fundamental challenge to the received notion of the self by subverting the opposition between subject and object. In this regard Hofmannsthal's works recall the theories of the Austrian critical empiricist philosopher and physicist Ernst Mach (1838–1916). Critical empiricism, the term favored by the Austrian practitioners of this school of thought, asserted that the only evidence for the existence of an object was that provided by our senses. Consequently, critical empiricists rejected both metaphysics and the dualism of subject and object.[34] Indeed, Mach held that both the percipient and the object perceived only existed in the act of perception. By invoking the critical empiricist worldview, Hofmannsthal's works overturn the basic demarcation between Self and Other that form the basis for the traditional orientalist and imperialist worldview.

The same peculiarly Austrian mixture of critical empiricism and imperialism informs my reading of Musil's novel *Die Verwirrungen des Zöglings Törleß* in chapter 2. While it is not surprising that Mach's theories should influence the novel, given that they formed the subject of Musil's dissertation, the context in which the novelist invokes Mach's thought is startling. Beineberg, one of Törleß's classmates, proposes a Machian dissolution of the subject/object divide in his sadistic "experiments" on a fellow pupil. Although Beineberg invokes Buddhist philosophy to justify his bizarre project, I contend that his warped notions reflect Western orientalism, rather than Eastern mysticism. Indeed, I read Beineberg's idiosyncratic ideas, which combine supposedly oriental mysticism with both traditional scientific empiricism and Mach's critical empiricist theories, as symptomatic of a wider crisis of moral and philosophical disorientation within Habsburg society.

The moral and logical aporia arising from Western empiricism and Enlightenment thought also figure prominently in the next section, which is devoted to three stories by Franz Kafka: *Description of a Struggle*, "Jackals and Arabs," and "In the Penal Colony." While these three works feature utterly disparate settings (a fantastic version of Prague, an Arabian desert, and a French island colony in the tropics, respectively), all three present disorientated, deracinated Western narrators who must confront exotic cultural practices with their supposedly superior logic. However, by undermining the narrators' pretensions to objectivity and rationality, Kafka excoriates the notion of scientific impartiality that provides the rationale for Western hegemony.

In the final chapter, on Kafka's Chinese stories "The Great Wall of China" and "An Old Manuscript," the fallacy of objectivity applies not only to the Other but also to the self. Neither of Kafka's Chinese narrators can disentangle himself from his cultural and political matrices to achieve a detached perspective on his empire. In this way, this study argues that the tendency among these Modernist writers to interrogate the subject/object divide attains a new political and cultural significance in the context of orientalist fiction, since it undermines both the pretensions to objectivity and the assertion of an insuperable divide between the Western percipient and the Eastern object that are fundamental to the conventional orientalist discourse.

Notes

[1] Edward Said, *Orientalism* (1978; repr., London: Penguin Books, 1991), 3.

[2] Ziauddin Sardar, *Orientalism.* (Philadelphia, PA: Open UP, 1999), 71–73.

[3] Lisa Lowe, *Critical Terrains: French and British Orientalisms* (Ithaca, NY: Cornell UP, 1991), 5.

[4] See Rolf Goebel, *Constructing China: Kafka's Orientalist Discourse* (Columbia, SC: Camden House, 1997), 3.

[5] This study is by no means the first to point out the etymology of the term "Österreich" in this regard. Cf. Glenda Sluga, "Bodies, Souls, and Sovereignty: The Austro-Hungarian Empire and the Legitimacy of Nations," *Ethnicities* 1.2 (2001): 215.

[6] Alan Sked, *The Decline and Fall of the Habsburg Empire, 1815–1918*, 2nd. ed. (London: Longman, 2001), 335.

[7] Again, these internal divisions between East and West within the Habsburg Empire were by no means a new phenomenon. Consider, for example, the famous observation made in the early nineteenth century by the Habsburg statesman Prince Metternich that Asia began at the Landstraße (i.e. as soon as one moved south and east of Vienna). Cited in Sluga, "Bodies, Souls, and Sovereignty," 215.

[8] Scholars based in the United States who have called for a postcolonial approach to Habsburg studies include Russell Berman, Valentina Glajar, Pieter Judson, and Scott Spector. Russell Berman, "German Colonialism: Another *Sonderweg*?" *European Studies Journal* 16.2 (Fall 1999); Valentina Glajar, *The German Legacy in East Central Europe as Recorded in Recent German-Language Literature* (Rochester: Camden House, 2004); Pieter Judson, "Inventing Germans: Class, Nationality, and Colonial Fantasy at the Margins of the Hapsburg Monarchy,"

in "Nations, Colonies, and Metropoles," ed. Daniel A. Segal and Richard Handler, special issue of *Social Analysis* 33 (1993): 47–67; Scott Spector, *Prague Territories: National Conflict and Cultural Innovation in Franz Kafka's* Fin-de-Siècle (Berkeley: U of California P, 2000). While these critics have made their case from a variety of standpoints, German-language scholarship on the topic displays more cohesion, largely because much of it is has been produced under the aegis of the *Kakanien Revisited* project (http://www.kakanien.ac.at/beitr). See the essay volumes in the series Kultur-Herrschaft-Differenz, published in Tübingen by A. Francke Verlag: *Kakanien Revisited: Das Eigene und das Fremde in der österreichischen-ungarischen Monarchie*, ed. Wolfgang Müller-Funk, Peter Plener, and Clemens Ruthner (2001), and *Zentren, Peripherien und kollektive Identitäten in Österreich-Ungarn*, ed. Endre Hárs, Wolfgang Müller-Funk, Ursula Reber, and Clemens Ruthner (2006), as well as Moritz Csáky, Johannes Feichtinger and Ursula Prutsch, eds., *Habsburg Postcolonial: Matchtstrukturen und kollektives Gedächtnis* (Innsbruck: Studien Verlag, 2003).

9 For example, both Ursula Prutsch and Clemens Ruthner raise doubts about the applicability of the term "colonial" to the Habsburg context in their contributions to Csáky et al., *Habsburg Postcolonial*. See Prutsch "Habsburg Postcolonial" in Csáky et al., *Habsburg Postcolonial*, 41, and Ruthner, "K.u.k. Kolonialismus als Befund, Begrifflichkeit, und Metapher" in Csáky et al., *Habsburg Postcolonial*, 111 and 114.

10 Robert Luft, "Machtansprüche und kulturelle Muster nichtperipherer Regionen: Die Kernlande Böhmen, Mähren und Schlesien in der späten Habsburger Monarchie," in Csáky et al., *Habsburg Postcolonial*, 165–87; here 168.

11 See Andrea Komlosy, "Innere Peripherien als Ersatz für Kolonien? Zentrenbildung und Peripherisierung in der Habsburgermonarchie," in *Zentren, Peripherien und kollektive Identitäten*, ed. Endre Hárs, Wolfgang Müller-Funk, Ursula Reber, and Clemens Ruthner (Tübingen: A. Francke Verlag, 2006), 71; and Heidemarie Uhl, "Zwischen "Habsburgischem Mythos" und (Post-)Kolonialismus: Zentraleuropa als Paradigma für Identititätskonstruktionen in der (Post-)Moderne," in Csáky et al., *Habsburg Postcolonial*, 49.

12 Komlosy, "Innere Peripherien," 57.

13 See Ruthner, "K.u.k. Kolonialismus," 116.

14 See Johannes Feichtinger, "Habsburg (Post-)Colonial: Anmerkungen zur Inneren Kolonisierung im Zentraleuropa," in Csáky et al., *Habsburg Postcolonial*, 13; Wolfgang Müller-Funk, "Kakanien Revisited: Über das Verhältnis von Herrschaft und Kultur," in Müller-Funk et al., *Kakanien Revisited: Das Eigene und das Fremde in der österreichischen-ungarischen Monarchie*, 18 and 19; and Clemens Ruthner, "Central Europe Goes Postcolonial," *New Approaches to the Habsburg Empire around 1900, Cultural Studies* 16.6 (2002): 881.

15 Sara Friedrichsmeyer, Sara Lennox, and Susanne Zantop, eds., *The Imperialist Imagination: German Colonialism and Its Legacy* (Ann Arbor: U of Michigan P, 1998), 1.

16 Axel Dunker, *Kontrapünktische Lektüren: Koloniale Strukturen in der deutschprachigen Literatur des 19. Jahrhunderts* (Munich: Wilhem Fink, 2008). For

Said's notion of "contrapuntal reading," see Edward Said, *Culture and Imperialism* (New York: Knopf, 1993), 66.

[17] Otto Spies, *Der Orient in der deutschen Literatur* (Kevelaer, Germany: Butzon & Bercker, 1949), 25.

[18] Franz Babinger, "Orient und die deutsche Literatur," *Deutsche Philologie im Aufriss* (1957): 333.

[19] See Ingrid Schuster, *China und Japan in der deutschen Literatur, 1890–1925* (Bern: Francke Verlag, 1977), and *Faszination Ostasien: Zur kuturellen Interaktion Europa-Japan-China; Aufsätze aus drei Jahrzenten* (Frankfurt am Main: Peter Lang, 2007).

[20] See Schuster, *China und Japan*, 159–65, and *Faszination Ostasien*, 69–75.

[21] Schuster, *China und Japan*, 165.

[22] Joo-Dong Lee, *Taoistiche Weltanschauung im Werke Franz Kafkas.* (Frankfurt am Main: Peter Lang, 1985).

[23] Dennis McCort, "Kafka and the East: The Case for Spiritual Affinity," *Symposium: A Quartery Journal in Modern Literatures* 55.4 (Winter 2002): 199.

[24] In contrast, Rolf Goebel argues in the same volume as McCort's essay that Kafka's "highly *subversive* attitude toward (cross)cultural authenticity" renders the issue of a spiritual affinity between Kafka and Eastern religion questionable. See Rolf Goebel, "Kafka and the East: The Case for Cultural Construction," *Symposium: A Quarterly Journal in Modern Literatures* 55.4 (Winter 2002): 194 (Goebel's emphasis).

[25] Andrea Fuchs-Sumiyoshi, *Orientalismus in der deutschen Literatur: Untersuchungen zu Werken des 19. und 20. Jahrhunderts, von Goethes 'West-östlichem Divan' bis Thomas Manns 'Joseph' Tetralogie* (Hildesheim: Olms, 1984), 5 (my italics).

[26] Andrea Polaschegg, *Der andere Orientalismus: Regeln deutsch-morgenländischer Imagination im 19. Jahrhundert* (Berlin: Walter de Gruyter, 2005), 3.

[27] Fuchs-Sumiyoshi, *Orientalismus*, 5, Polaschegg, *Der andere Orientalismus*, 5.

[28] See, for example, Nina Berman, "Orientalism, Imperialism, and Nationalism: Karl May's *Orientzyklus*," in *The Imperialist Imagination: German Colonialism and its Legacy*, ed. Sara Friedrichsmeyer, Sara Lennox, and Susanne Zantop (Ann Arbor: U of Michigan P, 1998), 52.

[29] Todd Kontje, *German Orientalisms* (Ann Arbor: U of Michigan P) 2004, 1.

[30] See Schuster, *China und Japan in der deutschen Literatur*, 5. Quoted by Wei-yan Meng in *Kafka und China* (Munich: Iudicium Verlag, 1986), 21.

[31] Nina Berman, *Orientalismus, Kolonialismus und Moderne: Zum Bild des Orients in der deutschsprachigen Literatur um 1900* (Stuttgart: M & P, Verlag für Wissenschaft & Foschung, 1996), and "K.u.k. Colonialism: Hofmannsthal in North Africa," *New German Critique* 75 (1998 Fall): 3–27; and Rolf Goebel, *Constructing China.*

[32] Susan Zantop, *Conquest, Family, and Nation in Precolonial Germany 1770–1870* (Durham, NC: Duke UP, 1997), 7. Quoted in Berman, "K.u.K. Colonialism," 8.

[33] Berman, "K.u.K. Colonialism," 25–26.

[34] Cf. Judith Ryan, *The Vanishing Subject: Early Psychology and Literary Modernism* (Chicago: U of Chicago P, 1991), 2. I have chosen to retain the term "critical empiricism," not only because of its Austrian provenance, but also to distinguish it from the broader connotations of "empiricism" in the history of philosophy.

1: Empiricist Empires: Hofmannsthal's Domestic Orientalism

Hofmannsthal's early works are imbued with a tremulous yet torpid aestheticism that seems at first glance far removed from the harsh reality of late nineteenth-century imperialism. It is therefore surprising to discover that some of his early texts, most noticeably "Das Märchen der 672. Nacht" (The Tale of Night 672, 1895) and the poetic monologue "Der Kaiser von China spricht" (The Emperor of China Speaks, 1897), draw upon orientalist topoi, and thus participate in the discourse that, according to Edward Said, consistently acts as the ideological cohort of Western colonialism. However, we must remember that, unlike the British and French empires that predominate in Said's *Orientalism*, Hofmannsthal's Austria-Hungary possessed no overseas colonies but was rather itself a contiguous, if somewhat fractious, European empire. My aim here is to consider how Hofmannsthal's tale and poem reflect on imperialism, not so much as a matter of overseas expansion, but rather of domestic policy. This chapter will demonstrate that rather than promoting Western hegemony, these texts question the basic viability of imperialism and challenge received notions of national identity.

Both the *Märchen* and the poem feature chimerical kingdoms, realms so vast that they can only exist as cohesive entities in the minds of their putative sovereigns. Although the monological form and monomaniacal speaker can only intimate this disturbing truth in "Der Kaiser von China spricht," the third-person narrative in the tale can address this topic more directly. Here the protagonist, the merchant's son, reads a historical narrative concerning a "great king of the past" and has the following realization:

> Er begriff, daß der große König der Vergangenheit hätte sterben müssen, wenn man ihm seine Länder genommen hätte, die er durchzogen und unterworfen hatte vom Meer im Westen bis zum Meer im Osten, die er zu beherrschen träumte und die doch so unendlich groß waren, daß er keine Macht über sie hatte und keinen Tribut von ihnen empfing, als den Gedanken, daß er sie unterworfen hatte und kein anderer als er ihr König war. (*MN*, 22)

> [He realized that the great king of the past would have died had he been deprived of the lands he had traversed and conquered from

the sea in the west to the sea in the east and had dreamed of ruling even though they were so infinitely large that that he had no
power over them and received no more tribute from them than the
thought that he had conquered them and he and he alone was their
king. (*TN*, 46)]

A note by Hofmannsthal written on the back of the manuscript makes
clear that the "great king of the past" that he has in mind is Alexander the
Great, whose empire extended from the Mediterranean to the Arabian
Sea. Not only was Alexander the first Western ruler to conquer Arabia and
Persia and to proclaim himself "king of Asia,"[1] he also inspired countless
subsequent imperialist expeditions from at least the second century B.C.E.
onwards that consciously followed in his footsteps. Hofmannsthal's inclusion of this inset narrative in a text whose title self-consciously alludes to
One Thousand and One Nights suggests a complex relationship with the
orientalist tradition. On the one hand, as we shall see, he appropriates the
literary topos that is a mainstay of Western orientalist fantasy and re-cre-
ates it in his own image; on the other, he reveals the futility of a Western
imperialist expansion in the East that produces no benefit other than the
mere thought of conquest and dominion in the mind of the purported
monarch. In this way, Hofmannsthal's references to Alexander the Great
signal a self-reflexive and critical approach to both the literary and military aspects of the orientalist legacy.

However, this passage, from an ostensibly exotic text set in the Orient, resonates with Hofmannsthal's domestic Austrian audience in that
the great king's situation reveals parallels with that of the contemporary
Habsburg emperor, Franz Josef. Following the *Ausgleich* or compromise
of 1867, which established that the Austrian and Hungarian regions
of the empire were to have separate parliaments and prime ministers,
Hungary acquired a considerable degree of autonomy in its domestic
affairs. This arrangement rendered Franz Josef's claim to rule over the
region more tenuous, if not quite imaginary. Further, at the time of the
tale's composition in the 1890s the "subject peoples" of Franz Josef's
diverse and sprawling kingdom were becoming more and more inclined
to challenge his "divine right" to rule over them. Finally, the connection between the life of the particular emperor on the throne and the
maintenance of the territories under his rule has a peculiar relevance for
the Dual Monarchy in the *fin-de-siècle*. While the great king would have
died had he been deprived of his lands (*MN*, 46), the formula must be
reversed for the Austria-Hungary of the 1890s. For the person of Franz
Josef, who ascended the throne back in 1848, had become synonymous
with the institution of the empire itself, and thus his demise might well
signal the end of the Dual Monarchy. (This is of course what happened
eventually following his death in 1916, with the catastrophe of the First

World War hastening the collapse of the empire.) Thus, in this early work Hofmannsthal, a writer more commonly associated with imperialist nostalgia, diagnoses with startling prescience the malaise at the heart of the Dual Monarchy.

This passage alludes not only to the political but also to the philosophical discourses peculiar to the Habsburg Empire. Throughout this excerpt Hofmannsthal subverts the customary dichotomy (and hierarchy) between subject and object in a manner that recalls the critical empiricism of Austrian philosophers/psychologists such as Ernst Mach. To illustrate this point, let us consider the ontological status of the great king's realm as described above. While empires normally owe their existence to their founding fathers, here the situation is reversed, as the emperor's life is apparently dependent on the maintenance of his realm. Moreover, although the emperor's subjects refuse to recognize his authority, Hofmannsthal ultimately privileges the monarch's highly dubious claim to rule the realm. The significance accorded to the emperor's subjective viewpoint recalls the critical empiricist arguments of Franz Brentano and Ernst Mach, who claimed that since both subject and object inhered in consciousness, the traditional distinction between them no longer pertained.[2] There were only various impressions and perceptions, prompted by various circumstances. As early as 1868, Mach claimed that to use the expression "sensory illusion" merely showed that one had failed to grasp that *"the senses represent things neither wrongly nor correctly."*[3] However, by expressing these ontological doubts through the figure of an emperor, Hofmannsthal endows this tenet of critical empiricist thought with subversive political significance, creating empires of doubtful substantiality three and a half decades before the appearance of Musil's Kakania in *Der Mann ohne Eigenschaften.*

By tracing the inflections and intersections of the orientalist, imperialist, and critical empiricist discourses in Hofmannsthal's "Tale of Night Six Hundred and Seventy-Two" and the poem "The Emperor of China Speaks," this study will position these works in a specifically Austrian cultural context. Thus this analysis aims to break with the majority of critical responses, which have generally subsumed "Das Märchen der 672. Nacht" under pan-European movements, such as decadence or aestheticism.

The tendency to read the *Märchen* solely in terms of aestheticism began with Richard Alewyn's groundbreaking study, "Hofmannsthals Wandlung" (1947), which defines the subject of the text as the "die Fragwürdigkeit des schönen Lebens und seine Überwindung" (the questionable nature of the beautiful life and overcoming it [the beautiful life]).[4] A brief synopsis of the plot reveals why this reading has held sway for so long. A handsome son of a merchant, who lives in splendid isolation with his four servants and a collection of beautiful ornaments, becomes convinced that his *objets d'art* provide a profound insight into the world he has rejected. When an anonymous letter threatens his idyll, he embarks on a series of misadventures in a dismal and menacing city, which culminate in a humiliating and agonizing death from a horse kick to the groin. In his death throes the merchant's son repudiates the solipsistic and aestheticist existence that has brought him to this pass (*MN*, 30). According to Alewyn, life conspires against the protagonist to exact revenge for having subordinated it to art (175).

However, this interpretation conforms so closely to that of the protagonist himself that it fails to recognize the inconsistencies in his attitude. For example, when the character blames his servants for bringing about his death, Alewyn follows suit, despite the servants' absence from the second half of the text. According to Alewyn, the four hold their master prisoner as if through a magical, invisible net, which they use to drag him down to his doom (172). We are thus left to ponder why the life of the everyday world should be so opposed to art and yet happy to have its agents employ supernatural means to achieve its aims.

One consequence of Alewyn's study is that subsequent interpretations in the same vein have tended to view the merchant's son as symbolic of the artist in general. Indeed, in a 1981 article, Jens Rieckmann argues that the protagonist's insufficiency is in fact the undefined, chameleon-like sense of self that enables the artist to inhabit the people or even objects he encounters through imaginative empathy.[5] According to Rieckmann, the death of the merchant's son, which freezes his features in an ugly rictus of pain, signifies "the extinction of the artistic existence as a consequence of individuation."[6] Unfortunately, the hero of the tale does not merely eschew creative endeavor but strives to avoid activity of any kind. Indeed, when describing his character as deriving great pride from the mirror, the verses of the poets, his wealth, and his cleverness (*MN*, 16), Hofmannsthal ironizes the protagonist's smug narcissism. How, one may ask, can someone draw personal pride from the poetry of others? This anomalous response suggests a profound confusion between the author and reader, between subject and object. Far from using his protagonist as an allegorical figure for the artist, Hofmannsthal emphasizes his passive and unproductive approach to both life and art.

In her Freudian reading of the *Märchen*, Dorrit Cohn makes a conscious attempt to break with aestheticist interpretations.[7] Her point of departure is Arthur Schnitzler's comment to Hofmannsthal that the latter's text represents a dream rather than a fairy tale (285). However, the notion that the second half of the text (that is, the hero's journey through the city and his untimely demise) "is all a dream" demands scrutiny. First, although the protagonist ends up in bed, he actually dies in agony there, rather than waking up in a cold sweat. Further, the only textual clue in the diegesis to suggest this oneiric reading is the adverb "traumhaft" or dream-like,[8] a term that indicates that this experience is similar to a dream, but not identical to it.

As the title suggests, Nina Berman's 1996 study of the *Märchen* in *Orientalismus, Kolonialismus und Moderne: Zum Bild des Orients in der deutschsprachigen Literatur um 1900* considers the place of the work in the context of the European orientalist discourse.[9] However, Berman's account of Austrian orientalism fails to distinguish it from that found in Wilhelmine Germany, which possessed overseas colonies. Moreover, her analysis of themes and motifs such as melancholy and the *femme fatale* reveals a flaw common to many New Historicist readings, in that it offers so many intertextual references that the work in question becomes lost in a welter of examples.

However, Berman is by no means alone in failing to address the implications of Hofmannsthal's complex and self-reflexive orientalism. Indeed, the connection between the title and the Arabian setting on the one hand and the narrative of the merchant's son on the other represents something of a blind spot in many critical responses to the text. For example, while Waltraud Wiethölter raises some very valid points regarding the self's lack of autonomy and sovereignty in the text[10] and the predominance of visuality, of actions relating to seeing and being seen (28–29), she does not notice when her own analysis slips into orientalist cliché. When she describes the extent to which Hofmannsthal identifies with the character of the merchant's son, she claims that the author has seen the ambiguous and horrifying world of the Orient with his own eyes (49). This startling comment is all the more remarkable for the fact that Hofmannsthal did not visit the Orient until 1925, when he made his first visit to North Africa. On other occasions, critics simply fail to acknowledge that Hofmannsthal's text is at least in part inspired by *The Arabian Nights* and is set in a stylized version of the East. For example, in her 2006 article on the *Märchen*, Ingrid Haag cites the Western *fin-de-siècle* artists, including Böcklin, Stuck, and Beardsley, listed by Wiethölter as sources of inspiration for Hofmannsthal's description of a pair of statues.[11] However, neither critic takes note of the fact that the statues represent *Indian* deities, and that presumably Hofmannsthal drew his visual inspiration for their description from further afield. Finally, in a 2008 address, Imke Meyer links the uncanny and threatening environment of the cityscape in the second half of Hofmannsthal's tale with Metternich's famous comment that "Asien beginnt an der Landstraße" (Asia begins on the outskirts of Vienna), without noting the fact that the merchant's son is himself an Asian character.[12] These moments of orientalist stereotyping, in which critics casually cast the Orient as horrifying or uncanny, or simply ignore it, seem at odds with a text that undermines the customary orientalist dichotomy and hierarchy between East and West by combining an oriental literary topos with a pungent evocation of the domestic realm of *fin-de-siècle* Vienna.

Helpfully, Hofmannsthal himself has provided a means of linking the macrocosmic issues of orientalism, imperialism, and East/West relations to the microcosm of the merchant's son's narrative in a comment written on the back of his manuscript. With regard to the merchant's son, Hofmannsthal writes this terse, telegraphic statement: "Diener so sein eigenstes, wie für Vater Waren, für Alexander eroberte Länder und kühnere Träume" (*MN*, 204: Servants his most personal possessions, like goods for the father, like conquered lands and bolder dreams for Alexander; my translation). Here the concept of possession, denoted by the adjective "eigen" (own), connects the father and son's cherished goods and servants with the conquests of Alexander the Great, the first Western leader to dominate territory in the Middle East and Asia. Clearly, the fact that individuals and even whole peoples can be equated with inanimate objects indicates the reification that is essential to imperialism. However, the unusual superlative "eigenstes" suggests that the most characteristic and intrinsic qualities of the son, father, and emperor can somehow be represented by other people, external objects, and remote territories. This notion recalls the critical empiricist rejection of the dualism between subject and object. And since the split between subject and object forms the basis for all hierarchization, including imperialism, such an interrogation of the subject/object divide subverts claims to hegemony in the very act of their enunciation.

Within the text itself, Hofmannsthal's depiction of the relationship between the protagonist and his four servants inverts the customary power dynamic by subverting the relationship between the percipient and the perceived. This reversal occurs on the visual level as the merchant's son is subjected to the panoptic gaze of his four servants.

> Manchmal mußte er mitten in der Beschreibung, wie die Tausende Reiter der feindlichen Könige schreiend ihre Pferde umwenden oder ihre Kriegswagen den steilen Rand eines Flusses hinabgerissen werden, plötzlich innehalten, denn er fühlte, daß die Augen seiner vier Diener auf ihn geheftet waren. Er wußte, ohne den Kopf zu heben, daß sie ihn ansahen, ohne ein Wort zu reden, jedes aus seinem Zimmer. (*MN*, 18)

> [Sometimes in the midst of a description of how thousands of the enemy kings' horsemen whooped and turned their chargers round or how the chariots hurtled down a steep riverbank he felt a sudden need to pause, sensing without looking that the eyes of the his four servants were upon him. He knew without lifting his head that they were watching him wordlessly, each from a different room. (*TN*, 43)]

Hofmannsthal ironizes his "hero's" timidity by juxtaposing the latter's hesitant reading of military history with the violent halts and reversals of the battle described therein. Here the syntax of the first sentence, with its encapsulated clause and delayed infinitive, reflects the protagonist's lack of resolution. In the context of his reading, a breathless account of military derring-do, the character's wavering borders on the comic. Moreover, the merchant's son finds his servants' presence so overwhelming that it threatens his own sense of self-identity.

> Er fühlte sie leben, stärker, eindringlicher, als er sich selber leben fühlte . . . Er fühlte mit der Deutlichkeit eines Alpdrucks, wie die beiden Alten dem Tod entgegenlebten, mit jeder Stunde, mit dem unaufhaltsamen leisen Anderswerden ihrer Züge und ihrer Gebärden, die er so gut kannte; und wie die beiden Mädchen in das öde, gleichsam lustlose Leben hineinlebten. Wie das Grauen und die tödliche Bitterkeit eines furchtbaren, beim Erwachen vergessenen Traumes, lag ihm die Schwere ihres Lebens, von der sie selber nichts wußten, in den Gliedern. (*MN*, 18–19)

> [He felt their lives more strongly, more vividly, than he felt his own. . . . With the clarity of a nightmare he sensed the lives of the two older servants moving hour by hour towards death in the slight yet inexorable modifications in the features and gestures he knew so well, sensed the two girls slipping into lives of [listless], as it were, desolation. Like the horror and deadly pungency of a frightening dream forgotten upon awakening, the onerous quality of their lives, of which they themselves were unaware, weighed heavily upon him. (*TN*, 43, translation slightly amended)]

The first sentence of the original German text literally reads: "He felt them living, more strongly, more vividly, than he felt himself living." As such it creates an ambiguity that is not preserved in the translation, for it is not clear whether the comparative adjectives "stärker" and "eindringlicher" (more strongly and more vividly) refer to the verb "fühlte" (felt), that is to the intensity with which the protagonist perceives the servants' lives, or to the verb "leben" (living), that is to the intensity with which the servants live their lives. This syntactical ambiguity again hints at the dissolution of the subject/object distinction. Whatever the case may be, the first sentence invokes the cliché that the lower orders possess greater vitality than their social superiors, only to undercut it with the subsequent description of the servants' dismal lives. One can only wonder at the protagonist's attenuated sense of his own life, that he should find so compelling an existence in which approaching death and entering life seem equally dreary prospects. However, while he claims to be able to intuit, as in a nightmare, "die Schwere ihres Lebens" (the onerousness of their lives or, more literally, the heaviness of their lives), the merchant's son assumes that the servants themselves know nothing of their own hardship (*MN*, 43). His presumptiveness evokes a sense of intellectual superiority and recalls the West's paternalistic attitude towards the Orient and its supposed ignorance of itself, an attitude that Said sums up with a quotation from Marx: "Sie können sich nicht vertreten, sie müssen vertreten werden" (They cannot represent themselves, they must be represented).[13] Thus Hofmannsthal's protagonist embodies a decadent form of orientalism, one in which the Western subject asserts its innate superiority over the Other, even as its sense of integrity crumbles.

Since the title of the *Märchen* alludes to the *Arabian Nights*, we tend to assume that the setting and characters are oriental, and that any traditionally negative orientalist attitudes towards the East will be found in the author's handling of his material, rather than within the diegesis itself. However, through clear cultural references Hofmannsthal imbues the merchant's son with recognizably Western traits. As we have seen, the protagonist's choice of reading matter links him to the West, since the "great king" whose exploits fascinate him is Alexander the Great, a Western leader who declared himself "lord of Asia."[14] Further, the merchant's son displays the ambivalent attitudes associated with Western orientalism when he considers the cultural artifacts of other Eastern cultures. For example, he ascribes great wisdom to Turkish mottoes (*MN*, 16)[15] and yet is frightened by statues of Indian deities (*MN*, 20). In this regard he displays the contradictory responses typical of the Western orientalist, which can range from admiring mystification to outright revulsion. By depicting the reactions of an ostensibly oriental character to other Eastern cultures, Hofmannsthal suggests a relativistic notion of the Orient, in which the exotic east is to be found not on maps, but in minds.

Indeed, Hofmannsthal links his protagonist not merely to the West in general, but more specifically to the author's own contemporary cultural milieu. The protagonist conforms to a type commonly found in *fin-de-siècle* Viennese society: the aesthete who is the son of a businessman. (As critics have remarked, this description equally applies to Hofmannsthal himself.[16]) Carl Schorske encapsulates the different attitudes exhibited by the succeeding generations of businessmen in the following: "Art becomes transformed from an ornament to an essence, from an expression of value to a source of value."[17] However, in the case of the merchant's son, the fact that he is only identified in relation to his father's occupation indicates his failure to dissociate himself from the previous generation and their attitudes.

Hofmannsthal's deployment of orientalist stereotypes in his depiction of the servants further aligns their master, the merchant's son, with the West. The importance of the relationship between the young master and his servants is revealed by the fact that the story was first published with the subtitle "Geschichte des jungen Kaufmannssohnes *und seiner vier Diener*" or "The Story of the Young Merchant's Son *and His Four Servants*" (*MN*, 202, my emphasis). The first servant described, an aged woman, evokes memories of the protagonist's late mother (*MN*, 16) and thus represents not only the antiquity of the Orient, but also the orientalist view of the East as the "cradle of humanity." While her presence is reassuring, the distant relative she brings to serve in the house disturbs the master profoundly. The description of this fifteen-year-old girl as hard on herself and difficult to understand seems a grotesque understatement, given that she throws herself out of a high window for no apparent reason (*MN*, 16–17). Moreover, when the master visits her after her suicide attempt, she gives him a cold and angry look and turns away onto her wounded side, even though the pain of doing so makes her faint (*MN*, 17). Her implacable, and to the protagonist baffling, hatred, combined with her youth, recalls Kipling's description of the colonized as "Your new-caught sullen peoples / Half devil and half child" in the poem "The White Man's Burden" (1899).[18] In stark contrast, the older male servant shows a great attachment to his master and excels in his role as valet (*MN*, 17), thus suggesting the innate amenability and obsequiousness often imputed to the so-called subject races by Western colonialists. Finally, the older servant girl represents the confusion between the erotic and the exotic that abounds in Western images of the East. In his description of this young woman, Hofmannsthal invokes the oriental body as the site of both sexual promise and arcane mystery:

> Dieses junge Mädchen war von jenen, die man von weitem, oder wenn man sie als Tänzerinnen beim Licht der Fackeln auftreten sieht, kaum für sich schön gelten ließe, weil da die Feinheit der Züge verloren geht; da er sie aber in der Nähe und täglich sah, ergriff ihn die unvergleichliche Schönheit ihrer Augenlider und ihrer Lippen und die trägen, freudlosen Bewegungen ihres schönen Leibes waren ihm die rätselhafte Sprache einer verschlossenen und wundervollen Welt. (*MN*, 18)

> [This girl was of the sort who, if seen from afar or by torchlight as a dancer on stage, would hardly be regarded as beautiful, because the delicacy of her features would be lost, but since he saw her close up and daily, he was taken with the incomparable beauty of her eyelids and lips, and the languid, joyless motion of her body was the enigmatic language of a wondrous world beyond his reach. (*TN* 42)]

Here Hofmannsthal invokes the notion of the veil, that symbol of the oriental erotic, by indicating that some kind of invisible barrier must be passed in order to appreciate the woman's charms fully. Clearly the merchant's son views her as an aesthetic object rather than a human being, as evinced by his lack of curiosity as to why she is "languid" and "joyless." However, he not only reifies but also mystifies his servant, interpreting her movements as symbols of an enticing and fabulous world that must remain closed to him. This fantasy, which recalls the colonizers' fetishization of the colonized, is predicated on the impossibility of its fulfillment, since any actual rapprochement between the merchant's son and his servant would threaten his hermetic vision. Thus through the servants Hofmannsthal depicts the oriental as a repository of contradictory images: a reassuring maternal figure *and* a mysterious temptress, a rebel filled with implacable hatred *and* a loyal servant.

The contradictions found in these stereotypes recall Homi Bhabha's discussion of the stereotypes surrounding blacks in *The Location of Culture*:

> The black is both savage (cannibal) and yet the most obedient and dignified of servants, (the bearer of food); he is the embodiment of rampant sexuality and yet as innocent as a child; he is mystical, simple-minded and yet the most worldly and accomplished liar, and manipulator of social forces.[19]

For Bhabha, stereotyping is by no means a rigid codification of supposed differences, but rather "a complex, ambivalent, contradictory mode of representation, as anxious as it assertive."[20] I do not wish to hail Hofmannsthal as a post-colonial critic *avant la lettre*, but it is apparent that such contradictions abound, not only among the servants, but also within each individual character. In the case of the old woman, the association with the Orient is qualified by ambiguous references to her white face and hands (*MN*, 16). Moreover, her connection with his mother is revealed to be both tenuous and suspect on closer inspection. Her presence merely evokes the *memory* of his mother's *voice*, (*MN*, 16; my emphasis) a formulation that excludes the attainment of plenitude at the moment of its evocation. The spurious source of this maternal connection is the fact that the servant's late daughter was the protagonist's wet-nurse. Thus the old woman is revealed as a substitute for the woman who supplanted his mother initially — hardly the most intimate of connections. On the other hand, while the younger servant girl seems to represent the absolute antithesis of her timid master, the merchant's son comes to resemble her in his final moments, slipping in and out of consciousness with a "fremden, bösen Ausdruck" (a strange and angry expression) on his face (*MN*, 30). The fact that the fate suffered by the servant deemed the most alien and incomprehensible prefigures that of the protagonist suggests that any claims of difference must always be provisional and contingent. In the case of the manservant, this paragon of obedience is accused of an unspeakable crime, an allegation that causes the merchant's son to fly into a rage and impels him on his ill-starred journey to the city (*MN*,

21). The behavior of the merchant's son thus recalls the mixture of anxiety and assertiveness that Bhabha discerns in the formation of stereotypes and suggests the cathexis that characterizes the protagonist's relationship with his servants. As for the older girl, the fact that he espies her in a mirror indicates that her image represents a projection of his own desires and fears, a notion that is confirmed when, in spite of her absence, he again glimpses her in the jeweler's mirror (*MN*, 23).[21]

Hofmannsthal imbues both of the serving girl's appearances with the ambivalence that Bhabha associates with the stereotype. On the first occasion, she holds two statues, which "bewegten sich neben den atmenden Wangen und streiften die schönen Schläfen ihrer Wangen" (*MN*, 20; move[d] next to her breathing cheeks, grazing her fair temples in time with her slow gait: *TN*, 44) and thus suggest the master's sensual attraction to his servant. However, the fact that she wears her hair "wie eine Königin im Kriege" (*MN*, 20; literally "like a queen at war,") indicates that her enticing adornment can suddenly seem more akin to protective armor. This dialectic between submission and aggression resurfaces with her second appearance, when he envisages a gold chain wound around her neck, "kindlich und doch an einen Panzer gemahnend" (*MN*, 23; childlike and yet like a coat of mail: *TN*, 48). Although the chain itself connotes slavery and the adjective "kindlich" (childlike) invokes the West's paternalistic attitude toward other peoples, the resemblance to armor recalls the notion of aggression found in the earlier image of the warrior queen. However, the implicit threat contained in these personal adornments appears positively comforting in comparison with the two statues carried by the serving girl. These Indian deities, with their three eyes, mouths full of serpents, and uncanny jewelry in their cold, hard hair (*MN*, 20) are most reminiscent of Kali,[22] the hideous bloodthirsty Hindu goddess, to whom only male children were sacrificed in Vedic India.[23] Hofmannsthal's reference to the goddess's "uncanny jewelry" only hints at the fact that she is normally festooned with a garland of skulls or freshly decapitated heads.[24] Here the text seems to prefigure Freud's notion of the uncanny, for that which the merchant's son represses, that is, the precise nature of Kali's headdress, returns with a vengeance in his ultimate castration and death.[25] However, we must note that the protagonist quells these disturbing elements by viewing the servant's own head as a form of adornment and thus reifying her as an *objet d'art*: "Eigentlich schien sie nicht an den Göttinnen schwer und feierlich zu tragen, sondern an der Schönheit *ihres eigenen Hauptes*" (*MN*, 20, my emphasis; However, it was not so much the goddesses' weight and solemnity that was a burden to her as the beauty *of her own head*, *TN*, 45–46). Thus a text that supposedly depicts the chasm between the art and life in fact reveals the complicity of aesthetics in one of the basic ideological impetuses of the imperialist project: the objectification of non-Western peoples.

Yet the son's reification of his servant does not imply a desire to possess her sexually. He is well aware that it would mean nothing to him to hold her in his arms (*MN*, 20). Instead, filled with a strange restlessness, he embarks on what he knows will be a fruitless quest for the particular fragrance of a flower, or the drifting aroma of a spice, that would provide him with the same sweet sensation of possessing the serving girl's beauty that he finds so unnerving (*MN*, 20). Here the aestheticist predilection for the evanescent ensures that the search will be futile and that his yearning will perpetuate itself. However, it is this need to possess people as objects that first disturbs his equilibrium and propels him out of the house, just as it does when he receives the anonymous accusation against his manservant (*MN*, 21). We can thus infer that the hero's crisis is already apparent in the first part of the text and, more importantly, stems from his own peculiarly possessive attitude toward his servants.[26]

If the merchant's son shows confusion over the distinction between objects and people, he comes by it honestly, since his late father not only personified his possessions but also lavished love on them. Only when an anonymous letter threatens his idyll does the merchant's son understand his father's anxious love for the objects that he had acquired for the "beautiful, insensitive children of his seeking and caring, the mysterious offspring of the vague but deepest wishes of his life" (*MN*, 22; *TN*, 46). The fact that the father's deepest wishes can find such satisfying expression in these lifeless progeny indicates the degree to which he is consumed by materialistic desires. Once again, the distinction between subject and object (in both senses of the word) no longer pertains.

Moreover, the father's love for his ornaments has an extra-diegetic referent: the contemporary Viennese mania for the *Schatzkammer* (literally "treasure chamber"), that is, highly decorated interiors brimming with antiques. In his 1893 essay devoted to the poet Gabriele D'Annunzio, Hofmannsthal comments acerbically on this trend, claiming that the legacy his generation has received from their grandfathers consists solely of "hübsche Möbel und überfeine Nerven" (pretty furniture and oversensitive nerves).[27] In Hofmannsthal's view this predilection for historical objects not only induces neurasthenia in the current generation but also drains them of their imaginative lifeblood:

> Es ist, als hätte die ganze Arbeit dieses feinfühligen, eklektischen Jahrhunderts darin bestanden, den vergangen Dingen ein unheimliches Eigenleben einzuflößen. Jetzt umflattern sie uns, Vampire, lebendige Leichen, beseelte Besen des unglücklichen Zauberlehrlings! Wir haben aus den Toten unsere Abgötter gemacht; alles, was sie haben, haben sie von uns; wir haben ihnen unser bestes Blut in die Adern geleitet; wir haben diese Schatten umgegürtet mit höherer Schönheit und wundervollerer Kraft als das Leben erträgt; mit der Schönheit unserer Sehnsucht und der Kraft unserer Träume.[28]

[It is as if all the work of this sensitive, eclectic century consisted of imbuing the things of the past with an uncanny life of their own. Now they flutter around us — vampires, living corpses, and animated broomsticks of the unfortunate magician's apprentice! We have made our idols out of the dead; everything that they have they have from us; we have poured our best blood into their veins; we have engirdled these shadows with a higher beauty and a more wonderful power than life itself can bear, with the beauty of our yearning and the power of our dreams.]

Clearly the merchant's son epitomizes this desire to revivify the past, for on the very first page of the *Märchen* he contemplates his ornaments in a mystical fashion and gradually perceives "how all the shapes and colors in the world *lived* in his artifacts" (*MN*, 15; *TN*, 39, my emphasis). While Jens Rieckmann perceives this ability to animate historical objects as evidence of the protagonist's artistic creativity and imaginative empathy,[29] Hofmannsthal's essay on D'Annunzio invokes vampires and zombies to argue that resurrecting the past in fact robs life in the present of its creative vitality.

For Nina Berman, the historicist *Schatzkammer* favored by the late nineteenth-century Viennese has political as well as aesthetic significance. In her analysis of the Austrian historicist painter Hans Makart, she identifies in his depictions of ancient Rome and Egypt an apocalyptic teleology, in which the faltering Dual Monarchy represents the final empire in a long series.[30] In my view, the *Märchen* itself alludes to this notion of history when the protagonist becomes convinced that his possessions are no longer dead or lowly but rather a great inheritance that represents the divine work of all the "Geschlechter" (*MN*, 16). This last term appears in Michael Henry Heim's translation as "nations" (*TN*, 40), but "Geschlechter," which can also denote "races" and "genders," is best rendered here as "generations." For although the protagonist perceives a whole world in his collection of *objets d'art*, the term "generations" indicates his own attitude toward the generative and creative processes. By claiming that his father's collection represents the work of *all* generations, the merchant's son places himself at the end of history, and he thereby confirms his own decision to withdraw from the world and neither create nor procreate. In this way Hofmannsthal suggests that the cultivation of the past stems from a rejection of the future.

When we consider the bleak and meager cityscape depicted in the second half of the *Märchen*, then the protagonist's rejection of modernity and retreat into an opulent past seems eminently understandable. As the first draft of the tale indicates, the original setting for these contrasting public and private spaces was not the Arabia of *The Thousand and One Nights*, but rather Vienna itself.[31] The fact that the locale for the story was originally local acquires greater significance when we consider Hofmannsthal's

1906 essay "Tausendundeine Nacht" in relation to his 1895 *Märchen*. From a cursory reading of the opening of the essay, in which Hofmannsthal describes his response to *The Thousand and One Nights* as a twenty-year-old, it is clear why critics cite the following in order to draw a thematic connection with the earlier work:[32]

> In der Jugend unseres Herzens, in der Einsamkeit unserer Seele fanden wir uns in einer sehr großen Stadt, die geheimnisvoll und drohend und verlockend war, wie Bagdad und Basra. Die Lockungen und die Drohungen waren seltsam vermischt; uns war unheimlich zu Herzen und sehnsüchtig; uns grauste vor innerer Einsamkeit, vor Verlorenheit, und doch trieb ein Mut und Verlangen uns vorwärts und trieb uns einen labyrinthischen Weg.[33]

> [In the youth of our heart, in the loneliness of our soul we found ourselves in a very big city, which was mysterious and threatening and enticing, like Baghdad and Basra. The enticements and the threats were mixed in a strange manner; we had an uncanny feeling in our hearts and a longing; we dreaded an inner loneliness and isolation, and yet courage and desire propelled us forward, down a labyrinthine path.]

Certainly, the city in the second half of the *Märchen* is both mysterious and threatening, and the path taken by the merchant's son is thoroughly labyrinthine. Furthermore, since Hofmannsthal was twenty-one at the time of the tale's composition,[34] the above reference to his twenty-year-old self seems to allude clearly to the earlier text. However, I would argue that the direction taken by the 1906 essay is antithetical to the process of composition used in the *Märchen*. For not only does the 1906 essay conclude by repeatedly and explicitly disavowing the idea of the uncanniness of the *One Thousand and One Nights*,[35] but it also adapts the initially disturbing notion of losing oneself in Middle Eastern streets to convey the pleasure and knowledge of immersing oneself in the world of the text: "je länger wir lesen, desto schöner geben wir dieser Welt uns hin, verlieren uns im Medium der unfaßlichsten, naivsten Poesie und besitzen uns erst recht" (the more we read, the more beautifully we give ourselves over to this world, lose ourselves in the medium of the most unfathomable and naive poetry and thus only then truly possess ourselves).[36] In stark contrast to the pleasurable self-knowledge that can be obtained through *The Arabian Nights*, the *Märchen* concludes with an uncanny, anguished moment of self-estrangement, as the contorted face of the dying merchant's son assumes a strange and angry expression (*MN*, 30). More importantly, the fact that the story was originally set in Vienna and retains many of the features of that city suggests that far from seeking to immerse the reader in a strange, magical, and captivating world, the text aims to break the spell cast by exotic literature. On the one hand, it imbues its ostensibly Arabian locale with all the dreariness of the proletarian quarters of Vienna, and on the other it renders the domestic environment *unheimlich* (uncanny, or literally "un-homely") through its adoption of oriental trappings.

The cityscape in the *Märchen* represents an urban modernity divested of all the energy and vitality that one might associate with the bourgeoning metropolises of the *fin de siècle*. Indeed, the city described in the *Märchen* recalls the listless yet sinister landscape depicted in Hofmannsthal's "Ballade des äußeren Lebens," (Ballad of External Life) which was also written in 1895. The contrast between the luxurious home of the merchant's son and the dismal city becomes especially apparent when he reaches his final destination, the soldiers' barracks. Unlike the merchant's son, who has his serving girl bring delicacies on a platter, the soldiers are engaged in the Sisyphean task of lugging endless sacks of bread around. The soldiers carry their bread in sacks, like those that clothe "die Traurigkeit ihres Leibes" (*MN*, 28; the sadness of their bodies). After the merchant's son has received the fateful kick from the horse, he sees three loaves or *Laibe* on a shelf (*MN*, 29). Thus Hofmannsthal plays on the homophones *Laib* and *Leib* (loaf and body) to emphasize how the soldiers' labor determines every aspect of their existence, including the shape of their bodies, and that the merchant's son is equally unable to escape the physicality of his existence.

Although the soldiers' poverty seems to border on self-parody in its extremity, we must bear in mind that like the protagonist's collection of ornaments, the depiction of the barracks refers to the reality of life in the Habsburg capital. There was indeed a strong military presence in the city, for as Carl Schorske points out, the Ringstrasse modernization included "an imposing new arsenal complex and two barracks."[37] Moreover, the contrast between the protagonist's luxurious home and the soldiers' squalid quarters recalls the nomenclature used for the civilian accommodation in the Ringstrasse development with its *Mietpaläste* (rental palaces) for the elite and *Mietkasernen* (rental barracks) for the rest.[38] Finally, even the soldiers' sacks of bread suggest the monotonous fare of the average Viennese worker, as described by Allan Janik and Stephen Toulmin: "He had a breakfast of coffee and a roll, a mid-morning snack of bread and butter, a main meal of soup, vegetable(s), bread, and perhaps coffee or beer; in the afternoon, he had a snack of bread, and an evening meal which was bread, with the occasional sausage."[39] Hofmannsthal's oriental façade therefore serves as a thin disguise for an albeit stylized portrait of the socioeconomic inequality prevalent in Vienna at the time.

The transition from the opulent home of the merchant's son to the dismal city also marks an important stylistic shift in the text. For whereas the protagonist's contemplation of his possessions is rendered in long, rhapsodic sentences in which abstract nouns are ascribed to concrete terms via the genitive as in, for example, "die Seligkeit der Bewegung und die Erhabenheit der Ruhe" (*MN*, 15; the bliss of movement and the grandeur of stillness), his experiences in the city are largely conveyed in short, active sentences that offer very little description. Thus Hofmannsthal's text divests itself of ornamentation in a performative manner that reinforces the contrast between the internal and external environments. Indeed, this transition recalls the shift from a highly ornamental *Jugendstil* idiom to a spare, unadorned prose such as critics have discerned in Kafka's writings.[40]

However, the contrast between the protagonist's home and the threatening city has philosophical as well as aesthetic import, since it reflects the antithetical consequences of the critical empiricist interrogation of the subject/object relationship. First, if the divide between subject and object no longer pertains, one can experience a *unio mystica* with the cosmos, such as that afforded the merchant's son when he contemplates his ornaments:

> er fand die Farben der Blumen und Blätter, die Farben der Felle und der wilden Tiere und der Gesichter der Völker, die Farbe der Edelsteine, die Farbe des stürmischen und des ruhig leuchtenden Meeres; ja, er fand den Mond und die Sterne, die mystische Kugel, die mystischen Ringe und an ihnen festgewachsen die Flügel der Seraphim. (*MN*, 16)

> [he noted the colors of flowers and trees, the colors of hides and of animals and the faces of [different] people[s], the color of precious stones, the color of the stormy sea and of the sea calm and luminous; and yes, he noted the moon and the stars, the mystic globe, the mystic rings, and the wings of the seraphim [grown fast to] them. (*TN*, 40)][41]

Here the breathless, ecstatic style leads the reader to forget, just as the protagonist does, that this cosmogonic insight is obtained from contemplating representations of nature, rather than the real thing. Moreover, Hofmannsthal intimates the tenuousness of this union by placing the adjective "festgewachsen" (grown fast to), which suggests the closest and most organic of connections, at the point of the vision, the link between the seraphim and the "mystic rings," that is most ethereal and least earthbound. Nevertheless, even this *ersatz* mysticism is preferable to the other consequence of the critical empiricist worldview proposed by Austrian thinkers such as Ernst Mach. For if there is no division between subject and object, then the self is reduced to "a mass of loosely connected sensations,"[42] and any sense of logic or continuity within the self or the outside world is annihilated in an endless flux of bewildering and disorientating impressions. This latter scenario accurately describes the harrowing experiences of the merchant's son in the city.

Moreover, Hofmannsthal suggests that cosmic union and individual disintegration are two sides of the same phenomenon by recapitulating motifs from the first part of the text in the second. Whereas the merchant's son is delighted to discern the shapes of animals and flowers and the metamorphosis of flora into fauna in his ornaments (*MN*, 15), he is disturbed when these protean forms, which recall *Jugendstil* designs, reappear in reality. This is evident from his uncanny experience in a greenhouse in the city: "die Formen der Pflanzen fingen an, sonderbar zu werden. In einiger Entfernung traten aus dem Halbdunkel schwarze, sinnlos drohende Zweige unangenehm hervor" (*MN*, 26; the shapes of the plants began to look strange. At some distance, black, senselessly menacing branches emerged unpleasantly from the half darkness). Although this sentence may simply describe the threatening appearance of some trees in the half-light rather than their actual movement, subsequent references endow the plants with a greater degree of animation. In his anxiousness to reach an exit, the merchant's son feels the branches and tops of the trees collapsing above and behind him in a "ghostly" fashion, and when he reaches the door he hears how the snapped stems and crushed leaves rise up as after a storm (*MN*, 26). By recapitulating the motif of animated plants Hofmannsthal suggests that the annihilation of boundaries envisioned in the protagonist's mystical vision is in fact an uncanny and frightening experience, rather than a liberating moment of enlightenment.

Given the close third-person viewpoint, it is impossible for the reader to verify whether the plants have indeed acquired the power to move or whether the merchant's son merely thinks they have. However, his death offers the reader a chance to evaluate interconnected motifs without the intervening filter of the protagonist's subjectivity. We are told that he dies "with deformed features, the lips so torn that the teeth and gums were exposed, lending him a strange, evil expression" (*MN*, 30; *TN*, 55). His distorted features recall those of the soldiers' horses, which are ugly and have an evil air as a result of their raised lips, which expose their canine teeth (*MN*, 28). We are also informed that one of the horses reminds the merchant's son of a poor man he once saw in his father's shop (*MN*, 29). This man's already unattractive features were twisted further with fear, since he had been accused of stealing the large gold coin he had in his possession. (*MN*, 29) If we read these motifs in the associative manner in which the merchant's son interprets his ornaments, then the protagonist, this somewhat epicene figure of refined sensibility and curiously esoteric desires, is linked with a wild beast and a common thief. The thief's connection with the father's shop undermines the son further by insinuating that he has not earned his fortune legitimately, either. Moreover, as we have already seen, the protagonist's dying expression recalls the icy and angry ("eisig und bös") stare he receives from the younger female servant after she tries to commit suicide (*MN*, 17). In turn, this motif is recapitulated not only in the four-year-old girl whom the merchant's son encounters in the greenhouse, but also in the rage he himself experienced as a child toward a father who lavished love upon his ornaments rather than his offspring (*MN*, 21). Through these interconnected motifs Hofmannsthal subverts the protagonist's "occidental" claim to superior rationality by revealing that he is equally subject to the "innere Wildheit" (inner wildness) he finds so alienating in others (*MN*, 30). Taking the broader view, however, this network of intra-textual allusions places the reader in an antithetical position to that of the merchant's son at the opening of the tale. For whereas the merchant's son claims to achieve an understanding of the cosmic order by meditating on aesthetic motifs, the reader is confronted with interconnected images of ugliness, rage, and fear that reveal a very different and much less comprehensible universe.

This does not prevent the merchant's son from discerning a pattern in his fate shortly before his death. He perceives a grand conspiracy among his servants who have brought him to this pass (*MN*, 30). In keeping with all conspiracy theories, this construct provides some measure of comfort in ascribing agency to a particular group rather than to a chaotic and incomprehensible universe. Moreover, we must recognize that the protagonist's condemnation of his servants stems, not from any new insight, but from the same solipsistic thought processes evident throughout the text. In accusing his servants of bringing about his downfall, the merchant's son confuses his own personal associations and impressions with reality. He alone decides to visit the embassy to verify the allegations made against his manservant (*MN*, 22); he alone links the beryl jewel with the old woman (*MN*, 23); he alone perceives the younger serving girl in the jeweler's mirror (*MN*, 23); and he alone discerns an uncanny resemblance between the four-year-old and the younger serving girl (*MN*, 24–25). Curiously, his attempt to blame his servants for his fate recalls Freud's notion of the "omnipotence of thoughts," the animistic mode of thinking that assumes that mental processes can have direct, physical effects.[43] This is apparent, not in the servants' alleged curse on their master, but rather in his belief that his own associations must be grounded in external causality. In this way, the protagonist reveals the archaic, primitive mode of thought that belies his almost over-civilized appearance.

It is the primacy of associative connections over causal logic in the *Märchen* that distinguishes it from the *Arabian Nights* invoked by the title. In contrast to Hofmannsthal's passive and withdrawn protagonist, Scheherazade's orphaned heroes eagerly go out to seek their fortunes and actively shape events. Within the frame narrative of the *Arabian Nights*, the linear plots of Scheherazade's tales generate sufficient suspense to ensure that the tale will continue the next evening and her life will be spared. In contrast, the refusal of the merchant's son to engage in action and thus enter a conventional narrative seems to invite death. Right at the beginning of the tale the protagonist's decision to withdraw from the world indicates a preoccupation with death that is confirmed by his morbid taste in mottoes (*MN*, 16). However, it is not so much the content of these maxims as the images that the merchant's son associates with them that reveal his character:

> Er sagte: "Wo du sterben sollst, dahin tragen dich deine Füße" und sah sich schön, wie ein auf der Jagd verirrter König, in einem unbekannten Wald unter seltsamen Bäumen einem fremden wunderbaren Geschick entgegengehen. Er sagte: "Wenn das Haus fertig ist, kommt der Tod" und sah jenen langsam heraufkommen über die von geflügelten Löwen getragene Brücke des Palastes, des fertigen Hauses, angefüllt mit der wundervollen Beute des Lebens. (*MN*, 16)

> ["Your feet will take you to where you are to die" he would say, and saw himself, elegant, like a lost king on a hunt under exotic trees, meet a strange and wondrous fate. "Death will come when the house is done," he would say and saw Death plod across a bridge resting on the backs of wingèd lions and leading to a palace, a house newly furnished and filled with life's [wonderful] spoils. (*TN*, 40)]

Of course, the young man's tendency to romanticize death is ironized by his actual, agonizing demise. While he envisages himself meeting death bravely in a strange forest, he in fact cowers in the undergrowth to avoid his servants' gaze (*MN*, 19) and later panics when he encounters a four-year-old child in a greenhouse (*MN*, 24–26). The ornate palace which he associates with the second saying is revealed to be the dismal barracks in which he dies an ignominious death, and the "the wonderful spoils of life" turn out to be three small loaves of bread (*MN*, 29).[44] However, if we ignore the image that the protagonist superimposes upon the second saying, then another meaning emerges. As in English, the word "Haus" (house) can refer to a familial dynasty as well as one's home. In this regard the second motto indicates that when there are no more heirs, death will eventually claim the family. Indeed, one can argue that the low blow from the horse's hoof did not so much cut off the merchant's son in his prime as merely confirm his original decision to withdraw from the world and thus end the family line. Whatever the case, it is clear that the merchant's son fails to understand the import of his favorite maxims: that death is not only inevitable but also arbitrary in its timing. Instead he views it as the fitting culmination of an active and successful life, despite the fact that he resolutely refuses to have one. Thus Hofmannsthal suggests the self-deception necessary for the merchant's son to maintain his romantic fantasies.

Nowhere is this self-deception more apparent than in his attachment to the Great King's story. Whenever it appears in the text, this embedded account of Alexander the Great's life casts an ironic light on the main narrative. As we have seen, a stirring description of a battle is juxtaposed with the protagonist's timidity toward his servants (*MN*, 18). Further, the merchant's son earnestly likens the fall of the great king's empire to the possible loss of his own much more modest "kingdom" (*MN*, 22). However, the young man's illusions regarding his idol are most apparent when he thinks of a mass wedding organized by the great king.

> Es verlangte ihn sehr nach einem Bette. Mit einer kindischen Sehn-
> sucht erinnerte er sich an die Schönheit seines eigenen breiten Bet-
> tes, und auch die Betten fielen ihm ein, die der große König der
> Vergangenheit für sich und seine Gefährten errichtet hatte, als sie
> Hochzeit hielten mit den Töchtern der unterworfenen Könige, für
> sich ein Bett von Gold, für die anderen von Silber, getragen von
> Greifen und geflügelten Stieren. (*MN*, 27)

> [Oh how he craved a bed! With childlike longing he recalled the
> beauty of his own wide bed; he thought too of beds that the great
> king of the past had made for himself and his companions when cel-
> ebrating their weddings to the daughters of subservient kings: a bed
> of gold for himself and of silver for the others, carried by griffins and
> winged bulls. (*TN*, 52)]

The use of the adjective "kindisch"("childlike") to describe the protagonist's longing for his own bed is certainly apt, given that he associates Alexander's nuptial beds with sleep rather than sex. His insouciant attitude towards the "daughters of the subjugated kings" reveals his failure to grasp the nature of these proceedings, that is, that these coerced sexual unions reinforce *en masse* the dominance of the invading army. Conversely, they also suggest the limitations of colonization, since the success of imperial rule in this case demands that one abandon any notions of racial purity and become integrated with the subjugated peoples through marriage. This motif recalls the mass wedding held in Susa in 324, in which Alexander and ninety-one of his companions and friends took Persian wives.[45] In the case of the merchant's son, this conflation of military and sexual conquests emphasizes his abject failure in both realms. Indeed, his martial and marital inadequacies are amply demonstrated by the fact that the ignominious and ludicrous struggle with a four-year-old girl remains his only physical encounter with a female throughout the text (*MN*, 24–25). However, we should note that the merchant's son does not misunderstand Alexander's mass wedding merely out of preternatural innocence and immaturity, but rather because he privileges the spectacular decorations surrounding the event over its actual content. Hofmannsthal subtly suggests that this preoccupation with ornament over essence is a fatal flaw, by having the decorative griffons and winged steers recapitulate the winged lions that the merchant's son associates with the motto "Death will come when the house is done" (*MN*, 16). More importantly, the author reveals the role of aesthetics in masking the violence implicit in the imperial project and thereby rendering it palatable.

However, the Alexandrian motifs in the *Märchen* are not confined to the embedded narrative of the Great King. The horrific statues of Kali that prefigure the demise of the merchant's son also remind us of Alexander's campaign in India, which saw thousands of Indians killed, the conquering hero wounded, and Alexander's appointed governor eventually withdrawn to a safer location.[46] A mere three years later, in 326, Alexander was dead. However, before he left India, Alexander named a city after his beloved horse Bucephalus, who died there. Hofmannsthal's references to the story of Bucephalus represent a hitherto unrecognized allusion to the Alexandrian legend. When the merchant's son encounters the horses and grooms in the barracks, the description of the animals emphasizes their ugliness, their strength, and their intractable nature. This is particularly true of the last horse in the row, which repeatedly tries to bite its groom's shoulder (*MN*, 28). This description recalls Alexander's legendary biography, in that when he first met Bucephalus the horse was considered utterly wild and intractable. Indeed, Pseudo-Callisthenes' account of this episode describes the horse as a literal man-eater or *anthrophagus*.[47] Furthermore, the horse that kills the merchant's son has a white mark on its forehead, a feature that the historian Arrian mentions in his eulogy to Bucephalus.[48] These allusions emphasize the disparity between the merchant's son and the great king whom he idealizes. While Alexander passes his initiation with flying colors by taming Bucephalus at a prodigious age, the merchant's son, who admits to the shopkeeper that he cannot even ride (*MN*, 23), is killed by the animal. Further, while Alexander elevates Bucephalus to the status of an illustrious human being by giving him a state funeral and naming a city in his honor, Hofmannsthal reduces his protagonist to the level of a beast by describing his dying in a manner that recalls the previous description of the horse, in that both have expressions that expose tooth and gum and both have "evil" looks about them (*MN*, 30). Taken in conjunction, the figures of Bucephalus, who rises from untamable animal to honorary human, and of the merchant's son, who travels in the opposite direction, suggest a continuum, rather than a dichotomy, between man and beast. In this way, the merchant's son's initial vision of cosmic interconnectedness receives one final horrifying twist.

Finally, the motif of the wild horses points not only to Alexander's ancient empire but also to the contemporary realm of Viennese politics. Hofmannsthal's unbroken horses and hapless grooms represent a parodic version of the two heroic horse tamers who have stood guard outside the Austrian *Reichsrat* since 1883.[49] While these statues were intended to represent the repression of passion in the interest of parliamentary cooperation, in the context of the 1880s and 1890s they could equally stand for the patrician class's determination to quell the proletariat. However, Hofmannsthal reverses this schema by stressing the ultimate similarity between his patrician protagonist and the savage steed. Thus the author suggests that irrational passions govern the ruling elite as much as their proletarian adversaries. Moreover, as we have seen, in his final agony the merchant's son also recalls the alleged thief discovered in his father's shop and the suicidal servant girl. Thus Hofmannsthal's network of internal and extradiegetic allusions subvert the cherished dichotomies between master and servant, reason and passion, adult and child, and even human and animal that have informed the West's images of itself and the Other since the days of Alexander.

Given its monological form and its egocentric speaker, it seems difficult to imagine a similarly subversive rhetorical practice in the poem "Der Kaiser von China spricht." However, on closer inspection, the poem can be shown to undermine the speaker's grandiose pretensions and reveal his unreliability as a narrator in a manner that recalls Browning's verse monologues. The reader is therefore obliged to place due emphasis on the title of the poem and regard it as a subjective utterance from a highly partial source rather than as a statement of fact. In order to make references to the primary text easier to follow, I will provide the poem in full, followed by my own translation:

> In der Mitte aller Dinge
> Wohne Ich, der Sohn des Himmels.
> Meine Frauen, meine Bäume,
> Meine Tiere, meine Teiche
> 5 Schließt die erste Mauer ein.
> Drunten liegen meine Ahnen:
> Aufgebahrt mit ihren Waffen,
> Ihre Kronen auf den Häuptern,
> Wie es einem jeden ziemt,
> 10 Wohnen sie in den Gewölben.
> Bis ins Herz der Welt hinunter
> Dröhnt das Schreiten meiner Hoheit.
> Stumm von meinen Rasenbänken,
> Grünen Schemeln meiner Füße,
> 15 Gehen gleichgeteilte Ströme
> Osten-, west-, und süd- und nordwärts,
> Meine Gärten zu bewässern,
> Der die weite Erde ist.
> Spiegeln hier die dunkeln Augen,
> 20 Bunten Schwingen meiner Tiere,
> Spiegeln draußen bunte Städte,

Dunkle Mauern, dichte Wälder
Und Gesichter vieler Völker.
Meine Edlen, wie die Sterne,
25 Wohnen rings um mich, sie haben
Namen, die ich ihnen gab,
Namen nach der einen Stunde,
Da mir einer näher kam,
Frauen, die ich ihnen schenkte,
30 Und den Scharen ihrer Kinder,
Allen Edlen dieser Erde
Schuf ich Augen, Wuchs und Lippen,
Wie der Gärtner an den Blumen.
Aber zwischen äußern Mauern
35 Wohnen Völker meine Krieger
Völker meine Ackerbauer.
Neuen Mauern und dann wieder
Jene unterworf'nen Völker,
Völker immer dumpfern Blutes,
40 Bis ans Meer, die letzte Mauer,
Die mein Reich und mich umgibt.[50]

[In the middle of all things
I, the Son of Heaven, dwell.
My women, my trees,
My animals and my pond
5 Are enclosed by the first wall.
Below my ancestors lie
In state with their weapons,
Their crowns upon their heads,
As befits every one of them,
10 They dwell in the vaults.
Down into the heart of the earth
My majestic tread resounds.
Silently from my grassy banks,
My green footstools,
15 Flow the equally divided streams
North, south, east and west,
To irrigate my garden,
Which is the wide earth.
They reflect here my animals'
20 Dark eyes and motley wings
Outside they reflect the motley towns,
Dark walls, dense forests,
And the faces of many peoples.
My nobles, like the stars,

25 Live in my orbit, they have
   Names that I gave them
   In honor of the hour
   When they came into my presence,
   The women whom I bestowed on them,
30 And the hordes of children;
   For all the nobles in world
   I created eyes, stature, and lips,
   As the gardener does with his flowers.
   But between the outer walls
35 Dwell other peoples — my warriors,
   More peoples — my farmers,
   Followed by new walls and then again
   Those subjugated peoples,
   Peoples of ever more torpid blood,
40 On down to the sea, the last wall,
   Which surrounds my empire and me.]

The ambivalence that characterizes the rhetoric of this text extends even to its setting. Imperial China seems very far removed from Austria-Hungary, but as Weiyan Meng has demonstrated, nineteenth-century writers such as Ludwig Börne and Franz Grillparzer used China as a metaphor for the Habsburg Empire to satirize what they perceived as the despotism, dishonesty, backwardness, and torpor of Europe's "middle kingdom."[51] Hofmannsthal draws on this tradition, but for a different purpose: to express and explore the racial and cultural anxieties afflicting the German-speaking Viennese elite.

In this regard, Hofmannsthal's use of an oriental speaker has particular resonance. For as Ritchie Robertson explains, the word "oriental" was frequently applied to European Jewry and was a particularly contested term in the battle to define Jewish identity in the late nineteenth and early twentieth centuries:

> Some anti-Semites applied it to Jews in order to define them as unassimilably alien; some Jews, frustrated in their desire for assimilation, applied it to themselves in a spirit of self-contempt; and yet other Jews accepted the term but either changed its content or valued positively the implications that anti-Semites regarded negatively.[52]

Although Hofmannsthal was raised a Catholic and only had one Jewish grandparent, he remained acutely aware of his mixed ancestry.[53] In this way, just as the apparently exotic topos of "Das Märchen der 672. Nacht" reveals parallels with contemporary Vienna, so the emperor's China invokes the ethnic tensions, not only within Hofmannsthal's nation, but also within the author himself.

However, the opening of this poem does not participate in the contemporary ethnological discourse, but rather contributes to the critical empiricist philosophical debates that informed Hofmannsthal's *Märchen*. For this most egocentric of speakers places himself firmly at the epicenter of the universe in the very first line: "In der Mitte aller Dinge / Wohne Ich, der Sohn des Himmels" (In the middle of all things I, the Son of Heaven, dwell). Here the syntactic inversion performs the encapsulation of the subject "Ich" described in the sentence. However, it is the unusual capitalization of the word "ich" ("I") that invokes the realms of philosophy and psychology. For while the capital letter "I" denotes on the one hand the majestic status of the speaker, on the other it suggests the noun "das Ich" or the ego. Thus this bifurcated signifier elevates the speaker to a unique position of power, while simultaneously intimating that he is merely a fanciful metaphor for the self, a conceptual everyman. Throughout the poem Hofmannsthal preserves the tension between these variant readings to subvert his speaker's pretensions of omnipotence.

From his central position the emperor's vision of his domain radiates along horizontal and vertical axes. On the horizontal plane he enumerates the wives, trees, animals, and ponds surrounded by the first wall (lines 3–5). This paratactic list admits no hierarchy among animal, vegetable, mineral, or human, as if the emperor can conceive of no order in the universe other than his own dominating position. The inclusion of the emperor's wives in this list reifies and dehumanizes them in a manner that recalls the attitude of the merchant's son toward his servants. It is therefore fitting that the emperor should declare that he lives "at the center of all *things*," for he regards everything outside himself, including other people, as mere objects.

However, the reader might well ask why the emperor, given his assertions of omnipotence, should brook a wall, an impediment to his vision and a division in his empire (line 5). Lorna Martens makes the astute observation that the concentric walls come to resemble protective enclosures in the course of the poem.[54] Not surprisingly, the emperor is unwilling to dwell on the defensive function of the walls, and presents them instead as merely another natural phenomenon. Thus Hofmannsthal intimates from the outset the limitations of the emperor's power.

Looking up and down the vertical axis, we see more pronounced contradictions in the emperor's assertions. One moment he cites his divine lineage, declaring himself "the son of Heaven" (line 2), the next he gazes downward and describes the earthly ancestors who lie entombed beneath him (line 6). Here his desire to emphasize his ancestral right to rule undermines the divine pretensions of his title.[55] Furthermore, the weapons buried with the emperor's forefathers, which are presumably more than ceremonial, indicate that their power, and by extension, that of the current emperor, was not unassailable and had to be defended. Most importantly, the presence of the emperor's deceased ancestors inevitably invokes the speaker's own mortality. Nevertheless, the monarch's use of the verb "wohnen" to describe the corpses' present activity suggests that he is as yet unwilling to consider his own demise (line 10). By imbuing the emperor's discourse with such contradictions, Hofmannsthal hints at the monarch's repression of uncomfortable facts that threaten his egocentric worldview.

His subsequent claim that "Bis ins Herz der Welt hinunter / Dröhnt das Schreiten [s]einer Hoheit" (lines 11–12: Down into the heart of the earth / [His] majestic tread resounds) moves more violently up and down the vertical scale and contains another telling contradiction. First, the term "Herz der Welt" (heart of the earth) displaces the speaker from his self-ascribed position at the center of all things. Moreover, it is not some intrinsic quality in the emperor that supposedly makes his footsteps reverberate into the bowels of the earth, but rather a metaphorical attribute derived from his title, "Hoheit" (majesty). As with the phrase "Son of Heaven," Hofmannsthal suggests the emperor's confusion between titular and actual powers.

The poem then abandons its vertical axis in favor of the horizontal one. If the whole world belongs to the emperor, then the notion of exteriority no longer pertains. Thus the grass banks are likened to house furniture: "My green footstools" (line 14). However, the concepts of the interior and exterior are gradually reintroduced, first via his claim that the whole world is his garden (lines 17–18), which represents admittedly a very limited notion of exteriority, and then through his description of the "motley towns" that are somehow located "outside" (line 21). Given that the whole wide world is apparently the emperor's extended domestic space, where could this exterior exist? The inconsistencies in the emperor's spatial references highlight his difficulties in maintaining a truly solipsistic worldview.

In the next section the emperor's solipsism faces a more severe challenge. While the rivers that radiate north, south, east, and west in line 16 serve as conduits for his vision of the empire, the motif of reflection introduced in line 20 suggests that this grand overview is nothing more than a narcissistic projection. Like that other narcissist, the merchant's son, the monarch's vision of the cosmos admits no hierarchy or even differences between animals and humans, or between animate and inanimate objects.

> Spiegeln hier die dunkeln Augen,
> Bunten Schwingen meiner Tiere,
> Spiegeln draußen bunte Städte,
> Dunkle Mauern, dichte Wälder
> Und Gesichter vieler Völker. (lines 19–23)

[They reflect here my animals'
Dark eyes and motley wings
Outside they reflect the motley towns,
Dark walls, dense forests,
And the faces of many peoples.]

Here one would normally expect the reflexive form of the verb "spiegeln."
However, the truncated syntax of these lines deprives the "many peoples"
mentioned in line 23 of a fully reflective consciousness and thus suggests
that they are no more sentient than exotically plumed birds or dense forests. Furthermore, while the repeated adjectives "bunt" (brightly or mul-
ticolored, or motley) and "dunkel" (dark) appear antithetical, it seems
that the emperor regards the diversity represented by the various hues
as synonymous with obscurity. This becomes apparent when he is confronted with the "faces of many peoples" (line 23). Clearly, the Chinese
sovereign finds the notion of ethnic diversity deeply disturbing, for in the
next line he retreats swiftly to the comforting inner circle of nobility. The
poem therefore does not continually expand with the emperor' vision, but
rather pulsates, retreating to the center when confronted with an obstacle,
as when the emperor's gaze returns to the ancestors buried beneath his feet
on encountering the first wall (lines 5–6). More importantly, these lines
introduce the crucial concept of ethnic anxiety that comes to dominate the
poem by the time it reaches the periphery of the kingdom.

Before he reaches the outskirts of his domain, the emperor must reassert his authority. To achieve this, he again places himself at the center,
this time of a constellation of aristocrats: "My nobles, like the stars,/
Live in my orbit" (lines 24–25). Although the emperor clearly needs the
blue-blooded nobles to shield him against the ethnic diversity beyond, he
stresses the power he wields over them. Indeed, he claims that he not only
names them, but also creates their eyes, lips, and stature (lines 25–32).
On the one hand, these assertions recall the Judeo-Christian God of Genesis, who calls Creation into being by first naming its individual elements.
On the other, the emperor's suggestion that his nobles do not really exist
until he has met and named them recalls the old conundrum of whether
a tree really falls in the forest if no one is there to hear it. The emperor's
naive faith in his own subjective worldview reinforces the notion that he
is merely representative of the "Ich" or ego. Thus the sovereign comes to
epitomize the egocentrism associated with the philosophical concept of
the subject.

The emperor's claim that he can fashion his nobles' features certainly
undermines the customary dualism between subject and object in a manner reminiscent of the critical empiricist Ernst Mach. However, it seems
difficult to discern Mach's influence in this motif, given that his *Analyse der Empfindungen* (Analysis of Sensations) condemns solipsism as a

"monstrosity" even worse than an idealistic system.[56] Nevertheless, Mach stresses the influence of the subject's perceptions on the object perceived to such a great extent that his argument begins to slip back into solipsism. For example, Mach's observation that a gaming die becomes large when viewed close up or small when viewed at a distance, appears different to the right eye than to the left, and disappears altogether when the eyes are closed (7), endows us all with an ability to alter perceived objects that is similar to that claimed by the emperor. This slippage in Mach's argumentation is best illustrated by one of the author's own drawings: his monocular view of his study (15, fig. 1; see figure 1.1). Here we see, framed by the curves of the author's eyebrow, nose, and mustache, Mach's view of his foreshortened body and his surroundings. Thus the picture illustrates the limitations of the single subject's perspective. However, the right hand holding the pen in mid-air appears to be applying the finishing touches to the shading on the couch. This playfully self-referential gesture indicates that the artist is not merely reproducing the world but creating it. Moreover, as with Hofmannsthal's emperor, who claims to name and sculpt his noble subjects, this solipsism invokes the realm of the aesthetic in the self's "artistic" creation of the world.

However, the metaphor that Hofmannsthal's emperor employs to describe the creation of the nobles' features is curiously inappropriate: "Allen Edlen dieser Erde / Schuf ich Augen, Wuchs, und Lippen, / Wie der Gärtner an den Blumen" (For all the nobles in world / I created eyes, stature, and lips, / As the gardener does with his flowers (lines 31–33). A gardener cannot bring forth flowers with new shapes at will; the process is one of incremental change over generations. Moreover, such change can only be wrought through the interbreeding of different strains, but as the emperor's consternation at the "many peoples" indicates, the notions of diversity and hybridization are anathema to him. In the final section the emperor's preoccupation with ethnicity is demonstrated by the fact that the word "Völker" (peoples) is repeated four times in eight lines. Furthermore, the fact that the emperor retrospectively mentions his connection to these various peoples, as in the phrases "Völker meine Krieger, / Völker meine Ackerbauer" (Peoples — my warriors, / Peoples — my farmers; lines 35–36), suggests that his control of these groups is somewhat attenuated. The next sentence signals this loss of control syntactically through the absence of a main clause (lines 37–41). Here the reference to "jene unterworf'nen Völker" (those subjugated peoples) explains the need for the warrior peoples mentioned in line 36: that is, to conquer the rebellious tribes at the edge of the kingdom. More importantly, the emperor invokes his own ethnological theory to account for these peoples' previous resistance to his rule: they are "Völker immer dumpfern Blutes" (line 39; Peoples of ever more torpid blood). In this way the sovereign reinscribes his position at the center, but this time as the embodiment of

Fig. 1.1. Mach's monocular perspective.
Note the right hand completing the picture.

a racial purity that becomes more attenuated the more one moves to the periphery of his empire. Crucially, the emperor is unable to conceive of this phenomenon as anything but a progressive stultification of his own racial vitality; the notion of ethnic plurality, in which diverse groups assert their own identity from various "centers," does not appear to even cross his mind.

The final wall, the sea, suggests the ultimate dilution of the emperor's blood. At this moment the expansive movement that has characterized the poem collapses in on itself, retreating behind the concentric walls to the individual "mich" (me) of the emperor, who is no longer a sovereign subject, but rather a subjugated object.

But where does this motif of concentric walls come from? Hofmannsthal cannot be referring to the Great Wall of China in his topography,
since that is a single, linear fortification. On the contrary, the concentric walls of this poem invoke another imperial construction project much
closer to home: the Viennese *Ringstrasse* development, begun in 1857.
As Carl Schorske explains, while this project opened up the city to cir-
cular traffic through its concentric boulevards, the lack of a radial system effectively encircled the old city in the center (32–33). This apparent
anomaly can be explained by the perceived need to protect the emperor
Franz Josef at the center from the unruly proletariat in the suburbs. To
quell the potential threat from these revolutionary suburbanites, an arsenal complex and two barracks were constructed (30). On the other hand,
this project, which was inaugurated by imperial decree, saw the extension of the emperor's influence through the building of the *Votivkirche*
(1856–79), "a monument of patriotism and of the devotion of the people to the Imperial House"[57] that celebrated Franz Josef's safe delivery
from an assassination attempt, and through the construction of public
cultural institutes that bore the stamp of the Imperial Court: "the *Hof*-
burgtheater, the *Hof*oper," and the "*Hof*museen."[58] Thus the concentric
walls of Hofmannsthal's poem, which fulfill a dialectic of constriction and
expansion in the face of a threat from the periphery, correspond to the
extradiegetic reality of the *Ringstrasse*. Moreover, as we can see from a
leaflet announcing the development (see figure 1.2), the *Ringstrasse* was
conceived as an aesthetic as well as a civic project. On the left, above the
legend "Geschmückt durch Kunst" (Adorned through Art), the personi-
fication of Art engirds her mistress Vienna, while on the right, Law and
Peace ensure the continued strength of the empire. The emphasis that
the Viennese authorities place on the decorative, as opposed to defensive,
aspects of the project recall Hofmannsthal's emperor, who, until the end
of the poem, does not present the walls as guard posts, but rather as so
many garlands casually strewn about his empire. Moreover, this depiction of the *Ringstrasse* represents the antithesis of the necklace that the
merchant's son envisages buying for the servant girl, which is "vielfach
herumgeschlungen . . . und . . . an einen Panzer gemahnend" (wound
around many times . . . and . . . reminiscent of armor; 23). For while
that decorative jewel reveals defensive, martial attributes, the Viennese
development presents itself not as an encircling fortification of established
power but as an aesthetic adornment to the city.

Nevertheless, the disquiet that Hofmannsthal's emperor feels when
confronted with the ethnic diversity of his realm indicates the walls' defensive function. The Chinese sovereign's racial anxiety mirrors the alarm of
the German-speaking elite in Vienna, who in the 1880s and 1890s faced
an influx of Hungarians, Czechs, Poles, Serbs, *Ostjuden* (Eastern European Jews), and so on. This fear could reach apocalyptic proportions,

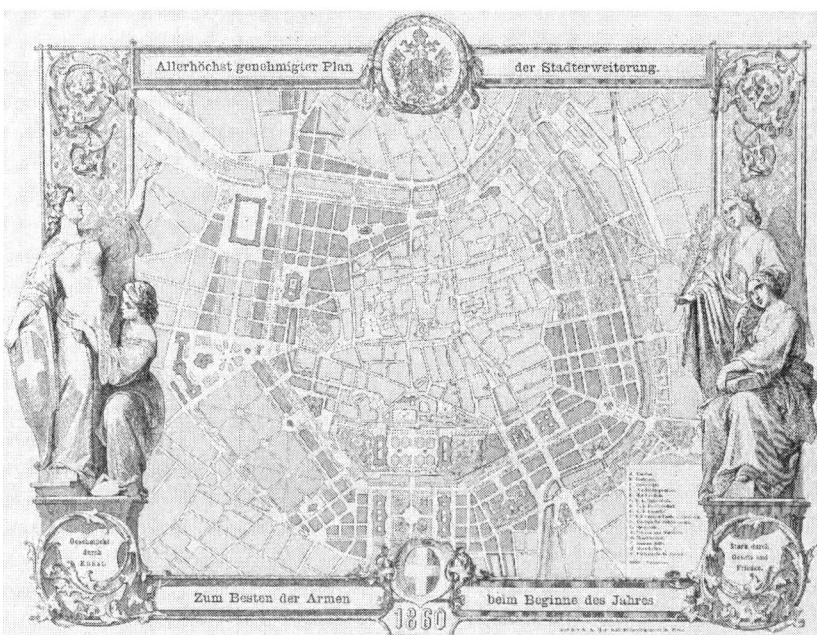

Fig. 1.2. Leaflet proclaiming the Ringstrasse development. Note the figure of Art on the left engirding the city. Reproduced with kind permission of the Wien Museum.

as demonstrated by Hofmannsthal's own diary entry for 13 May 1894. Here he describes walking with his friend Richard Beer-Hoffmann toward the Tivoli pleasure gardens amid a throng of drunks and craftsmen and little, poor people, when he is struck by the following thought:

> Wie merkwürdig auch das wieder ist, daß wir vielleicht in Wien die letzten denkenden, die letzten ganzen, beseelten Menschen sind, daß dann vielleicht eine große Barbarei kommt, eine slavisch-jüdische, sinnliche Welt. Das zerstörte Wien zu denken: alle Mauern verfallen, der innere Leib der Stadt bloßgelegt, die Wunden mit unendlichem Schlingkraut übersponnen, überall lichtgrüne Baumwipfel, Stille, plätscherndes Wasser, alles Leben tot; welch wundervolle Fern- und Durchsichten! Und Wächter zu sein in einem der Trajanstürme vor der Karlskirche, der noch aufrecht steht und mit Gedanken, die keiner mehr versteht, zwischen den Ruinen herumzugehen.[59]

> [How remarkable it is again that in Vienna we may be the last thinking, whole, and inspired people, that afterward there may be a great barbarism, a Slavic-Jewish, sensual world. To think of Vienna destroyed: all the walls collapsed, the inner body of the city exposed, the wounds covered over with endless tangles of creepers, everywhere

the light-green crowns of trees, silence, the plash of water, all life dead. But what wonderful vistas — into the distance and into the interior! And to stand guard in one of the columns of Trajan in front of St. Charles's Church, which still stands erect, and to wander among the ruins with thoughts that no one understands any more.]

It is fitting that Hofmannsthal should experience this vision at Whitsuntide, given that he considers himself a disciple of aestheticism who has received the holy spirit of Viennese culture. This outburst seems particularly intemperate, given that the proletarian crowd taking a Sunday stroll to a pleasure garden hardly fulfills the traditional image of the barbarians at the city gates. Indeed, this passage does not correspond to actual circumstances but rather provides, in an apparently unwitting fashion, a palimpsest of the projected fears haunting the Viennese elite in the areas of class, race, and culture. Thus Hofmannsthal's initial disquiet at the proletarians' proximity gives way to a vision of "eine große Barbarei, eine slavisch-jüdische, sinnliche Welt," (a great barbarism, a Slavic-Jewish, sensual world) which will result in the destruction of Viennese civilization. Here the dichotomy that Hofmannsthal attempts to establish between the Slavic-Jewish "sensual world" and the German-Austrian realm of the spirit is undermined by his own rhetoric, which revels in the material and sensory destruction of the city itself. Indeed, his description of "the inner body of the city exposed" incarnates the Habsburg capital, so that the "Slavic-Jewish" invasion appears akin to rape. However, what is most striking about this passage is the alacrity with which Hofmannsthal embraces this catastrophe. Unlike the Chinese emperor, whose gaze traverses his walls to encompass his empire, all the walls of Vienna must fall to afford Hofmannsthal panoramic and penetrating perspectives ("wundervolle Fern- und Durchsichten.") The overall impression is of an egocentric adolescent who envisages, to borrow Hermann Broch's phrase, "a joyful apocalypse"[60] that will confirm his innate sense of cultural superiority.

However, it would of course be misguided to characterize Hofmannsthal as simply a racist reactionary, whose vision of Slavic-Jewish "barbarism" represents an attempt to repress his own Jewish heritage. Indeed, less than a year before the diary entry above, at the end of June 1893, Hofmannsthal muses on the possibility that his Jewish blood acts as the "grit" in the oyster shell of his personality, provoking development through reaction and counter-reaction: "Wenn meine ganzen inneren Entwicklungen und Kämpfe nichts wären als Unruhen des ererbten Blutes, Aufstände der jüdischen Blutstropfen (Reflexion) gegen die germanischen und romanischen, und Reaktionen gegen diese Aufstände" (If all my inner developments and struggles were nothing more than the disturbances of my inherited blood, uprisings of the Jewish drops of blood (reflection) against Germanic and Romance ones, and counter-reactions against these uprisings).[61]

Hofmannsthal's hypothesis represents the antithesis of the procedure outlined by Carl Schorske in his analysis of Freud.[62] For according to Schorske, Freud subsumes the ethnic and political discord of his time under psychological categories, while Hofmannsthal employs the vocabulary of civil unrest ("disturbances . . . uprisings") to describe his internal, psychological conflict. Moreover, although the quotation from 1894 associates Jews with mindlessness, materialism, and depraved sexuality, here Hofmannsthal links them with an over-developed capacity for reflection that is inimical to the healthy, vital spontaneity of his Germanic and Italian blood. To complicate matters further, this association of the Jews with a capacity for rational reflection is derived from Richard Wagner's anti-Semitic essay "Das Judentum in der Musik" ("Judaism in Music," 1850).[63] Thus Hofmannsthal's image of the Jew, which was by no means peculiar to the author but rather endemic to the culture, displays the radical ambivalence that Homi Bhaba deems essential to the stereotype.

Hofmannsthal's reflections on his Jewish heritage complicate our reading of "Der Kaiser von China spricht." In the figure of the Chinese emperor, Hofmannsthal reverses the Eurocentric paradigm by depicting an oriental figure who asserts his racial purity. Indeed, if we consider the contemporary application of the term "oriental" to European Jewry, then we must conclude that Hofmannsthal's rather meager share of "oriental" blood would relegate him to the periphery of his imaginary China. However, if we accept the convention that China stands for the Habsburg Empire, then the Chinese emperor's concern with racial purity reflects the ethnic and cultural anxieties of the German-speaking elite. In this way Hofmannsthal's poem maintains a perfect equilibrium of ambivalence, encompassing contradictory readings.

In conclusion, "Das Märchen der 672. Nacht" and "Der Kaiser von China spricht" demonstrate the inadequacy of Said's notion of orientalism when applied to Austrian orientalist texts of the *fin-de-siècle*. For in these texts Hofmannsthal mobilizes the tropes and the topoi of the orientalist discourse, such as the *Arabian Nights* or Chinese autocracy, not in order to subjugate the oriental Other, but rather to investigate his own culture. But what is the status of these motifs, given the texts in which they appear? Certainly Hofmannsthal is not remotely interested in probing the "real" Arabia or China but rather erects these exotic facades in order to veil his critique of the Habsburg Empire in a discreet ambivalence. However, by employing orientalist clichés to address domestic concerns, Hofmannsthal's tale and poem emerge as peculiarly honest orientalist fictions: works that tacitly acknowledge that their images of the Other are hollow husks, the repositories of Western fantasy rather than Eastern reality.

Notes

[1] Alexander insisted that King Darius of Persia address him by this title following Alexander's defeat of the Persian ruler at the battle of Issos. See Guy Maclean Rogers, *Alexander: The Ambiguity of Greatness* (New York: Random House, 2004), 79. However, Alexander had earlier symbolically earned the right to rule Asia by dint of untying the Gordian knot (*Alexander*, 63).

[2] For a detailed account of Mach and Brentano's theories see Judith Ryan, *The Vanishing Subject: Early Psychology and Literary Modernism*, 6–22.

[3] Ernst Mach, *Analyse der Empfindungen* (Jena: Verlag von Gustav Fischer, 1885), 8, n 1. (Mach's emphasis.)

[4] Richard Alewyn, *Hofmannsthals Wandlung* (Frankfurt am Main: Klostermann, 1949), 170.

[5] Jens Rieckmann, "Von der menschlichen Unzulänglichkeit: Zu Hofmannsthals *Das Märchen der 672. Nacht*," *German Quarterly* 54.3 (1981): 302.

[6] Rieckmann, "Von der menschlichen Unzulänglichkeit," 309.

[7] Dorrit Cohn, "'Als Traum erzählt': The Case for a Freudian Reading of Hofmannsthal's 'Märchen der 672. Nacht,'" *Deutsche Vierteljahrsschrift für Literaturwissenschaft und Geistesgeschichte* 54 (1980): 284–305.

[8] Cohn, "Als Traum erzählt," 282.

[9] Nina Berman, "Hugo von Hofmannsthal: *Das Märchen der 672. Nacht*," in *Orientalismus, Kolonialismus und Moderne: Zum Bild des Orients in der deutschsprachigen Literatur um 1900* (Stuttgart: M & P, Verlag für Wissenschaft & Forschung, 1996), 165–269.

[10] Waltraud Wiethölter, *Hofmannsthal oder die Geometrie des Subjekts: Psychostrukturelle und ikonographische Studien zum Prosawerk* (Tübingen: Niemeyer Verlag, 1990), 6 and 18.

[11] Ingrid Haag, "Kryptogramme der Liebesangst: Zu Hofmannsthals *Märchen der 672. Nacht* und zu seinem *Andreas*-Fragment," *Cahiers d'Études Germaniques* 50 (2006): 132.

[12] Imke Meyer, "The Insider as Outsider: Representations of the Bourgeoisie in *Fin-de-Siècle* Vienna," *Pacific Coast Philology* 44.1 (2009): 7.

[13] Edward Said, *Orientalism*, 21. Said quotes Marx from *The Eighteenth Brumaire of Louis Bonaparte*.

[14] Cf. Maclean Rogers, *Alexander*, 79.

[15] For the Turkish provenance of the protagonist's favorite mottoes, see Hans-Jürgen Schings, "Allegorie des Lebens: Zum Formproblem von Hofmannsthals 'Märchen der 672. Nacht,'" *Zeitschrift für Deutsche Philologie* 86 (1967): 534, n. 15; and Lawrence O. Frye, "'Das Märchen der 672. Nacht' von Hofmannsthal: Todesgang als Kunstmärchen und Kunstkritik," *Zeitschrift für Deutsche Philologie* 108.4 (1989): 530.

[16] Waltraud Wiethölter insists most forcefully on the identity of the protagonist and the author (*Hofmannsthal oder die Geometrie des Subjekts*, 49).

[17] Carl E. Schorske, *Fin-de-siècle Vienna: Politics and Culture* (New York: Vintage, 1981), 10.

[18] Rudyard Kipling, "The White Man's Burden," in *Rudyard Kipling*, ed. Daniel Karlin, The Oxford Authors (Oxford: Oxford UP, 1999), 479–80.

[19] Homi K. Bhabha, *The Location of Culture* (London: Routledge, 1994), 82.

[20] Bhahba, *The Location of Culture*, 70.

[21] For a more detailed discussion of the optical interplay between the gaze of the merchant's son and those of his servants, see Waltraud Wiethölter, "Augen-Blicke: Das Märchen der 672. Nacht," in *Hofmannsthal oder die Geometrie des Subjekts*, 23–46. Wiethölter makes the point that the servants' gazes reflect back the protagonist's own desires, but ascribes this process to a spectral breaking of the Narcissistic spell rather than to simple projection (37).

[22] Cf. Frye, "'Das Märchen der 672. Nacht' von Hofmannsthal," 536.

[23] Cf. George M. Williams, *Handbook of Hindu Mythology* (Santa Barbara, CA: ABC-CLIO, 2003), 174.

[24] See Lynn Foulston and Stuart Abbott, *Hindu Goddesses: Beliefs and Practices* (Portland, OR: Sussex Academic, 2009), 37. Although Hofmannsthal's references to three eyes and "uncanny jewelry" are strongly suggestive of Kali, the mouthful of serpents may represent the author's embellishment of, or confusion about, Kali's customarily protruding tongue (Foulston and Abbott, *Hindu Goddesses*, 37).

[25] The goddess Kali is associated with the symbolic castration of her human sacrifices. See Williams, *Handbook of Hindu Mythology*, 174.

[26] For a fuller refutation of the view that the two parts of the text are distinct and contrasting, see Andrew W. Barker, "The Triumph of Life in Hofmannsthal's 'Das Märchen der 672. Nacht,'" *Modern Language Review* 74 (1979): 342–44.

[27] Hugo von Hofmannsthal, "Gabriele D'Annunzio," in *Gesammelte Werke in zehn Einzelbänden*, vol. 8, *Reden und Aufsätze I, 1891–1913* (Frankfurt am Main: Fischer Verlag. 1979), 174.

[28] Hofmannsthal, "Gabriele D'Annunzio," 174.

[29] Rieckmann, "Von der menschlichen Unzulänglichkeit," 302.

[30] Berman, *Orientalismus, Kolonialismus und Moderne*, 189.

[31] Cf. Hofmannsthal's first draft of the tale, *MN*, 203.

[32] See Wiethölter, *Hofmannsthal oder die Geometrie des Subjekts*, 49, and Haag, "Kryptogramme der Liebesangst, 127.

[33] Hugo von Hofmannsthal, "Tausendundeine Nacht" in *Gesammelte Werke in Einzelausgaben, Prosa 2*, ed. Herbert Steiner (Frankfurt am Main: S. Fischer Verlag, 1951), 311.

[34] Cf. Hofmannsthal, *MN*, 201.

[35] Hugo von Hofmannsthal, "Tausendundeine Nacht," 319 and 320.

[36] Hofmannsthal, "Tausendundeine Nacht," 314.

[37] Schorske, *Fin-de-siècle Vienna*, 30.

[38] Schorske, *Fin-de-siècle Vienna*, 47.

[39] Allan Janik and Stephen Toulmin, *Wittgenstein's Vienna* (New York: Simon & Schuster, 1973), 51.

[40] See Mark Anderson, *Kafka's Clothes: Ornament and Aestheticism in the Habsburg Fin de Siècle*, 1992).

[41] I have taken the liberty of slightly amending Michael Henry Heim's translation of this passage.

[42] Mach, *Analyse der Empfindungen*, 24, n. 1.

[43] Sigmund Freud, *Totem und Tabu*, in *Gesammelte Werke*, vol. 9, ed. Anna Freud, Edward Bibring, and Ernst Kris (Frankfurt am Main; S. Fischer Verlag, 1973), 93–121.

[44] Frye also notes the parallels between the greenhouse and the forest (542), and between the loaves and "the wonderful spoils of life" (545).

[45] Maclean Rogers, *Alexander*, 251–53.

[46] Maclean Rogers, *Alexander*, 226.

[47] Cf. Pseudo-Callisthenes, *The Romance of Alexander the Great*, trans. Albert Mugrdich Wolohojian (New York: Columbia UP, 1969), 38.

[48] Maclean Rogers, *Alexander*, 201.

[49] Schorske notes that because of a lack of any indigenous political symbols the Austrian parliament was obliged to borrow these figures from Rome's Capitol Hill (*Fin-de-siècle Vienna*, 43).

[50] All references to the poem are to Hugo von Hofmannsthal, "Der Kaiser von China spricht," in *Sämtliche Werke: Kritische Ausgabe, Gedichte I*, ed. Eugene Weber (Frankfurt am Main: S. Fischer Verlag, 1984), 72–73. This edition will henceforth be cited in the text.

[51] Weiyan Meng, *Kafka und China*, 17.

[52] Ritchie Robertson, "'Urheimat Asien': The Re-Orientation of German and Austrian Jews, 1900–1925," *German Life and Letters* 49.2 (1996): 182.

[53] For a more detailed account of Hofmannsthal's attitudes toward his Jewish heritage over the years, see Jens Rieckmann's perceptive and judicious article "Zwischen Bewußtsein und Verdrängung: Hofmannsthals jüdisches Erbe," *Deutsche Vierteljahrsschrift für Literaturwissenschaft und Geistesgeschichte* 67.3 (1993): 466–83.

[54] Lorna Martens, *Shadow Lines: Austrian Literature from Freud to Kafka* (Lincoln: U of Nebraska P, 1996), 118.

[55] The notion of the emperor's divinity is subverted further by the knowledge that the poem in which he appears was originally the first monologue in the puppet play *Das Kleine Welttheater* (The Little World Theater). The phrase "Sohn des Himmels" (son of heaven) thus suggests the parental puppeteer, pulling his strings from above. See Hofmannsthal, *Sämtliche Werke, Gedichte I*, 324.

[56] Ernst Mach, *Analyse der Empfindungen*, 28.

[57] Quoted in Schorske, *Fin-de-siècle Vienna*, 30.

[58] Schorske, *Fin-de-siècle Vienna*, 38.

[59] Hugo von Hofmannsthal, *Reden und Aufsätze III: Buch der Freunde; Aufzeich-nungen, 1889–1929*, in *Gesammelte Werke in zehn Einzelbänden*, ed. Bend Schoeller (Frankfurt am Main: S. Fischer Verlag, 1980), 383. Quoted in excerpted form in Rieckmann, "Zwischen Bewußtsein und Verdrängung," 477–78.

[60] Hermann Broch, *Hofmannsthal und seine Zeit*, ed. Paul Michael Lützeler (Frankfurt am Main: Suhrkamp, 2001), 46.

[61] Hugo von Hofmannsthal, Diaries and Notebooks, Houghton Library 147.11.3. Quoted in Rieckmann, "Zwischen Bewußtsein und Verdrängung," 466.

[62] Schorske, "Politics and Patricide in Freud's *Interpretation of Dreams*," in *Fin-de-siècle Vienna: Politics and Culture*, 181–207.

[63] Cf. Bernd Witte, "Dichtung aus dem Geiste des Judentums: Hugo von Hof-mannsthals Traum von Asien," *Links* 5 (2005): 64.

2: Empirical Mysticism and Imperial Mystique: Orientalism in Musil's *Die Verwirrungen des Zöglings Törleß*

"E INE KLEINE STATION AN DER STRECKE, welche nach Rußland führt" (*T*, 7; It was a small station on the long railroad to Russia, *YT*, 1). The first sentence of Robert Musil's first novel, *Die Verwirrungen des Zöglings Törleß* (translated as *Young Törless*, but literally The Confusions of the Boarding Student Törless*, 1906), opens up a vista to the East, which, although literally unexplored within the diegesis, nevertheless suggests a thematic trajectory for the work and for the following reading of it. In the early twentieth century German-speaking Central Europe often consigned Russia to Asia rather than Europe, and thereby to what it often perceived as oriental barbarism rather than occidental civilization.[1] However, Musil's opening motif of the track that traverses several borders on its way to Russia creates a continuum between East and West that undermines this traditional orientalist dichotomy. Although this eastern route represents the railroad less traveled by critics,[2] it is my thesis that orientalist preconceptions, whether evident in the attitudes of the schoolboy protagonist and his classmates toward the local "Eastern" Slavs, or in the supposedly Indian philosophy espoused by his peer Beineberg, are of vital significance to the novel as a whole. In this chapter I will demonstrate that by applying a postcolonial reading to the orientalist motifs, associations, and discourses portrayed in the novel we can begin to understand the global ramifications of one Austrian adolescent's internal confusion.

In drawing upon postcolonial theory, I am not applying a remote and disparate discourse to the text, but rather merely responding to the paracolonial imagery and rhetoric employed by the novel itself in its depictions of the German-speaking Törleß's response to the local Czech population. Although the novel is set in Moravia, a province adjacent to Lower Austria and Vienna, the protagonist views the local inhabitants as profoundly exotic and alien. In this, Törleß is typical of both his ethnicity and class, for despite the peculiar proximity between the Austro-Germans and the various Others of the Habsburg Empire, the ruling elite frequently resorted to exotic imagery in its depictions of its "subject peoples." As Moritz Csáky explains, this daily contact with different ethnicities and cultures in the empire's cities led to a compensatory desire to exaggerate the distinction between the Self and Other:

Um die vermeintliche eigene Identität immer wieder neu zu begründen und zu festigen, versuchte man folglich dieser Fremdheiten
zu vergewissern, was nichts anderes bedeutete, als daß man solche
Fremdheiten zuweilen künstlich hochzuspielen, zu konstruieren
oder zu "erfinden" begann, um sich dann ihrer zu entledigen.³

[In order to again and again justify and consolidate their own putative
identity anew, they consequently tried to make certain of these strange
or foreign aspects [of the Other], which meant nothing other than
that at times they began to inflate artificially, fabricate, or "invent"
such strange aspects, in order to then rid themselves of them.]

As we shall see, Robert Musil's *Die Verwirrungen des Zöglings Törleß*
invokes such heightened images of alterity in depicting the response of the
protagonist, an Austrian schoolboy, to the local Czech women. In so doing
it creates an associative link between the internal imperial relationship with
a very proximate Other, that is Czech women from what Robert Luft terms
the "Kernlandschaften" or "core territories" of Bohemia and Moravia,⁴ and
global overseas colonialism. Thus the imaginative terms of reference found
in the novel demand a reading informed by postcolonial theory.

In depictions of relationships that pair German Austrian men with
women from the so-called "subject peoples," critics perceive a conflu-
ence of mutually reinforcing hierarchies based on gender and ethnicity.⁵
However, such an approach tends to overlook the peculiar ambivalence
generated by works of fiction, as opposed to, for example, historical or
anthropological texts. A work such as Musil's novel presents images of
eastern exoticism as part of the imaginative process through which its
Austrian protagonist attempts to assimilate the alterity represented by the
ethnic and cultural Other to their own self-identity. By depicting this process of identity formation in a character who displays a tenuous sense of
self, this text eschews simple declarations of cultural hegemony in favor of
a more nuanced, multivalent, and ironic approach that provides opportunities not only for self-reflection but also for self-critique. This chapter will examine the subversive implications of these connections between
the internal colonialism of Austria-Hungary,⁶ global imperialism, and the
protagonist's internal development.

Musil's first novel might seem an odd choice for an exploration of the
link between Austrian self-identity and global visions of the exotic. After
all, the text is not set in some far-flung outpost of the empire but rather
in Moravia, a region bordering Lower Austria and Vienna, and most of
the action takes place in the cloistered realm of a boys' boarding school
for the Germanophone elite. However, visions of the exotic East play a
vital role in suggesting the broader significance of the eponymous hero's
confusion for both the Habsburg Empire and the wider world. To begin,
I will focus on the relationship between the Austrian schoolboys and the

local Czech women, including the prostitute Božena. I will then con-sider the supposedly Indian philosophy espoused by Törleß's schoolmate Beineberg, and its implications for the Western philosophical tradition. In this way I will explore the role of exoticist and orientalist motifs in connecting the ostensibly circumscribed plot — Törleß's involvement in the torture of his classmate Basini and his subsequent ethical and episte-mological crises — to a broad critique of both contemporary Habsburg society and the Western Enlightenment tradition.

This notion of self-critique is at variance with previous readings that address the inter-ethnic encounters in *Törleß*. J. P. Stern and Ritchie Robertson both conclude that the novel supports the hegemony of the Austro-German elite over the native Czech population. In his essay "The Education of the Master Race," Stern explores the novel's political con-text, arguing that the work represents one of a series expressing "the theme of German superiority and the Slav-German conflict" (80) and as such heralds the *Drang nach Osten* (eastward expansion) of the Third Reich and the concentration camps at Treblinka and Auschwitz (79–80). Quoting Stern's views with approval, Robertson situates the text within a broad history of German literary representations of Slavs, a history that shows the persistence of the antinomies intellect and nature, man and woman, German and Slavs.[7] Charles N. Genno also trades in well-worn dualities when he discerns in the text "the same East-West polarity found in the works of Mann, Hesse and other neo-Romantic writers concerned with the problem of nurturing the rational image of the world from irra-tional source" (271). Genno thus accepts uncritically the cliché that the West embodies rationality and the East irrationality, without considering that this opposition, along with the very notion of a dichotomy, is itself a product of orientalist thinking. Indeed, he even claims that "the debili-tating effect . . . of the Slavic atmosphere, with its mystical and decadent undercurrents" is the source of Törleß's involvement in the persecution and torture of Basini (271). However, my analysis will show how the novel probes rather than promotes both the notion of Austro-German supremacy and the assumption that the West stands for a healthy rational-ity and the East for its antithesis. Far from offering proto-Nazi sentiments and orientalist stereotypes, the novel in fact undermines pretensions to cultural superiority by delving into the psychosexual mechanisms of fan-tasy and repression behind Törleß's response to alterity.

These fantasies of alterity are apparent from the beginning of the text. Frau Hofrat von Törleß's anxiety at having to leave her son in "so ferner, unwirtlicher Fremde" (*T*, 8; this remote and inhospitable outlandish district, *YT*, 2) seems disproportionate, if we accept the Moravian town of Mährisch-Weisskirchen (now Hranice in the Czech Republic) as Musil's autobiographical inspiration for the fictional W.[8] First, even the narrator's claim that the area lies in the east of the empire

(8) seems exaggerated in view of Moravia's proximity to Lower Austria and Vienna. Further, given that Moravia had been allied with Austria since the Middle Ages, Frau Törleß's view of the region as exotic and peripheral shows the power of cultural stereotypes to overturn historical reality. More important, this passage reveals the paradoxes of Austro-German imperialism. For while the Viennese elite rejects the integral territories of the Bohemian Crown as irredeemably foreign, that very perception enables them to partake vicariously in the colonial experience denied by their lack of overseas possessions.

To understand this contested area, it is useful to refer to Mary Louise Pratt's notion of a "contact zone" as "the space of colonial encounters" between peoples, who "establish ongoing relations, usually involving conditions of coercion, radical inequality and intractable conflict."[9] This description applies to the space in which the German-speaking schoolboys encounter the local women, as demonstrated in the following confrontation:

> Waren sie [the Czech women] jung und drall, so flog ihnen manches derbe slawische Scherzwort zu. Sie stießen sich an und kicherten über die "jungen Herren"; manchmal schrie eine auf, wenn im Vor-übergehen allzu hart ihre Brüste gerstreift wurden, oder erwiderte mit einem lachenden Schimpfwort einen Schlag auf die Schenkel. Manche sah auch bloß mit zornigem Ernste hinter den Eilenden drein; und der Bauer lächelte verlegen, — halb unsicher, halb gut-mütig, — wenn er zufällig gekommen war. (*T*, 17)

> [If they [the Czech women] were young and buxom, some crude Slav jest would be flung at them, They would nudge each other and titter at "the young gentlemen"; sometimes, too, one would utter a shriek when her breasts were too vigorously brushed against in passing, or would answer a slap on the [thighs] with an insulting epithet and a burst of laughter. There were others who merely watched the swift passers-by with a grave and angry look; and the peasant himself, if he happened to have come on the scene, would smile awkwardly, half unsure what to make of it, half in good humour. (*YT*, 15–16)][10]

This scene depicts a literal "contact zone," in which the schoolboys' sexual harassment of the local women has become a regular ritual. The implication that this is a frequent occurrence that simply must be endured is only one of the strategies used by the narrator to condone their behavior. The passage partially absolves the boys of culpability by claiming that it is the youth and sturdy physique of the women that attract the pupils' coarse comments and by using the passive voice without an agent in the second sentence. Moreover, the formulation "wenn im Vorübergehen *allzu hart* ihre Brüste gestreift wurden" (*T*, 17, my italics; when her breasts were *too vigorously* brushed against in passing: *YT*, 15) intimates that there is an acceptably gentle manner in which such an assault might be committed. The narrator's tone suggests that the right to commit this casual sexual abuse represents one of the privileges granted to a ruling elite at the top of the ethnic, social, and sexual hierarchies.

However, by applying what Edward Said terms a "contrapuntal reading," that is, one that takes into account the historical processes of both imperialism and the resistance it engenders,[11] we can restore some agency to Musil's Moravians and uncover suggestions of counter-hegemonic tendencies among this group. Certainly, the local women do not all acquiesce passively to the boys' assault. In fact, their responses run the gamut from good-humored badinage through silent, indignant rage to yelling and swearing. The women's varied reactions and their menfolk's confusion arise from the liminal status of the "young gentlemen," For although the pupils enjoy privilege and power, their immaturity belies their sexual menace. In addition, the linguistic confusion of this scene undercuts any sense of absolute cultural domination. While the boys address the women with crude jokes in Czech, some of the women respond by making giggling references to "die jungen Herren" (young gentlemen) in German. This exchange of languages is significant in a region that in 1897 saw massive demonstrations by German speakers against minister-president Badeni's decision to grant Czech equal status with German as an official language.[12] The language of the boys and women's speech thus intimates a more liminal, hybrid space between the two cultures than the content of their addresses would at first suggest.

When considering Törleß's personal reaction to the Slavs, the text begins to explore in detail the fantasies that the Self projects onto the Other in the process of identity formation. In contrast to the nonchalant boorishness of his peers, Törleß experiences an intense, erotic reverie when he encounters the local people. Through narrow "Torwege" (doorways) he spies the following scene:

> Fast nackte Kinder wälzten sich in dem Kot der Höfe, da und dort gab der Rock eines arbeitenden Weibes die Kniekehlen frei oder drückte sich eine schwere Brust straff in die Falten der Leinwand. Und als ob dies sogar unter einer anderen tierischen, drückenden Atmosphäre sich abspielte, floß aus dem Flur der Häuser eine träge, schwere Luft, die Törleß begierig einatmete. (*T*, 17)

> [Almost naked children tumbled around in the mud of the yards: here and there as some woman bent over her work her skirt swung high, revealing the hollows at the back of her knees, or the bulge of a heavy breast showed as the linen tightened over it. It was as though all this were going on in some quite different, animal, oppressive atmosphere, and the cottages exuded a heavy, sluggish air which Törless eagerly breathed in. (*YT*, 16)]

Here Törleß fulfills the role of the colonial voyeur who is captivated by the scantily clad natives and the sultry, savage atmosphere of his surroundings. However, the reference to narrow doorways prior to this passage reminds us that the protagonist is called Tör*leß* and therefore by dint of his descriptive name will always lack a doorway to gain physical access to the scene.[13] Rather, the courtyard acts as the site of projection for his desire. The expression "als ob all dies sogar unter einer ganz anderen tierischen, drückenden Atmosphäre abspielte" (as though all this were going on in some quite different, animal, oppressive atmosphere) suggests through the subjunctive voice and the adverb "sogar" the disparity between reality and Törleß's fantasy. Finally, the adverb "begierig," used to describe the protagonist's heaving breathing and perhaps better rendered as "hungrily," confirms that this fantasy arises from his own desire, rather than from any qualities intrinsic to the oblivious Moravians.

Törleß's reaction to the villagers recalls the "monarch-of-all-I-survey" attitude that Mary Louise Pratt ascribes to the visually acquisitive colonialist. He aestheticizes the scene and endows it with extra meaning in the manner described by Pratt (204), even connecting it with paintings by old masters in museums (*T*, 17). For Pratt, such a pictorial attitude toward reality betokens a stable relationship between subject and object in which the "scene is deictically ordered with reference to his [the viewer's] vantage point, and is static" (205) as befits a "relation of *mastery* predicated between the seer and the seen" (205, original italics). However, instead of consuming the scene, Törleß wishes it would consume him:

> Er wartete auf irgend etwas, so wie er vor diesen Bildern immer auf etwas gewartet hatte, das sich nie ereignete. Worauf . . .? . . . . Auf ewas Überraschendes, noch nie Gesehenes; auf einen ungeheuerlichen Anblick, von dem er sich nicht die geringste Vorstellung machen konnte; auf irgend etwas von fürchterlicher, tierischer Sinnlichkeit; das ihn wie mit Krallen packe und von den Augen aus zerreiße; auf ein Erlebnis, das in irgendeiner noch ganz unklaren Weise mit den schmutzigen Kitteln der Weiber, mit ihren rauhen Händen, mit der Niedrigkeit ihrer Stuben, mit . . . mit einer Beschmutzung an dem Kot der Höfe . . . zusammenhängen müsse. . . . (*T*, 17–18)

> [He was waiting for something, just as, when he stood in front of those paintings, he had always been waiting for something that never happened. What was it . . .? It must be something surprising, something never beheld before, some monstrous sight of which he could not form the slightest notion; something of a terrifying, beast-like sensuality; something that would seize him and rend him starting with the eyes, an experience that in some still obscure way seemed to be associated with these women's soiled [aprons], with their rough-

ened hands, with the low ceilings of their little rooms, with . . . with a besmirching of himself with the filth of these yards . . . (*YT*, 16–17)]

While Pratt describes the imperialist taking possession of the landscape through his eyes, Musil's text reverses the schema by having the protagonist wish that the scene would seize him and annihilate him through his gaze. However, even in the realm of Törleß's imagination, the subversion of the hierarchy between subject and object does not reverse the power dynamic between Austro-Germans and Czechs. Indeed, he remains only dimly aware of the link between his desire to be devoured by art and the sight of the local women. In both the German original and the translation the ellipses of the final sentence enact this failure to make the connection. Instead, he fetishizes the signs of the women's impoverishment and squalid living conditions, their dirty aprons, rough hands, low houses, and filthy courtyards, in order to heighten the frisson of his imagined degradation. By eroticizing the differences between the Austro-German subject and Czech object, the schoolboy's fantasy ultimately reinforces the hierarchy between the ethnic groups.

If Törleß's voyeurism implicitly recalls that of the colonist, elsewhere Musil's text is explicit about the colonialist and racist fantasies that fuel his protagonist's imagination. Sitting in a café with Beineberg, Törleß finds that something as banal and literally everyday as nightfall can induce visions of race war:

> Es war eine Welt für sich, dieses Dunkel. Wie ein Schwarm schwarzer Feinde war es über die Erde gekommen und hatten die Menschen erschlagen oder vertrieben oder was immer getan, das jede Spur von ihnen auslöschte. Und Törleß schien es, daß er sich darüber freue. (*T*, 24)

> [This darkness was a world apart. It had descended upon the earth like a horde of black enemies, slaughtering or banishing human beings, or whatever it did, blotting out all trace of them. Und it seemed to Törless that he was glad of this. (*YT*, 27)]

His siding with the forces of darkness adds a bathetic note of teenage misanthropy, but it does not alter the dichotomy between "Menschen" (human beings) on the one hand and inhuman "schwarz[e] Feinde" (black enemies) on the other. Nor does it alter the fact that his vision projects the atrocities committed by white imperialists, such as mass expulsions and genocide, onto a fictitious black foe. Here the context for Törleß's reverie is crucial: Beineberg has just aired his views on Indian philosophy (*T*, 18) and shortly before that the boys had encountered the Czech women (*T*, 17). This sequence implies a link in the protagonist's mind between the Moravians, India, and his unspecified, imaginary black hordes. Through this chain of associations, the novel connects the internal imperialism of the Dual Monarchy with overseas colonialism in India and Africa. Thus Törleß's train of thought suggests that the Self does not admit gradations in alterity but rather casts even the most proximate Other as irredeemably alien and exotic.

As in the encounter with the local women, the text reveals the sexual insecurity behind Törleß's racist projections. At nightfall the world resembles a "somber, empty house" which he is to explore until "er der Herrin selbst der schwarzen Scharen gegenüberstünde" (*T*, 24; he would stand opposite the mistress of the black hordes herself: *YT*, 26). And after all the locks of the doors he passed through had snapped shut, far beyond the outside walls "die Schatten der Dunkelheit [würden] wie schwarze Eunuchen auf Wache stehen und die Nähe der Menschen fernhalten" (*T*, 25; the shades of darkness [would] stand on guard like black eunuchs, warding off any human approach, *YT*, 27). This passage exemplifies a tendency in Musil's text to elaborate Törleß's inner visions to the point where they efface the outer world of the diegesis. A Freudian reading of this passage would emphasize Törleß's castration complex, most obviously in the eunuch guards, but also in the sexually ambiguous "Herrin" who commands them. (The term "Herrin" is basically untranslatable, but resembles something like "lord-ess" in English in terms of its gender confusion.) However, if we turn our focus outward to the origin of these images, the latter figure recalls the eroticism and despotism stereotypically associated with the East, while her eunuch guards represent the standard entourage in the orientalist tableau. Thus this passage shows how racist, colonialist, and orientalist clichés inform and deform the protagonist's erotic imagination.

Törleß's erotic experiences are not limited to fantasy, since he, like his schoolmates, pays regular visits to the local prostitute Božena. The visit described in the text, however, represents the ironic fulfillment of his masochistic tendencies, since it offers humiliation and degradation without sex. Even before he and Beineberg arrive at the inn where Božena works, they are exposed to potential violence and shame in the form of a drunken and aggressive client, who threatens the prostitute and seems about to go after the boys (*T*, 27–28). Reflecting on this near miss, Törleß concludes that he would have been defenseless:

> Der zierliche Degen kam ihm entgegen diesen groben Fäusten wie ein Spott vor. Außerdem die Schande und die Strafe, die er zu gegenwärtigen hätte! Es bliebe ihm nur übrig zu fliehen oder sich aufs Bitten zu verlegen. Oder sich von Božena schützen zu lassen. Der Gedanke durchrieselte ihn. Aber das war es! Nur das! Nichts anderes! Diese Angst, dieses Sichaufgeben lockte ihn jedes Mal von

neuem. Dieses Heraustreten aus seiner bevorzugten Stellung unter die gemeinen Leute; unter sie, — tiefer als sie! (*T*, 30)

[By comparison with those big fists his dainty sword was a mockery. And apart from that, the disgrace and punishment that would follow! There would be nothing for it but to run, or plead for mercy. Or to let himself be protected by Božena. The thought went shuddering through him. But that was it! That was just it! Nothing else! This fear, this self-abandonment, was what seduced him anew every time. This stepping out of his privileged position and going among the common people — among them? No, lower than them! (*YT*, 36)]

While Stern's description of the Moravian proletariat as "drunken, foul-mouthed, and darkly threatening" (80) certainly applies to Božena's customer, it does not take into account the fact that Törleß imagines seeking protection from the Czech prostitute herself. In this regard, the dainty sword, which the Austrian schoolboy finds so risible when compared to the drunken Slav's fists, functions not only as a phallic symbol but also as the insignia of the Habsburg ruling class. It is indeed difficult to reconcile Stern's claim that the novel bolsters Austro-German superiority with the fact that here a young member of the elite culture envisages being entirely at the mercy of the lowly Moravians and is, moreover, excited erotically at the prospect of this degradation.

Yet at first sight the character of Božena seems to fulfill many of the stereotypes associated with Slavic women in the Austrian literature of the period. Wolfgang Müller-Funk defines this "Other woman" variously "as submissive, a whore, but also where possible a Mommy, a lover and an earthy breast-feeding mother/wetnurse."[14] Admittedly, Božena is a prostitute by trade, and during his visit she begins, to Törleß's great discomfort, to remind him of his own mother (*T*, 32–33). However, in this case the list of clichés described by Müller-Funk falls wide of the mark for two reasons. First, in her interaction with Törleß and Beineberg Božena is far from submissive. Indeed, in both her affect and her speech she emerges as a figure of resistance to the prevailing cultural order. Second, the text specifically presents the association between Božena and Törleß's mother as an idea that arises from the protagonist's own psyche and his own Oedipal tendencies, rather than as a response to any maternal quality in the prostitute (*T*, 32–33). By dissociating Božena's own discourse and behavior from the Viennese elite's perception of her, we can see her as a vehicle for social criticism rather than merely as a cultural stereotype.[15]

The brief account of Božena's life indicates the text's interest, not merely in reproducing such clichéd notions, but rather in consciously exploring their effects. Her descent into prostitution began while she was working as a chambermaid in Vienna and resulted at least in part from the associations that her bucolic background evoked in her urban employers: "Die bäurische Art, welche sie so wenig ganz abstreifte wie ihren breiten, festen Gang, sicherte ihr das Vertrauen ihrer Herrinnen, welche an dem Kuhstallduft ihres Wesens seine Einfalt liebten, und die Liebe ihrer Herren, welche daran das Parfum schätzten" (*T*, 28–29; Her peasant ways, which she never lost any more than her plodding, firm-footed walk, inspired confidence in her mistresses, who liked the whiff of the cow-shed about her and the simplicity they associated with it; it also inspired amorous desires in her masters, who liked the whiff of the cow shed for other reasons," *YT*, 34). Ironically, it is her rustic simplicity that precipitates her moral corruption. By combining the stereotype of the earthy, naive Czech maid with the equally shopworn figure of the cynical, metropolitan prostitute, the text subverts both clichés through their mutual incompatibility.[16]

Božena's contempt for the ruling class is apparent in her behavior toward her schoolboy clients, to whom she deliberately displays her crudest and ugliest characteristics, safe in the knowledge that they will still come crawling to her (*T*, 29). As someone who has lived in the capital and worked for the Germanophone elite, her rejection of the elegance of the genteel world earns her some kudos among the local farmers' sons.

> Sie spuckten zwar aus, wenn sie von ihr sprachen, und fühlten sich verpflichtet, mehr noch als gegen andere Mädchen grob gegen sie zu sein, im Grunde waren sie aber gewaltig stolz auf dieses «verfluchte Mensch», das aus ihnen hervorgegangen war und der Welt so durch den Lack geguckt hatte. (*T* 29)

> [True, they spat when they spoke of her, and felt obliged to treat her with even more coarseness than other girls, but at bottom they were really mightily proud of this "damned slut" who had issued from their own midst and who had so thoroughly seen through the veneer of the world. (*YT*, 35)]

Thus Božena suggests the limited scope for rebellion among the Czechs. Although she plies her trade with the Austro-German schoolboys, she has penetrated the façade of metropolitan Viennese society and thus enables her community to reject Habsburg domination vicariously.

In her conversation with Törleß and Beineberg, Božena demonstrates her contempt for the ruling class by airing the dirty laundry of her former employers, who happen to have been the Beinebergs (*T*, 31–32). She describes her liaison with the uncle who courted Beineberg's mother and how the ladies of the family expressed disgust at the cook's pregnancy shortly before Beineberg's aunt fell pregnant herself (*T*, 32). Although the narrator condemns her words as impertinent and her facial expression as intent on sullying everything, the veracity of her account remains unchallenged (*T*, 32). With the incisiveness of Schnitzler, Božena's vignette of life "below stairs" exposes the sexual hypocrisy of Viennese society and thereby paradoxically provides this "woman of ill repute" with a moral basis for her rejection of the imperial metropolis's mores.

Törleß's response is instructive: in his imagination he replaces Beineberg's mother with his own (*T*, 32). Discomfited by this mental association, he seeks reassurance in the memory of his parents. He recalls their well-cared for, immaculate, and unapproachable faces filling him with awe at dinner, and their "vornehmen, kühlen Hände, die sich selbst beim Essen nichts zu vergeben schienen" (*T*, 32; the cultivated cool hands that seemed to lose none of their dignity even while handling knife and fork, *YT*, 40). Here of course the unapproachable faces and dignified hands of his parents intimate his inability to imagine their sexuality. These images ironically reinforce Božena's view of the Austro-German upper class as repressed and hypocritical with regard to sex. Indeed, Törleß's attempt to seek refuge in the superiority of his class raises questions about their ethics: "Die Erinnerung an die vollendete Manier dieser nie formvergessenen Gesellschaft wirkte stärker auf ihn als alle moralische Überlegung" (*T*, 32; His memory of the perfected manners of that society, which never for an instant allowed itself any slip out of its own style, had a stronger effect on him than any moral considerations, *YT*, 40). By privileging style and form over morality, Törleß inadvertently confirms Božena's assertion that Viennese society is more devoted to the maintenance of appearances than to ethical precepts.

In fact, one could argue that the trajectory of the whole novel subtly reinforces Božena's cynical view of the Austro-German elite. Let us consider how Törleß's attitudes toward the prostitute and his parents shift in the course of the narrative. When he visits Božena with Beineberg he is transfixed by her account of Beineberg's family and feels compelled to associate his own mother with the prostitute (*T*, 32–33). However, by the end of the novel, as he leaves the school and the town with Frau von Törleß, he finds that his enthrallment with Božena has dissipated: now the wood in which her house stands appears insignificant and harmless (*T*, 140). Further, while he remembers how unimaginable his parents' life, that is, their sexuality, had seemed back then, Törleß now steals sidelong glances at his mother and samples the scent emanating from her body (*T*, 140). The ending suggests that the protagonist has belatedly absorbed the message of the prostitute's narrative, since he now finds himself able to conduct a conversation with his mother while furtively indulging his Oedipal, sensual appetites. If we consider that throughout the text he is concerned with this disparity between the everyday realm of experience and another one, beyond language, in which unconscionable acts such as consorting with Božena or abusing Basini can occur, then the significance of this conclusion become clear. Törleß's newfound acceptance of these contradictory impulses signals his "maturity," that is, a readiness to enter a society marked by moral duplicity.[17] It is thus Božena, the social and cultural Other of Habsburg imperial society, who inadvertently instructs Törleß in the ways of his own world.

This development is confirmed by the proleptic passage in which the adult Törleß appears as an enervated aesthete, uninterested in moral questions (*T*, 111–12). What makes this outcome all the more disappointing is that as a teenager he shows the moral clarity to disavow the torture of Basini, the schoolboy whom he, Beineberg, and Reiting discover stealing. Having first witnessed and then participated in this abuse, Törleß finally musters the *Zivilcourage* or courage of his convictions to intervene, warning Basini that Reiting and Beineberg plan to hand him over to the class (*T*, 129). This episode runs counter to Stern's claim that the novel does not "disassociate itself from the ethos of the death camps" (91). Rather, the fact that the adult Törleß shows no interest in the fate of Basini and even claims that the experience left his soul more discriminating (*T*, 112) raises disturbing questions about the moral obtuseness of society in general.

The ending of the novel confirms the broader social significance of the boys' persecution of Basini. As he envisages handing the thief over to a class whose outrage he has carefully cultivated, Reiting, the Machiavellian manipulator, declares that he enjoys these mass movements and that instigating a scenario like this affords him particular pleasure (*T*, 115). This reference to "mass movements" prefigures Musil's diary entry, made between 1937 and 1941, in which he describes the characters of Reiting and Beineberg as "today's dictators *in nucleo*" and mentions the idea of the masses as susceptible to coercion.[18] Here we should consider these comments in light of the statement that "jede Klasse ist in einem solchen Institute ein kleiner Staat für sich" (*T*, 41; in such a school each class constitutes a small State in itself: *YT*, 52). This political analogy draws force from the fact that the pupils will join the ranks of the military and civil elite in Habsburg society (*T*, 8). Taken in conjunction with the boys' treatment of the Slavic villagers and the Other Basini, the text can be seen to presage, rather than propagate, the fascist mentality.

However, it is not the shrewd manipulator Reiting but rather the mystic fanatic Beineberg who comes to dominate the text, both as Törleß's main interlocutor and as a motivator of the plot. The novel not only provides Beineberg with the opportunity to expound his "philosophy" at length and to visit it upon the hapless Basini (*T*, 116–25) but also gives the provenance of these ideas, offering a detailed description of how Beineberg's father developed an interest in Buddhist mysticism while serving with the British Army in India (*T*, 19–20). Given the number of pages devoted to Beineberg *père* and *fils* and their respective philosophies, it is surprising that no critics have addressed these figures in any detail.

The description of Beineberg senior's obsession with Indian philosophy undercuts the notion that mysticism is a category of experience that transcends the political and social world. Indeed, the text undermines the senior Beineberg's religious conversion by likening it to the acquisition of exotic knick-knacks produced for tourists: "Nicht nur hatte er wie sonstige Europäer Schnitzereien, Gewebe und kleine Industriegötzen mit herübergebracht, sondern auch etwas von dem geheimnisvollen, bizarren Dämmern des esoterischen Buddhismus gefühlt und sich bewahrt" (*T*, 19: he had brought back not only what any other European brought back with him, but something of a feeling, which he had never lost, for the mysterious, bizarre glimmerings of esoteric Buddhism," *YT*, 18). Moreover, the fact that the senior Beineberg develops this interest while serving as an imperial soldier is of great significance. We are reminded of one Edward Said's central claims in *Orientalism*, that all knowledge of the Orient "is somehow tinged and impressed with, violated by, the gross political fact [of European imperialism]."[19] Yet the figure of Beineberg's father suggests an implicit criticism of Western civilization, since this European colonist turns his back on his own culture to embrace that of the colonized Other.

Although Beineberg *père*'s understanding of Indian Buddhism is highly attenuated, his encounter with the religion has a profound effect.

> Seine Gedanken [verloren] sich in ein Dämmern wohliger Melancholie . . . wenn er an den geheimen Kult dachte, der sich an die Originale der vor ihm liegenden Schriften knüpfte, an die Wunder, die von ihnen ausgegangen waren und Tausende ergriffen hatten, Tausende von Menschen, die ihm wegen der großen Entfernung, die ihn von ihnen trennte, nun wie Brüder erschienen, während er doch die Menschen seiner Umgebung, die er mit allen Details sah, verachtete. (*T*, 19)

> [His thoughts los[t] themselves in a twilit state of agreeable melancholy . . . when he thought of the esoteric cult bound up with the originals of the writings open before him, of the miracles that had emanated from them, stirring thousands, thousands of human beings, who now, despite the vast distance separating him from them, appeared to him like brothers, while he despised the people round about him, whom he saw in all their detail. (*Y* 19–20)]

The repetition of the term "Dämmern," which was used initially to describe Beineberg senior's comprehension of Buddhist philosophy and denotes a glimmering knowledge or a twilit state of mind, reminds us that the colonial soldier is far from attaining enlightenment in the Buddhist sense. Equally, his pursuit of mystical knowledge has taken him far from the bright rationalism of Western Enlightenment thought. This passage also makes it clear that Officer Beineberg sees his fellow worshippers in far-off lands as brothers only because of the distance separating him from them. Were he closer to them, the misanthropy he shows towards his fellow countrymen, whom he can perceive clearly, would doubtless reassert itself. Nevertheless, Beineberg senior's conversion to Buddhism suggests the tenuousness of the Western tradition. For even a highly mediated and attenuated form of Buddhism has succeeded in alienating him from his own culture and faith, in colonizing the colonist.

The reference to Buddhist scriptures in the above passage offers an insight into the process of orientalization as applied to Eastern religions. According to Richard King, Western scholars' approach to Buddhism reflects several presuppositions: "the post-Reformation location of religion in the printed word, the literary and philological roots of orientalist scholarship, and Christian assumptions about the nature of religion and the importance of a canon of authoritative works."[20] For all his rejection of his native society, Beineberg senior's preoccupation with texts reveals the continued influence of the Western tradition. This inconsistency is understandable if we consider that Western scholars strove to erase any trace of their involvement in the formation of this orientalized "Buddhism." As King explains, "The authorial presence of the Western orientalists in the construction of this textualized 'Buddhism' was safely hidden from view by a philological positivism, which claimed to be revealing, through the medium of translation, nothing more than the meaning embodied in the original text itself" (150). Beineberg's father goes a step further than the philologists in failing to admit the fact of translation. Although the German verb "übersetzen" has the same literal meaning of "to ferry or carry across" as its Latinate equivalent ("to translate"), Beineberg *père* ignores this primary transference, insisting that his religious tomes are works in which "no single word could be shifted without disturbing the secret significance" (*T*, 19; *YT*, 19]). Indeed, for him, these texts are no longer mere books but "revelations, something real — keys" like "the alchemical and magical books of the Middle Ages" (*T*, 19; *YT*, 19). By comparing Herr Beineberg's textual fetishism with the occult practices of the European Dark Ages, Musil avoids imputing such claims to the Buddhist texts themselves and thus suggests that the "Aberwitz religiöser Ekstase" (*T*, 20; the lunacy of religious ecstasy) exhibited by Beineberg's father is an occidental phenomenon.

Beineberg senior's veneration of Buddhist scriptures recalls the Törleß family's attitude toward the philosopher Kant and his works. The very name "Kant" is intoned in Törleß's home "wie der eines unheimlichen Heiligen" (*T*, 78; like that of an uncanny saint). Thus the central proponent of the Enlightenment suffers the indignity of becoming an object of occult superstition. Furthermore, unlike Beineberg's father, Törleß's parents have no desire to read the texts they fetishize, regarding them as the "Heiligtum einer Gottheit, der man nicht gerne naht und die man nur verehrt, weil man froh ist, daß man sich dank ihrer Existenz um gewisse

Dinge nicht mehr zu kümmern braucht" (*T*, 78–79; the shrine of some divinity to which one does not readily draw nigh and which one venerates only because one is glad that thanks to its existence there are certain things that one need no longer bother about, *YT*, 115). While the devotee of Indian mysticism pursues Buddhist enlightenment with zeal, Törleß's family is content, thanks ironically to Kant's efforts, to remain in precisely that state of "selbstverschuldeten Unmündigkeit" (self-induced dependence) that the philosopher exhorts his readers to abandon in the essay "Beantwortung der Frage: Was ist Aufklärung?" (A Response to the Question: What is Enlightenment? 1783).[21]

From the perspective of today's reader, Musil's depiction of attitudes toward philosophy illustrates one of the tenets of Max Horkheimer and Theodor Adorno's *Dialektik der Aufklärung* (1944): that the Enlightenment tends to revert to the superstitious and mythological modes of thought that it was intended to supersede.[22] As Adorno and Horkheimer explain, this regression does not arise from modern myths (such as nationalism) extinguishing the Enlightenment, but rather from the petrification of the movement itself (3). The attitudes displayed by Törleß's parents thus appear representative of the intellectual atrophy afflicting their class a whole. Where once *Bildungsbürger* cultivated an active interest in philosophy and the arts, now Törleß's education seems to have stopped around 1832, leaving him with the distinct impression that after Kant, Goethe, and Schiller there is no point in tackling philosophical problems or writing poetry (*T*, 78). While Adorno and Horkheimer conduct a forensic enquiry into the dialectical demise of the Enlightenment in 1944, Musil diagnoses the patient's nascent symptoms in 1906.

Törleß's parents' inert admiration for Kant leads their son to develop the radical notion of actually *reading* one of the philosopher's works, an experience that the protagonist finds tortuous (*T*, 80). Similarly, Beineberg's "Eastern" philosophy emerges as a radicalized and hypostasized version of his father's:

> Jene Eigenheit seines Vaters, die für diesen im Grunde genommen vielleicht doch nur den letzten Schlupfwinkel der Individualität bedeutete, den sich jeder Mensch — und sei es auch nur durch die Wahl seiner Kleider — schaffen muß, das ihn vor anderen auszeichne, war in ihm [Beineberg *fils*] zu dem festen Glauben geworden, sich mittels ungewöhnlicher seelischer Kräfte eine Herrschaft sichern zu können. (*T*, 20)

> [That peculiarity of his father's, which for the older man was at bottom perhaps no more than the last refuge for individuality which every human being — and even if it is only through his choice of clothes — must provide himself with in order to have something to distinguish himself from others, had in him turned into the firm

belief that that he could achieve dominion over others by means of more than ordinary spiritual powers.] (*Y* 21)

What was an idiosyncrasy in the father has become the son's *raison d'être*. To borrow Carl Schorske's description of the transvaluation wrought by the aestheticists, orientalism, rather than art, becomes for Beineberg *fils* an essence, rather than a mere ornament, and a source of value rather than an expression of value.[23] Here we should not confuse the younger Beineberg's firm belief with a more profound understanding of Buddhism. The fact that he seeks "spiritual" powers to gain mastery over others demonstrates his failure to grasp the basic tenet of renouncing worldly desires. Indeed, Beineberg's philosophical program distorts the Buddhist spirit of renunciation to the point that it comes to resemble the Nietzschean will to power. Thus when J. P. Stern describes Beineberg's ideas as "Indian mystical claptrap" (90), he fails to distinguish oriental from orientalist thought.

Whereas the passage above portrays Beineberg senior's interest as ornamental, likening it to a quirky taste in clothes, Beineberg junior's beliefs are presented as essential, the defining feature of the schoolboy's corporeal self: "Er sog zwischen dem Sprechen an einem langen Tschibuk, saß mit orientalisch gekreuzten Beinen und sah mit seinen abstehenden Ohren . . . wie ein groteskes Götzenbild aus" (*T*, 48; He sat there cross-legged in an oriental style, sucking at long chibouk, and with his protruding ears . . . he looked like a grotesque idol, *YT*, 64). Thus Musil depicts Beineberg, with a Turkish pipe, oriental posture, and the head of an idol, as a bricolage of orientalist tropes. This composite image recalls the orientalist's tendency to regard the East as "a series of textual fragments, which he thereafter edited and arranged as a restorer of old sketches might put a series of them together for the cumulative picture they represent."[24] Further, the diverse oriental motifs that Beineberg embodies suggest the Western orientalists' willingness to ignore the distinctions between the various cultures of the Middle East and Asia in their construction of a fictitious "Orient." For example, Beineberg's head, which resembles that of an idol, sits awkwardly with the Turkish pipe, given the Islamic tradition's dim view of graven images. In this way Beineberg embodies the contradictions inherent in the Western notion of "the Orient."

Such inconsistencies also misinform Beineberg's discourse. As he ponders what action to take with the thief Basini, he declares that he is not concerned about the money or justice, pointing out that "'In Indien würde man ihm einen gespitzten Bambus durch den Darm treiben; das wäre wenigstens ein Vegnügen'" (*T*, 48: In India they would drive a pointed bamboo pole through his guts. There'd be some fun in that, anyway, *YT*, 64). He concludes his remarks with the imprecation "'Allah schenke eurem Urteil seine Gnade!'" (*T*, 48; May Allah bestow his grace upon your verdict! *YT*, 64). The obscure reference to Indian torture practices and the exhortation to Allah give the impression of an orientalist arbitrarily constructing a composite "Eastern" belief system to justify his own sadistic proclivities.

Beineberg's attempt to hypnotize Basini invokes the popular orientalist image of the snake charmer, with Basini swaying from side to side in a serpentine manner (*T*, 120). Depending on whether one identifies with the charmer or the snake, this image conjures up either the mesmerizing tyranny of the Orient or the abnegation of the individual will that such power induces. This image recurs during Törleß's tribunal before his teachers at the end of the novel. The headmaster of the school explains the protagonist's need to witness Basini's humiliation with the rationale that the sight of vice held him in his thrall as a serpent's gaze does its victim (*T*, 134). This analogy gives a new meaning to the term "snake charming" by pointing out that the snake is itself capable of hypnotizing its victim. Thus Musil's use of the trope of snake charming enacts the subject/object confusion that afflicts both Törleß and Beineberg.

Moreover, Musil ascribes the image of the snake to the repertoire of orientalist clichés by relating, in free indirect discourse, the associations that Beineberg's "mystical" utterances evoke for Törleß:

> Seine Worte würden zu einem zerbröckelnden indischen Tempel gehören, in die Gesellschaft unheimlicher Götzenbilder und zauberkundiger Schlangen in tiefen Verstecken; was sollten sie aber am Tage, im Konvikte, im modernen Europa? (*T*, 62)

> [His way of talking would not have been out of place in some crumbling Indian temple, among uncanny idols, where wizard serpents lay hidden in deep crannies. But what place had such talk in broad daylight, in this school, in Europe? (*YT*, 87)]

Here Törleß calls upon various stereotypical notions of the East as ruined, uncanny, magical and hidden. The irony is that these clichéd associations originated, not in the ancient Orient, but rather in modern Europe, which invented the notion of the mysterious, magical East in order to justify the hegemony of Western logic and reason. Moreover, Törleß's naive expression of orientalist tropes is ironic given that its is precisely in this school in central Europe that one finds deep and uncanny recesses, whether literally in the structure of the building itself, or figuratively in the minds of its pupils.

While Beineberg cites Indian Buddhism as the inspiration for his "philosophy," the fact that he conducts experiments to prove his theories betrays the influence of Western scientific empiricism. His empiricist mysticism is doomed to failure, since the empirical method cannot comprehend an experience that is often "said to be devoid of the subject-object distinction."[25] Indeed, Beineberg remains perpetually confused over whether he or Basini is the object of experimental enquiry. On the one hand, he intends to rid himself of the "'miserable desires directed towards the external world'" such as compassion for one's fellow man, which he believes prevent him from comprehending his own soul and the cosmos (*T*, 59; *YT*, 82). On the other, he seeks to destroy Basini's will, reducing him to an automaton that unthinkingly obeys his commands (*T*, 121–22). This oscillation between subject and object recalls the neo-empiricism of the Austrian physicist Ernst Mach,[26] who was the subject of Musil's dissertation. Mach claimed that once we grasp that the apparent unities of the self and other bodies are merely makeshift measures that provide a means of orientation, the subject/object distinction will no longer pertain: "*Der Gegensatz zwischen Ich und Welt, Empfindung oder Erscheinung und Ding fällt dann weg*" (*The antithesis between ego and world between sensation (or appearance) and thing then no longer applies.*)[27] Through the character of Beineberg, who invokes the dissolution of the self to justify his "experiments," the novel suggests that the destabilization of self-identity described in Mach's theories can lead to a violent desire to reimpose the subject/object hierarchy. In this way Beineberg's theories and his experiments on the hapless Basini serve to illustrate the lesson that the self-absorbed adult Törleß singularly fails to grasp: that the struggle for self-identity can have profound consequences for the Other co-opted into the process.

Beineberg's violent experiments on the difference between Self and Other thus provide a double critique of the Western philosophical tradition. On the one hand, a scion of the European elite has been captivated by a distorted and debased version of Indian mysticism. On the other, the empirical philosophical tradition of the West has become unmoored from morality and devolved into a sickening series of arbitrary experiments conducted on a fellow human being. In this way the figure of Beineberg expands the context of the novel, rendering the confusions of its schoolboy protagonist emblematic of an entire civilization.

In conclusion, this examination of Musil's novel contradicts the common critical assumption that a work that invokes the notion of the exotic Eastern Other automatically represents a declaration of cultural hegemony. Certainly, one must concede that this text perpetuates in the figure of Božena the common contemporary stereotype of the sexually licentious and morally duplicitous Czech woman and that Beineberg's philosophy, despite its many Western influences, still draws on the traditional orientalist association of India and mysticism. However, the novel subjects the protagonist's view of the Other to both internal and external criticism. Internally, we see how his struggle to assimilate alterity reflects his own precarious sense of self, especially in the projection of fantasies that oscillate between fear and desire. Externally, the invocation of a global context and of a conventional colonial scenario through the figures of Beineberg and his father ironizes the Austro-German view of their Czech neighbors as exotic and alien Others, while also expanding the scope of the novel's critique to encompass not only Habsburg society but also Western civilization in general. It is only through the lens of postcolonial theory that we can perceive this self-critical tendency in Musil's novel.

Notes

[1] Cf. Effi Böhlke, "Rußlandbilder aus dem 18. und 19. Jahrhundert, entworfen in der deutschen und französischen politisch-philosophischen Literatur," *Osteuropa. Zeitschrift für Gegenwartsfragen des Ostens* 52.5 (May 2002): 578–79. According to Böhlke, Russia occupied three possible positions in the symbolic geography of German and French intellectual discourse from the eighteenth and nineteenth centuries: a peripheral position on the northern and eastern fringe of Europe; a position entirely within Asia; or that of a half European and half Asian country through which the border between the two continents ran (578–79).

[2] To my knowledge, three critics, J. P. Stern, Charles N. Genno, and Tim Beasley-Murray, refer to the liminal setting of the novel between East and West. See J. P. Stern, "The Education of the Master Race," in *In The Heart of Europe: Essays on Literature and Ideology* (Oxford: Blackwell, 1992), 78–93; Charles Genno, "The Nexus between Mathematics and Reality and Phantasy in Musil's Works," *Neophilologus* 70.2 (1986 Apr.): 270–78; Tim Beasley-Murray, "German-Language Culture and the Slav Stranger Within," *Central Europe* 4.2 (Nov. 2006): 131–45. However, none of the above readings employs postcolonial theory or attempts to connect the novel's depiction of internal colonialism (i.e., relations between Austro-Germans and Czechs) and the broader issue of Western imperialism suggested by the "Indian" philosophy of Beinenberg and his colonialist father.

[3] Moritz Csáky, "'Was man Nation und Rasse heißt, sind Ergebnisse und keine Ursachen': Zur Konstruktion kollektiver Identitäten in Zentraleuropa," in *Kakanien Revisited: Das Eigene und das Fremde (in) der österreichisch-ungarischen Monarchie*, vol. 1 of *Kultur-Herrschaft-Differenz*, ed. Wolfgang Müller-Funk, Peter Plener, and Clemens Ruthner (Tübingen: A. Francke Verlag, 2002), 41.

[4] Robert Luft, "Machtansprüche und kulturelle Muster nichtperipherer Regionen: Die Kernlande Böhmen, Mähren und Schlesien in der späten Habsburger Monarchie," 168.

[5] See Wolfgang Müller-Funk, "Kakanien Revisited: Über das Verhältnis von Herrschaft und Kultur" in Müller-Funk, Plener, and Ruthner, *Kakanien Revisited: Das Eigene und das Fremde in der österreichischen-ungarischen Monarchie*, 26; and Georg Escher, "Prager *Femmes Fatales* — Stadt, Geschlecht, Identität," *Kakanien Revisited*, 6 Jun. 2004, http://www.kakanien.ac.at/beitr/fallstudieGEscher1.pdf, 4.

[6] For a definition of "internal colonialism," see Michael Hechter, *Internal Colonialism: The Celtic Fringe in British National Development, 1536–1966* (Berkeley: U of California P, 1975). Joe Metz has recently applied this term to relations

between Germanic and non-Germanic peoples in Austria-Hungary in "Austrian Inner Colonialism and the Visibility of Difference in Stifter's *Die Narrenburg*," *PMLA* 121.5 (Oct. 2006): 1475.

[7] Ritchie Robertson, "Zum deutschen Slawenbild von Herder bis Musil," in *Das Eigene und das Fremde*, ed. Urs Faes and Béatrice Ziegler (Zurich: NZ Verlag, 2000), 140.

[8] Cf. Beasley-Murray, "German-Language Culture," 142, n. 43.

[9] Mary Louise Pratt, *Imperial Eyes: Travel Writing and Transculturation* (London: Routledge, 1992), 6.

[10] I have taken the liberty of slightly emending Wilkins and Kaiser's translation here, since the German "Schenkel" denotes thighs rather than buttocks.

[11] Edward Said, *Culture and Imperialism*, 66–67.

[12] See Hugh LeCaine Agnew, *The Czechs and the Lands of the Bohemian Crown* (Stanford, CA: Hoover Institution Press, Stanford University, 2004), 149.

[13] Stanley Corngold takes the analysis of Törleß's *sprechender Name* or descriptive name further by describing the character as "the being from which there is no exit" in "Patterns of Justification in *Young Törleß*," in *Neverending Stories: Toward a Critical Narratology*, ed. Ann Fehn, Ingeborg Hoesterey, and Maria Tatar (Princeton, NJ: Princeton UP, 1992), 142. One could equally argue that he is the being to whom there is no access, given that the teachers find his explanation of his response to Basini's crime utterly impenetrable (*T*, 134–38).

[14] Müller-Funk, "Kakanien Revisited," 27. Also quoted in Beasley-Murray, "German-Language Culture," 135, n. 16.

[15] As Ruth Amossy explains, while the stereotype is itself "necessarily reductive," this does not mean that it is always involved in "reductive enterprises." The fact that the text explicitly examines the repercussions of this stereotype for Božena's later life removes this figure from the realm of the purely reductive. Ruth Amossy, "Stereotypes and Representation in Fiction," trans. Therese Heidingsfeld, *Poetics Today*, 5.4 (1984): 689–700.

[16] For a survey of some other Austrian texts by Musil, Max Brod, and Hermann Broch that combine the two stereotypes of the rustic maid and urban prostitute in their depictions of Czech women, see my article, "Imperial Mystique and Empiricist Mysticism: Exoticism and Inner Colonialism in Musil's *Törleß*," *Modern Austrian Literature* 42.1 (2009): 1–23, esp. 14–19.

[17] See Patrizia McBride's recent assessment of the novel: "In *Törless* the gap between an ordinary and an ineffable realm is portrayed not as an anomalous condition that should be reversed, but rather as the state of mind of adulthood, a state of mind one deals with by accepting the incommensurability of the two realms." McBride, *The Void of Ethics: Robert Musil and the Experience of Modernity* (Evanston, IL: Northwestern UP, 2006), 52.

[18] Robert Musil, *Tagebücher I*, ed. Adolf Frisé (Reinbek bei Hamburg: Rowohlt, 1983), 914.

[19] Edward Said, *Orientalism*, 11.

[20] Richard King, *Orientalism and Religion: Post-Colonial Theory, India and "the Mystic East"* (London: Routledge, 1999), 146.

[21] Immanuel Kant, "Beantwortung der Frage: Was ist Aufklärung?" (1783), in *Was ist Aufklärung? Thesen und Definitionen*, ed. Ehrhard Bahr (Stuttgart: Philipp Reclam Jr., 1974), 9.

[22] Theodor Adorno and Max Horkheimer, *Dialektik der Aufklärung* (Frankfurt am Main: S. Fischer Verlag, 1969), 3. Todd Kontje is to my knowledge the only other critic who mentions Adorno and Horkheimer's text in relation to *Törleß*. See Kontje, "Organized Violence/Violating Order: Robert Musil's *Die Verwirrungen des Zöglings Törless*," *Seminar: A Journal of Germanic Studies* 24.3 (1988): 252.

[23] Carl Schorske, *Fin-de-siècle Vienna: Politics and Culture*, 10.

[24] Said, *Orientalism*, 176.

[25] King, *Orientalism and Religion*, 20.

[26] For a full account of Mach's influence in *Törleß* see Judith Ryan, *The Vanishing Subject: Early Psychology and Literary Modernism*, 208–11.

[27] Ernst Mach, *Analyse der Empfindungen*, 11. (Mach's emphasis.)

3: The Sovereign Subject under Siege: Ethnology and Ethnocentrism in Kafka's "Description of a Struggle," "Jackals und Arabs," and "In the Penal Colony"

I N THE SEMINAL ESSAY "Structure, Sign, and Play in the Discourse of the Human Sciences" (1969), Jacques Derrida makes the following aside concerning the origin of ethnology:

> One can assume that ethnology could have been born as a science only at the moment when a decentering had come about: at the moment when European culture — and, in consequence, the history of metaphysics and of its concepts — had been *dislocated*, driven from its locus and forced to stop considering itself as the culture of reference.[1]

Conversely, as a practitioner of a "primarily . . . European science employing traditional concepts," the ethnologist "accepts into his discourse the premises of ethnocentrism at the very moment when he denounces them" (282). For Derrida, ethnology emerges as a divided subject that must constantly contend with the contradictory acentric and ethnocentric impulses that gave rise to the discipline.

The contradiction that Derrida perceives in the theory of ethnology also influences the practice of ethnology's modern successor, anthropology. On the one hand, as Clifford Geertz explains, the anthropologist conducting fieldwork while living among the objects of his enquiry must contend with the "difficulties of being at one and the same time an involved actor and a detached observer."[2] Conversely, the mere presence of an alien researcher in a community may radically alter the behavior of those subjects and thus produce the anthropological analogue to the Heisenberg Uncertainty Principle, that is, a situation in which the very act of observation impinges upon the phenomena observed and thus precludes any objective findings.

The effect of intercultural encounters on both the Western percipient and the exotic objects of his scrutiny was a theme of abiding interest for Franz Kafka. In his earliest major prose work, the first version of the novella "Beschreibung eines Kampfes" (1904–7), and in the short stories "Schakale und Araber" (1917) and "In der Strafkolonie" (1919), Kafka portrays Western protagonists who find their sovereign subjectivity and rationality besieged by disturbing, alien cultural practices. The primary narrator of "Beschreibung eines Kampfes" must contend with the appearance of the oriental Fat Man and his bearers in the midst of a Prague landscape; the narrator/protagonist of "Schakale und Araber" becomes embroiled in the conflict raging in the desert between the two eponymous parties; the explorer of the penal colony is confronted with the island's bizarre judicial procedures. Moreover, in all three texts these characters discover that they exert an undue influence on the phenomena they seek to observe. Thus Kafka presents in these stories Western protagonists who find that their automatic presumptions of logic and objectivity no longer pertain in these disorienting ethnological encounters.

Of course, these stories are by no means anthropological field studies, but rather works of fiction that include elements of the fantastic: the protagonist can rearrange the landscape on a whim in "Beschreibung eines Kampfes," the eponymous jackals have the ability to speak in "Schakale und Araber," and "In der Strafkolonie" depicts an execution machine that is capable of starting up of its own accord. Nevertheless, by embedding these fantastic elements in stories that portray ethnological encounters, Kafka suggests that the imagination invariably impinges upon intercultural exchanges by projecting its own fears and desires onto the Other, thus precluding the experience of genuine alterity.

At this point it is instructive to refer to Homi Bhabha's discussion of Edward Said's use of the term "discourse" in *Orientalism*, in order to clarify what is at stake in Kafka's depictions of ethnological encounters. For Bhabha, there is an inherent contradiction in Said's combination of on the one hand the Foucauldian terminology of discourse and power, that is, a terminology that refuses "an epistemology which opposes essence/appearance, ideology/science,"[3] and on the other a Freudian, binary opposition between "the *form* of manifest Orientalism as the historically and discursively determined, diachronic aspect" and the latent "*content* . . . as the unconscious repository of fantasy, imaginative writings and essential ideas" (71–72, his italics). According to Bhabha, Said's theoretical impasse can be solved with recourse to the notion of "representation as a concept that articulates the historical and fantasy . . . in the production of the 'political' effects of discourse" (72). In this regard Kafka's depictions of ethnological encounters in "Beschreibung eines Kampfes," "Schakale und Araber," and "In der Strafkolonie" correspond to Bhabha's concept of "representation." For while these texts draw upon the discursively and historically determined orientalist stereotypes of, for example, Eastern cruelty and irrationality, the figures and motifs that appear to embody oriental alterity, (the Fat Man in "Beschreibung," the eponymous jackals of "Schakale und Araber," and the bizarre juridical customs of the penal colony) are ultimately revealed to be emanations of occidental fantasy. Thus these works offer a self-reflective and self-critical orientalism that indicates both the historical and imaginative processes behind the production of the discourse.

In "Beschreibung eines Kampfes" Kafka signals that he is concerned with orientalism rather than with the Orient *per se*, through his first reference to the East: a well-worn oriental carpet owned by the main narrator of the text (*NS*, 59). A commodity reflecting Western taste rather than its Eastern culture of origin, this ragged rug invokes the popular orientalist image of the magic carpet from *The Thousand and One Nights*, suggesting that this motif and its associated topos have become threadbare through overuse. Moreover, the narrator's oriental rug presages the character's own decrepit physical state. While walking with his companion through the snowy streets of Prague, the narrator ventriloquizes the younger man, imagining how the latter will describe the narrator to his girlfriend:

> Er sieht aus, — wie soll ich es beschreiben — wie eine Stange in baumelnder Bewegung auf die ein gelbhäutiger und schwarzbehaarter Schädel ein wenig ungeschickt aufgespießt ist. Sein Körper ist mit vielen, ziemlich kleinen, grellen, gelblichen Stoffstücken behängt, die ihn gestern vollständig bedeckten, denn in der Windstille dieser Nacht lagen sie glatt an. (*NS*, 62)

> [He looks — how can I describe him to you? — like a dangling stick on which a yellow-skinned and black-haired skull has been a little clumsily skewered. His body is hung with many fairly small lurid, yellowish patches of cloth which yesterday covered him completely because in the still air of this night they hung to him closely. (*CS*, 14, translation modified)]

In the first sentence the narrator likens himself to the trophy of a barbaric headhunting tribe, his skull speared on a bobbing stick. Here he also casts himself as an Oriental, through the references to his yellow skin and black hair. In this way Kafka creates an image of the narrator that recalls the West's contradictory notions of the Orient as primitive and savage but also decadent, insubstantial, and enfeebled.[4] The second sentence indicates the degree to which the narrator's acquisition of an oriental appearance is determined by his own corporeal insubstantiality, the yellowish rags serving as an ineffective covering, not for the narrator's body, but rather for his lack of one. Orientalism becomes a façade through which the Western subject attempts to mask his eroded self-identity.

In contrast, the ample figure of the Fat Man, along with the bodies of the four naked servants who bear him aloft (*NS*, 78), appears to lend some corporeal substance to the representations of the Orient. Indeed, these figures embody a plethora of orientalist stereotypes: the combination of the Fat Man's gargantuan and inert girth, which effortlessly clears a path through thorny bushes (*NS*, 79) and the absolute devotion of his servants, who drown while attempting to carry him across the river (*NS*, 83), casts the East as "a fantastic realm of degenerate sensuality, immobility, and feudalistic power" according to Rolf Goebel (37). However, the imagery used to describe the Fat Man's physical appearance recalls that of the emaciated narrator: "Seine faltigen Fettmassen waren so sorgfältig ausgebreitet, daß sie zwar die ganze Tragbahre bedeckten und noch an den Seiten gleich dem Saume eines gelblichen Teppichs hinunterhiengen, und ihn dennoch nicht störten" (*NS*, 79: His folds of fat were so carefully spread out that although they covered the whole litter and even hung down its side like the hem of a yellowish carpet, they did not hamper him, *CS*, 25). By likening the folds of flesh to the narrator's oriental rug and employing the adjective "yellow*ish*," which recalls the narrator's skull and ragged clothing, Kafka suggests that the very person of the Fat Man, despite his considerable corporeal mass, exhibits the same insubstantiality as the narrator.

The ontological doubts surrounding the Fat man extend to his identity as an Oriental. Indeed, he resembles the character of Beineberg in Robert Musil's novel *Die Verwirrungen des Zöglings Törleß* in his inauthentic adoption of an oriental persona. While Beineberg sits "with his legs crossed in an Oriental fashion" (*T*, 48), Kafka's character adopts "an oriental posture" (*NS*, 78). More importantly, the Fat Man's narrative concerning the Supplicant (*NS*, 84–95) casts doubt upon the former's ostensibly oriental character, since it is very difficult to imagine him attending a Prague church in the same garb (or lack of it) and in the same company without attracting considerable attention. However, before we ascribe authenticity to the church-going Fat Man, as opposed to his orientalized self, we must consider that the former only appears in the character's embedded tale, rather than in the frame narrative. Thus Kafka transposes the customary locations of fantasy and reality in orientalist fiction: while the fabulous, gargantuan, and magical figure of the Fat Man inhabits the diegetic "reality" of the text, his mundane, local, church-going self belongs to the realm of inserted fictional narrative. Through this reversal Kafka ironizes the West's tendency to associate the Orient with the realm of fantasy and fiction.

The Fat Man is by no means alone in his desire to narrate. Indeed, Kafka's text contains a bewildering variety of nested narratives[5] that come to resemble Chinese boxes. "Beschreibung eines Kampfes" begins with the narrator, who introduces the Fat Man, who in turn describes the Supplicant, who then relates his encounter with the Drunkard. However, none of these figures reveals as profound a disparity between narrating and narrated personae as the Fat Man. By combining such an outlandishly

oriental persona with an unobtrusively occidental alter ego, this character
undermines the East/West dichotomy that is fundamental to orientalist
thought. Moreover, the oriental persona, which combines vaguely Buddhist mysticism with a despotic indifference toward his bearers, embodies
the contradictions that abound in orientalist fantasies of the East. However, the most important facet of the Fat Man's schizoid existence is his
failure to recognize the discrepancy between his Western and Eastern
personae. In this way the Fat Man's hybrid personality not only suggests
the occluded and contradictory nature of the Western orientalist vision
but also challenges the basic notion of a unified subject.

As we have seen in chapter 1, the critical empiricist dissolution of the
subject/object distinction leads to one of two antithetical outcomes: a
mystical union with the cosmos or the annihilation of the self. While the
Fat Man magically rearranges the landscape on a whim (NS, 81), he must
also suffer the indignity of having a gull fly through his stomach (NS,
84). Moreover, he is not alone in finding that although he can command
the elements, his own body proves more recalcitrant. The first speaker
can on the one hand create mountains and prevent the moon from rising
(NS, 75), yet on the other is unable to stop his own body developing,
as it were, a mind of its own. In his conversation with the rapidly sinking Fat Man, the first narrator's body exhibits an alarming elasticity: his
arms and legs grow to gargantuan proportions, while his head shrinks to
the size of an ant egg (NS, 112). By placing these fantastic events in the
context of a pseudo-ethnological encounter between the Western speaker
and the ostensibly Eastern Fat Man, the text undermines the notion of a
deictically ordered subject/object relationship that is the basis not only of
ethnology but of all scientific endeavor.

However, in his reading of "Beschreibung eines Kampfes" Walter Sokel links the fantastic powers displayed by Kafka's characters with
Freud's claim that "primitive peoples" hold a narcissistic belief in "the
omnipotence of thoughts."[6] In this way Sokel's reading seeks to rein-
scribe a binary opposition between the civilized and the primitive on a
text that, in its subversion of both orientalist stereotypes and conventional
subject/object relations, refutes such dualistic thought.

The characters' confusion over subject/object relations, coupled with
their own dubious ontological status, points to a broader epistemological
crisis. The controlling metaphor for this crisis emerges in the conversation
between the Fat Man and the Supplicant ("der Beter"). The latter con-
fesses that he prays in an ostentatiously loud manner, "'um angeschaut
zu werden und Körper zu bekommen'" (NS, 109; in order to be looked
at and acquire a body, CS, 44), that is, in order to attract the attention
of other worshippers and thus confirm his own existence. The Fat Man
dubs this condition "eine Seekrankheit auf festem Lande" (NS, 89; a
seasickness on dry, or literally, solid land). Indeed, throughout the text

Kafka literalizes the absence of a common epistemological foundation by referring to his characters' unsure footing.[7] This metaphor recurs with increasing intensity: the opening verse epigraph describes people strolling "schwankend auf dem Kies" (*NS*, 54; swaying over the gravel, *CS*, 9), the first narrator and his companion both fall on the slippery, icy streets of Prague (*NS*, 67 and 74) and the Fat Man forsakes *terra firma* altogether for a watery grave (*NS*, 111). Moreover, this instability extends to the characters' surroundings: a monument to Charles IV collapses in Prague (*NS*, 69) and tall buildings are said to tumble for no apparent reason in Paris (*NS*, 92). However, it is not until almost the end of the Supplicant's conversation with the Fat Man that he reveals the meaning of this trope: "'Denn schon sind wir auf dieser Erde eingerichtet und leben auf Grund unseres Einverständnisses'" (*NS*, 109; for we are already established on this earth and live by virtue of an agreement, *CS*, 45). This sentence plays on the link between the epistemological ground and that beneath our feet. (The German "Grund," like its English cognate, signifies both "reason" and "earth.") The proliferation of images associated with the lack of a secure ground suggests that this epistemic crisis has reached epidemic proportions, engulfing Western civilization.

Indeed, although he refers to the Orient with regard to the first narrator and the Fat Man, the main object of Kafka's ethnological scrutiny in this text is the West. Again, Kafka literalizes a metaphor to intimate his thematic concerns. At one point the narrator and his companion arrive "in das Innere einer großen, aber noch unfertigen Gegend, *in der es Abend war*" (*NS*, 73, my italics; in the interior of a large yet still unfinished region, *in which it was evening*). By conflating the spatial and temporal in a region of perpetual evening, Kafka creates a literal *Abendland*. (This is the German term for the geographical west that literally signifies "evening land," because of course the sun sets in the west.) In so doing Kafka participates in the literary and cultural discourse of Western decadence. From the 1890s onwards cultural critics asserted, with paradoxical vigor, that the sun was setting on Western civilization, and by the end of the First World War this view had achieved pseudo-scientific respectability with the publication of Oswald Spengler's treatise on racial destiny *Der Untergang des Abendlandes* (The Decline of the West, 1918–22). Thus Kafka's *Abendland* transforms the trope of Western entropy into a topos.

However, the motif of the *Abendland* indicates a specific intertextual allusion to a poem by one of the foremost Austrian Decadents, Hugo von Hofmannsthal. The first verse of Hofmannsthal's "Ballade des äußeren Lebens" (Ballad of the External Life, 1896) reads

Und Kinder wachsen auf mit tiefen Augen,
Die von nichts wissen, wachsen auf und sterben,
Und alle Menschen gehen ihre Wege[8]

[And children grow up with deeply wondering eyes
That know of nothing, grow a while and die,
And every one of us goes his own way.]⁹

Thus begins a listless list of images that evoke a sense of entropy, decay, and futility, offering a modernist variation on the baroque theme of *vanitas*. The unusual verse epigraph at the beginning of Kafka's "Beschreibung eines Kampfes" parodies both the tone and the content of Hofmannsthal's poem:[10]

Und die Menschen gehn in Kleidern
schwankend auf dem Kies spazieren
unter diesem großen Himmel,
der von Hügeln in der Ferne
sich zu fernen Hügeln breitet. (*NS*, 54)

[And people, in their [clothes]
Stroll about, swaying over the gravel
Under the enormous sky
Which, from hills in the distance,
Stretches to distant hills. (*CS*, 9)][11]

Kafka's verse mocks "Ballade des äußeren Lebens" through the banal detail "Und die Menschen gehn in Kleidern . . . spazieren" (And the people stroll about in their clothes) and the tedious uniformity of a landscape featuring nothing but distant hills. Later, Kafka offers a more specific parody of Hofmannsthal's poem. While Hofmannthal's third verse reads

Und süße Früchte werden aus den herben
Und fallen nachts wie tote Vögel nieder
Und liegen wenig Tage und verderben,

[And bitter fruit will sweeten by and by
And like dead birds come hurtling down at night
and for a few days fester when they lie][12]

Kafka has unripe fruit falling senselessly to the ground (*NS*, 78). However, the most important intertextual link is apparent in Hofmannsthal's final tercet:

Was frommts, dergleichen viel gesehn haben?
Und dennoch sagt der viel, der "Abend" sagt,
Ein Wort, daraus Tiefsinn und Trauer rinnt
Wie schwerer Honig aus den hohlen Waben.[13]

[To see such things do travelers leave their homes?
Yet he says much who utters "evening,"

A word from which grave thought and sadness flow
Like rich dark honey from the hollow combs.][14]

Through his allusions to Hofmannsthal's poem, particularly to its valorization of the term "Abend" (evening) Kafka both parodies and perpetuates the notion of Western decadence. In the motif of the *Abendland* he literalizes the concept of a cultural landscape, producing a multi-layered topos that can simultaneously embody the notion of Western decadence and satirize it as one aspect of the contemporary *Zeitgeist*.

Kafka's ability to express empathy with, and yet maintain an ironic distance from, the Western cultural malaise is also evident in his treatment of philosophical and linguistic issues. For example, the forest of pines ("Fichtenwald") that is located in the *Abendland* (*NS*, 74), evokes the name of the German Idealist philosopher Johann Gottlieb Fichte, who asserted that the phenomenal world (the "Nicht-Ich" or "Not-I") was merely the creation of the noumenal ego (the "Ich" or "ego"). With self-referential irony Kafka confirms this solipsistic worldview by having his protagonist call the pine forests into being on a whim (*NS*, 74). Kafka's irreverent, parodic attitude toward the Western philosophical tradition is also apparent in the casual reference to the approaching crash of falling trees, which the first narrator and his companion hear on entering the forest and which evokes the hoary conundrum concerning the fate of the tree that falls in the forest when no one is there to hear it (*NS*, 76). Finally, Kafka evokes one of the central problems of Western philosophy in the Supplicant's confession to the Fat Man:

> Es hat niemals eine Zeit gegeben, in der ich durch mich selbst von meinem Leben überzeugt war. Ich erfasse nämlich die Dinge um mich nur in so hinfälligen Vorstellungen, daß ich immer glaube, die Dinge hätten einmal gelebt, jetzt aber seien sie versinkend. Immer, lieber Herr, habe ich eine so quälende Lust, die Dinge so zu sehn, wie sie sich geben mögen, ehe sie sich zu mir zeigen. Sie sind da wohl schön und ruhig, denn ich höre oft Leute in dieser Weise von ihnen reden. (*NS*, 91)

> [There has never been a time in which I was convinced of my life through my own efforts. You see, I grasp the things around me in ideas that are so weak that I always think that the things must have lived once, but are now sinking into oblivion. My dear sir, I always have such a tormenting desire to see things as they behave before they show themselves to me. They are probably nice and calm then, because I often hear people talk about them in this way.][15]

Here Kafka connects the general, epistemological crisis with a personal existential problematic: the Supplicant's lack of faith in his own existence deprives his ideas concerning the outside world of their vitality and validity. The use of the adjectives "hinfällig" (frail or invalid, but with the literal sense of prone to falls) and "versinkend" (sinking) links the Supplicant's personal dilemma to the broader metaphor of the unstable epistemological ground and the unsure footing it provides. More importantly, the character's problematic relationship with the outside world encapsulates a vital development in the history of Western philosophy. On the one hand, the Supplicant's faith in the existence of "the thing in itself" recalls not only Kant but also the Platonic foundations of Western thought. On the other, his skepticism regarding his own ability to perceive these Platonic essences recalls Nietzsche's description of the tenuous relationship between subject and object in the essay "Über Wahrheit und Lüge im aussermoralischen Sinne" (On Truth and Lying in an Extra-Moral Sense, 1873):[16]

> Überhaupt aber scheint mir die richtige Perception — das würde heissen der adäquate Ausdruck eines Objekts im Subjekt — ein widerspruchvolles Unding: denn zwischen zwei absolut verschiedenen Sphären wie zwischen Subjekt und Objekt giebt es keine Causalität, keine Richtigkeit, keinen Ausdruck, sondern höchstens ein ästhetisches Verhalten, ich meine eine andeutende Übertragung, eine nachstammelnde Übersetzung in eine ganz fremde Sprache.[17]

> [Basically, the right perception — that would mean the adequate expression of an object in the subject — seems to me to be a self-contradictory absurdity. For between two absolutely different spheres such as subject and object, there can be [no causality, no correctness] no expression, but at most an *aesthetic stance*, I mean an allusive transference, a stammering translation into a completely foreign medium.][18]

Here Nietzsche's use of the metaphor of language to describe the subject/object relationship recalls his main thesis in the essay: that the "truths" structuring our language and thought are nothing more than illusions that have gained general acceptance, "eine gleichmässig gültige und verbindliche Bezeichnung der Dinge" (877; a uniformly valid and binding terminology for things, 247). It is precisely this unexamined faith in the commensurability of signifier and signified that Nietzsche wishes to critique and which Kafka's Supplicant envies in others. Kafka places in the mouth of the naive Supplicant a condensed history of Western thought, from Platonic essences to the contemporary Nietzschean *Sprachkrise*. In the process Kafka emphasizes the fact that the individual subjective consciousness, which represented the bedrock for all philosophical truth claims in the Western tradition, has now become the source of epistemological uncertainty.

This loss of faith in the validity of the subjective viewpoint leads to a destabilization of values, particularly with regard to the characters' sexual, religious, and cultural identities. A link between homoerotic desire and the dissolution of the rationalist worldview is implied by the appearance, apropos of nothing, of the Fat Man and his four naked bearers on a Prague riverbank (*NS*, 8). Although the Western protagonist invokes the racist stereotype of East Asian inscrutability, claiming that he can discern "nichts genaues" in "dem dunklen Viereck ihrer Gesichter" (*NS*, 81; [no] details in the dark square of their faces, *CS*, 27), he nevertheless shows considerable interest in their gleaming, sweaty bodies and unusually prominent muscles (*NS*, 82). This response is particularly important in the context of the ethnological encounter between the Western speaker and the ostensibly oriental Fat Man. While the sado-masochistic relationship between the Fat Man and his bearers suggests the deviant sexuality routinely associated with the Orient, the speaker's evident arousal at this scene undermines the notion of the Western observer as dispassionate and objective. Like Musil's Törleß, Kafka's protagonist views the encounter with the exotic Other as an opportunity for libidinal projection rather than logical interpretation.

However, as with Musil's novel *Törleß*, it would be wrong to attribute the speaker's homosexual inclinations to the supposedly deleterious influence of an eastern, alien culture. From the outset Kafka's text makes plain that the narrator/protagonist of the first section harbors an erotic interest in his younger companion. The protagonist regards his acquaintance with "eyes filled with love" (*NS*, 61), declares that his companion's life is dearer to him than his own (*NS*, 61), and sees the young man respond by embracing him and kissing his clothes (*NS*, 71). They then engage in homoerotic horseplay in the section aptly entitled "A Ride," in which the narrator jumps on his companion's back and gallops around on him (*NS*, 72–74). Moreover, this homoerotic behavior is not confined to the frame narrative but rather pervades the inset narratives as well. The Fat Man relates how the Supplicant propositions him, while denying him the opportunity to disavow his alleged homosexuality: "'Er sagte, daß ich hübsch gekleidet sei, und daß ihm meine Halsbinde sehr gefalle. Und was für eine feine Haut ich hätte. Und Geständnisse wurden am klarsten, wenn man sie wiederriefe'" (*NS*, 94–95; He said I was dressed nicely and that he very much liked my tie. And what a fine complexion I had. And that confessions become clearest when they are retracted, *CS*, 36). Such a double bind is hardly necessary in a text in which all the male characters, the frame narrator and his companion, the Fat Man and the Supplicant, and the Supplicant and the drunkard, either embrace or kiss each other. However, the fact that many critics have until recently ignored the homoerotic component in this text suggests that no confession can be clear enough for some readers.[19]

Taken in conjunction with the speaker's discussion of his yellow skin (*NS*, 62), his sexual orientation serves to undermine the automatic assumption that any first person narrator must be a white heterosexual male. Only the presumption of male gender remains intact. In this way the text disorients the Western, heterosexual, male reader by thwarting his desire to identify with the narrating protagonist. This reader, who unthinkingly identifies with the first-person narrator, is thus obliged to experience this destabilization of identity.

The disorientation experienced by Kafka's characters in "Beschreibung eines Kampfes" affects not only their sexuality but also their sense of national and cultural self-identity. Ironically, it is the monuments to national figures, which should provide the most stable, concrete link to the past, that prove most susceptible to the characters' perceptions. In the eyes of the first speaker the statue of Emperor Charles IV in Prague degenerates from a fixed point of reference to a source of disorientation.

> Ich schwankte und mußte das Standbild Karl des Vierten fest ansehn um meines Standpunktes sicher zu sein. Aber das Mondlicht war ungeschickt und brachte auch Karl den Vierten in Bewegung. Ich staunte darüber und meine Füße wurden viel kräftiger aus Angst, Karl der Vierte möchte umstürzen, wenn ich nicht in beruhigender Haltung ware. Später schien mir meine Anstrengung nutzlos, denn Karl der Vierte fiel herunter, gerade als es mir einfiel, daß ich geliebt würde von einem Mädchen in einem schönen weißen Kleid. (*NS*, 69)

> [I began to sway, and had to look firmly at the statue of Charles IV to be sure of my position. But the moonlight was clumsy and started moving Charles IV too. I was amazed by this and my feet became much stronger out of fear that Charles IV might topple over if I did not maintain a calming posture. Later my efforts seemed futile, because Charles IV fell down just as it occurred to me that I was loved by a girl in a white dress.][20]

Here Kafka rapidly reverses the perceptual relationship between the observer and the object: instead of relying on the fixed position of the statue, the speaker must remain still in order to prevent the monument from toppling. (The German term "*Stand*bild," which literally combines "standing" with "image," emphasizes the paradox of an unstable statue.) Kafka conveys the interdependence of the internal and external worlds through the play on "fallen" (to fall) and "einfallen" (to occur to someone) in the final sentence. Moreover, the figure of Charles IV, whose name is repeated four times to coincide with his title, suggests that the leitmotif of instability has a political resonance. This monarch established in 1364 the treaties of succession with the Austrian Habsburgs and

Hungarian Árpáds that would form the basis of the Austro-Hungarian Empire.[21] Two pages later, the statue of Saint Ludmila, the Czech martyr and patron of Bohemia, quivers under the amorous attentions of the acquaintance. Gesturing toward the statue, the acquaintance announces that he had always loved the sculpture's hands until this evening, when he kissed the hands of his new, living sweetheart (NS, 71). Thus the protagonist and his companion reject two important historical figures on unlikely erotic whims. By invoking a Czech saint along with a German prince who united the Habsburgs and the Hungarians, Kafka implicates all the major ethnic groups of the empire in the contemporary state of instability and instability of the state.

The statue of the Virgin Mary proves no more steadfast than that of Saint Ludmila, its cloak billowing and whipping about in the wind (NS, 94). Indeed, in the course of the text Kafka indicates the destabilization of the whole Judeo-Christian tradition. When the Fat Man diagnoses the Supplicant's condition as "eine Seekrankheit auf festem Lande" (NS, 89; a seasickness on dry, or more literally, solid land), he defines the malady by twice invoking the Old Testament:

> Deren Wesen ist so, daß Ihr den wahrhaftigen Namen der Dinge vergessen habt, und über sie in einer Eile zufällige Namen schüttet. . . . Aber kaum seid Ihr von ihnen weggelaufen, habt Ihr wieder den Namen vergessen. Die Pappel in den Feldern, die Ihr den "Thurm von Babel" genannt habt, denn Ihr wußtet nicht oder wolltet nicht wissen, daß es eine Pappel war, schaukelt wieder namenlos und Ihr müßt sie nennen "Noah, wie er betrunken war." (NS, 89)

> [Its nature is such that you have forgotten the true names of things and are now pelting them with random names in a hurry. . . . But you've hardly run away from them before you've forgotten their names again. The poplar in the field, which you have named "The Tower of Babel" because you didn't know or didn't want to know that it was a poplar, is again swaying namelessly and you have to call it "Noah in his cups."]

Clearly, the names that the Fat Man devises for the poplar tree are anything but "zufällig" (random). As Rolf Goebel argues, the figure of the Tower of Babel suggests a "linguistic malaise" that predates the contemporary *Sprachkrise* by millennia (44), while both the tower and the inebriated Noah's nudity signify "a violation of patriarchal authority" (45).[22] God punishes humanity with linguistic confusion and geographic dispersal for daring to unite and reach heavenward with the tower (Gen. 11:7–11:9). Noah curses Ham's progeny to servitude because Ham saw him in a state of drunken undress (Gen. 9:25). However, one could argue that the Tower of Babel itself, as opposed to God's response to it, signifies humanity's positive desire to unite and strive upwards, and that Noah gets drunk to celebrate his new covenant with God.[23] My point here is not to engage in cabbalistic exegeses of the Bible, but rather to indicate how the rich suggestiveness of these metaphors is lost when they are applied to a tree. For the poplar tree, tower, and patriarch share only one salient feature: a swaying motion that again invokes the loss of a stable epistemological ground. Through his manipulation of Old Testament motifs Kafka suggests that the Bible has lost its auratic authority and become merely a repository of common images that can be decontextualized and appropriated without regard for their source.

In this way Kafka's irreverent attitude toward the Western Judeo-Christian tradition mirrors that of the orientalist toward Eastern cultures. In order to produce a textualized Orient, Westerners freely excerpted, adapted, and recombined motifs from the East. As Edward Said explains, orientalists developed the specialized genre of the chrestomathy, a compilation of excerpted fragments from oriental texts, which in the eyes of many Western readers did not merely represent, but rather became, the Orient itself.[24]

> In time, the reader forgets the Orientalist's efforts and takes the restructuring of the Orient signified by a chrestomathy as the Orient *tout court*. Objective structure (designation of the Orient) and subjective restructure (representation of Orient by Orientalist) become interchangeable. The Orient is overlaid with the Orientalist's rationality; its principles become his. (129)

"Beschreibung eines Kampfes" undoes the work of the self-effacing orientalist by drawing attention not only to the process of textual orientalization but also to its fundamental irrationality. The text ironizes the orientalist approach by subjecting Western religion and local cultural history to the processes of decontextualization and appropriation visited upon Eastern traditions. Moreover, in the figure of the Fat Man, Kafka parodies the orientalist predilection for *bricolage*. On the one hand, as James Whitlark points out, the Fat Man recalls the obese Chinese monk Pu-Tai of the Taoist tradition.[25] During the European vogue for chinoiserie in the eighteenth and nineteenth centuries, Pu-Tai became a favorite subject for porcelain figurines, but was often confused with the Gautama Buddha (100). On the other hand, Max Brod claims that Kafka drew inspiration from a popular picture postcard, an *uki-yoe* woodcut by the Japanese artist Ando Hiroshige.[26] According to Rolf Goebel, the most likely source for Kafka's image of the Fat Man and the bearers is the woodcut entitled *Okitsu* from the "Tokkaido"[27] (see fig. 3.1). As an amalgam of China and Japan, Taoism and Buddhism, the figure of the Fat Man reflects ironically on the Western tendency to disregard important cultural differences in the production of a homogenized Orient. Indeed,

Fig. 3.1. The ukiyo-e woodcut Okitsu *by Ando Hiroshige.*
Reproduced with kind permission of the Honolulu Academy of Arts.

by incorporating two mass-produced orientalist artifacts, the Pu-Tai figurine and the postcard, into his depiction of the Fat Man, Kafka creates representations of representations, a hall of mirrors that reveals the purpose of orientalism as narcissistic self-reflection rather than the objective interpretation of Eastern cultures.

In this regard the narrator's response to the Fat Man is instructive. Initially he likens the Fat man to "ein Götterbild aus hellem Holz, das überflüssig geworden war und das man daher in den Fluß geworfen hatte" (*NS,* 83; a yellow wooden idol which had become useless [literally: superfluous] and so had been cast into the river, *CS,* 29). Kafka renders the term "überflüssig" (superfluous) literal by having the wooden idol thrown into a "Fluß" (river), which is the root of the adjective "flüssig" (fluid or here the suffix -fluous) and where it will inevitably become "*unter*flüssig" (*sub*fluous) as it sinks into the water. As a specimen of religious and cultural flotsam and jetsam, this oriental idol appears to exemplify the idolatry and credulity of the East, which apparently adopts and rejects gods with alacrity. However, in the very next paragraph the narrator describes crawling up a riverbank to accompany the Fat Man on the latter's final journey because he truly loves the Fat Man and hopes to learn from him "etwas . . . über die Gefährlichkeit dieses scheinbar sicheren Landes" (*NS,* 83–84; something about the dangers of this apparently safe country, *CS,* 28). Thus the Westerner declares his devotion to the Eastern mystic and looks to him for guidance through the epistemologically treacherous terrain. Here the text drops several hints that the Eastern mystic holding the Western narrator in his thrall is in fact an Occidental creation. First, the reflective surface of the river becomes a site of narcissistic self-contemplation as the Fat Man sails along on the reflection of a raincloud (*NS*, 83). Furthermore, this passage recapitulates the literalized motif of the *Abendland* by describing the emergence of the "abendlichen Sonne" (*NS*, 83; evening sun) to accompany the Fat Man's downfall. Through this detail Kafka portrays the orientalist clichés embodied in the figure of the Fat Man as symptomatic of Western decadence in general. Finally, Kafka uses an extra-diegetic device to suggest the allure of the Fat Man for the Western observer. The character's lengthy, interpolated narrative, entitled "b. Begonnenes Gespräch mit dem Beter" (literally B. A Begun Conversation with the Supplicant), contains within it the inset narratives "c. Geschichte des Beters" (*NS*, 95–107; C. The Story of the Supplicant) and "D. Fortgesetztes Gespräch zwischen dem Dicken und dem Beter" (*NS*, 107–11; Continued Conversation between the Fat Man and the Supplicant), with each successive story revealing a new narrative nested within it like a set of Russian dolls. This sequence suspends the corpulent narrator's imminent demise in the protracted narrative time or *Erzählzeit* required to recount these various stories, and goes to show that it isn't over until the fat gentleman sinks. Like a gargantuan Sheherezade, the Fat Man defers his death through storytelling, and in so doing holds not only the primary narrator but also the reader in his thrall. In this way Kafka emphasizes Western credulity by showing how easily the occidental observer succumbs to the orientalist images of his own creation. Like Musil's Törleß, Kafka's protagonist reveals the power of the orientalist discourse to captivate the Western imagination. Kafka embodies the clichéd notions of Eastern despotism, decadence, and mysticism in the surreal figure of the Fat Man to suggest that such notions derive from Occidental fantasy rather than oriental reality.

The Fat Man's ultimate submergence in the first version of "Beschreibung eines Kampfes" (A, written 1904–7) ironically prefigures his complete disappearance from Kafka's revised text (B, written 1909–11). Kafka's deletion of the scenes involving the Fat Man and his interlocutor, the Supplicant, reduces the polyvocal narrative of the first version to the single first-person narration of the second. As Judith Ryan explains, Kafka's narrowing of the narrative to a single viewpoint in Fassung B denies the reader the overview afforded by the fragmentary perspectives of the first version,[28] and thus lays the groundwork for the limited perspective imposed on narrators and/ or protagonists in subsequent narratives.[29] However, while this revision points beyond the text, to the future development of Kafka's narrative technique, his writerly practice with the text(s) of "Beschreibung eines Kampfes" resonates with the theme of orientalism found in the first version. According to Wolf Kittler, Kafka incorporated motifs from his correspondence with Max Brod into the work[30] and then freely excerpted passages from the resulting novella to publish them as independent texts (52–53). Kafka took the prose pieces "Kleider" (Clothes) and "Die Bäume" (The Trees) from the first version and published them in *Hyperion* in 1908. The prose pieces "Kinder auf der Landstraße" (Children on the Country Road) and "Der Ausflug ins Gebirge" (The Excursion into the Mountains) arose out of the revised work and appeared, along with the texts from Fassung A, in Kafka's first book *Betrachtung* (Meditation) in 1912. The author's own textual practice starts to resemble that of the orientalist who freely cites, collates, and recombines Eastern texts from diverse sources to create his chrestomathy. Thus Kafka turns the European ethnologist's gaze inward by applying orientalist assumptions and practices not only to his Western cultural milieu but also to his own literary creations.

In contrast to the self-critical stance of "Beschreibung eines Kampfes," the opening of Kafka's 1917 story "Schakale und Araber" seems at first glance to offer a compendium of unalloyed orientalist clichés: a lone Westerner traveling through the desert rests at an oasis accompanied by the obligatory retinue of Arabs and a caravan of camels. However, the European speaker soon finds his sovereignty and rationality challenged as he becomes embroiled in a conflict between the eponymous jackals and Arabs. This analysis will demonstrate how these jackals, which are endowed with the power of speech as in a fable, embody a whole range of illogical and contradictory stereotypes that nevertheless hold sway over the narrator. By thus undermining the speaker's pretensions to objectivity and logic, Kafka's text not only critiques the European construction of the "Other," but also the "enlightened" empiricism that provides the rationale for Western ethnocentrism.

Kafka's subverts the speaker's subject position from the very beginning of "Schakale und Araber." The narrator starts his account by differentiating himself from his traveling companions: "Wir lagerten in der Oase. Die Gefährten schliefen. Ein Araber, hoch und weiß, kam an mir vorüber" (We were camping in the oasis. My companions were asleep. The tall, white figure of an Arab passed [me] by, *CS*, 407). The grammatical subject moves from the collective pronoun "wir" (we) to a separate group defined by its relation to the speaker, "Die Gefährten" (the companions), and finally to "Ein Araber" (an Arab), a single representative of a group to whom, we may infer, the speaker does not belong. Thus the narrator merely defines himself *ex negativo* as a non-Arab, assuming that his European identity will be understood as a matter of course. The description of the Arab as "hoch und weiß" ("tall," but also "high" and "white") most probably refers to his stature and attire. However, the fact that the texts ascribes to an Arab literal and figurative qualities traditionally associated with Europe, that is, height and an elevated position, along with white skin and purity, suggests that these characteristics are not the exclusive property of the West, and that simplistic binary oppositions between ethnic groups no longer pertain.

The narrator divulges his ethnic origins after the jackals have introduced themselves and declared him to be their long-awaited Messiah (*DL*, 270). Far from being a man with a divine mission, he reveals himself to be an accidental as well as an occidental tourist: "'Nur zufällig komme ich aus dem hohen Norden'" (*DL*, 270; It is by pure chance that I have come here from the far North, *CS*, 409). If we consider the connotations of the phrase "aus dem hohen Norden," (from the far north) then an interesting discrepancy emerges. Figuratively, the expression suggests the speaker's assumption that the higher latitude of the "hohe[ ] Norden" (literally the high north) reflects the inherent superiority of Europe over the more southerly and consequently lowlier areas. However, the term also indicates the speaker's disorientation, since it is clear that he no longer aligns himself with his homeland, which he marginalizes as the far north, but rather with his current position. Kafka complicates his critique of the protagonist's ethnocentrism by showing that while travel affects the speaker's relation to his homeland, his vision of the world remains a thoroughly egocentric one.

Ironically, the jackals invoke the European's supposedly superior powers of reason to persuade him to undertake the highly irrational mission of annihilating the Arab race (*DL*, 274). The head jackal compares the intellectual capabilities of European and Arabs thus: "Dort [in the North or Europe] ist der Verstand, der hier unter den Arabern nicht zu finden ist. Aus diesem kalten Hochmut . . . ist kein Funken Verstand zu schlagen" (*DL*, 271; You Northerners have the kind of intelligence that is not to be found among the Arabs. Not a spark of intelligence . . . can be struck from their cold arrogance, *CS*, 408). The association of *Verstand* (intelligence or reason) with a spark ironizes the protagonist, who, in the initial confusion of the jackal's address, literally lacks a spark when he forgets to light the torch that he was supposed to use to fend off the animals (*DL*, 270). Moreover, in the setting of a nighttime oasis, the only light mentioned is the "Irrlicht" or will-o'-the-wisp. When the Arab caravan leader whips the jackals into shape, they form such a tight and rigid pack "daß es aussah wie eine schmale Hürde, von Irrlichtern umflogen" (*DL*, 274: that they looked as if penned in a small fold girt by flickering will-o'-the-wisps, *CS*, 410). The German term "Irrlicht," which combines the words "Irre" (astray) and "Licht" (light), indicates more directly than the English equivalent the metaphorical meaning of the term: a misleading illusion. Yet the only optical illusion one would expect to encounter in the desert is a mirage. By invoking the flickering lights of European marshland in this desert setting, Kafka suggests that the jackals represent a peculiarly Western illusion.

In this unenlightened and vulnerable state, the traveler does not perceive the irony of inherently illogical creatures (that is, the loquacious jackals) attempting to enlist his powers of reason. Indeed, the European's readiness to accept these absurd creatures is apparent in his response to their first speech: "'das wundert mich sehr zu hören'" (*DL*, 270; I'm surprised to hear that). The narrator, for all his much-vaunted rationalism, is not surprised at the fact of the jackal's speech but by its content. By placing the case for an exclusively Western Enlightenment in the maws of talking beasts, Kafka suggests that this notion is a mere fable.

Nevertheless, the narrator appeals to his occidental rationality when he argues that he cannot venture an opinion on the conflict between jackals and Arabs: "'Ich maße mir kein Urteil an in Dingen, die mir so fern liegen'" (*DL*, 271; I do not presume to make judgments on matters so far outside my province). However, the speaker's physical situation subverts his rhetorical position. Firstly, the jackals have encircled him and their chief has insinuated his way into the speaker's personal space (*DL*, 270). More importantly, when the narrator is told of his mission to eliminate the Arabs, he is naturally outraged and attempts to stand up in order to assert his physical superiority over the pack, only to find that two jackals are holding him down, their teeth firmly clamped on the hems of his jacket and shirt (*DL*, 272). In this way the narrators's physical proximity to, and literal entanglement with, the jackals undermine his rhetorical claims to distance, objectivity, and a lack of involvement with regard to their situation.

While Walter Sokel acknowledges in his reading of this passage that the narrator has been captured by the object of his interest, he nevertheless claims that the power exerted by the perceived over the percipient presents no danger, for unlike other Kafkan protagonists (such as Josef K.) the narrator of "Schakale und Araber" is free of inner contradictions.[31] Indeed, Sokel ignores the speaker's perilous position vis-à-vis the jackals and restates the character's claim to objectivity: "The rational self wants however to remain impartial. It does not presume to judge, and insists on being a neutral observer" (288). Further, Sokel makes the claim that the narrator never becomes emotionally involved in the events of the story and preserves his inner distance from them, and thus represents nothing more than "schauende Intelligenz" (292; an observing intellect). Interestingly, Sokel cites the jackals' argument that the narrator represents reason (281) and asserts that this story shows the victory of the "rational perspective of the modern European" over the jackals' irrational asceticism, which arises from "the repressed and out-of-the-way regions of the world" (289). Thus Sokel combines the truth claims of both the jackals and the narrator to present the text as a triumph of Western rationality over Eastern unreason.

It will come as no surprise that my interpretation of this text is diametrically opposed to that described above. Indeed, in the following I will argue that it is precisely these assumptions of impartiality, objectivity, rationality, and consistency that the text interrogates and ultimately subverts. The fact that the narrator's and the jackals' claims on behalf of these supposedly Western virtues have gone unchallenged until now attests to the durability of these cultural assumptions.

Despite his professed impartiality, the European does ultimately intervene in the conflict on behalf of the jackals, curtailing the whipping administered by the Arab caravan leader (*DL,* 275). Significantly, this intervention only occurs after the Arab has demonstrated his mastery over the jackals by distracting them from their murderous plan with a camel carcass (*DL,* 275). With the hierarchy between man and beast restored, the traveler can afford to show compassion to the unfortunate animals. But this magnanimous concern for the jackals stands in stark contrast to his indifference toward his fellow human beings, that is, his Arab companions. Indeed, rather than warning the Arabs of the threat posed by the jackals, the narrator helpfully informs the jackals that the Arabs are sleeping nearby and that they will defend themselves stoutly in the event of an attack, shooting the jackals in droves with their shotguns (*DL,* 272). Why does the European display so little loyalty to his species? Certainly, as we have already seen, the jackals intimidate him physically. However, the speaker's own statements indicate a more sinister reason for his compliant attitude towards the jackals' murderous scheme. When he describes the situation thus: "'Es scheint ein sehr alter Streit; liegt also wohl im Blut; wird also vielleicht erst mit dem Blut enden'" (*DL,* 271; It seems to me a very old quarrel; I suppose it's in the blood, and perhaps will only end with it, *CS,* 408), he posits a conflict that is endemic to the jackals and the Arabs. Moreover, as the original German conjunctions "also . . . also . . ." (therefore . . . therefore . . .) suggest, this conflict will only cease with great bloodshed, a final solution involving the eradication of one of these groups. Here I take issue with the claim made by Walter Sokel and repeated by Ruth Gross that the narrator merely envisages the eventual dying out of one or other of the groups and that only the jackals interpret the phrase as a literal bloodbath.[32] The expression used by the narrator/protagonist "es wird mit Blut enden" (it will end with blood) indicates a violent end rather than a gradual extinction, and suggests a callous indifference behind his protestations of impartiality. Ironically, the narrator's prophecy finds its fulfillment in the reeking carcass of a camel rather than in a bloody war. Nevertheless, the narrator's response to the conflict reveals that this supposedly enlightened European subscribes to the same racist and ultimately genocidal logic as his animal interlocutors.

Thus far this study has differed from most critical responses to Kafka's text by focusing on the narrator's viewpoint rather than attempting an allegorical interpretation of the jackals. In view of the fact that the story was published in Martin Buber's periodical *Der Jude* in October 1917, a general critical consensus has arisen around the notion that the jackals represent the Jews.[33] In an article entitled "Unsere Literaten und die Gemeinschaft" (Our Writers and the Community), published in a previous edition of *Der Jude,* Max Brod prompted such allegorical readings by introducing the then largely unknown Kafka thus: "Although the word

'Jew' never appears in his works, they belong with the most Jewish docu-
ments of our era."[34] Paradoxically, the very absence of the word "Jew"
supports this allegorical interpretation, since allegory depends on the
absolute separation of the diegetic sign from its extra-diegetic referent.
However, while subsequent critics broadly agree that the jackals represent
the Jews, they differ markedly on which aspects of Judaism and the Jewish
community these creatures embody. For example, William C. Rubinstein
concentrates on the jackals' acclamation of the narrator as their savior,
and consequently reads the text as a satire on Old Testament teachings
regarding the coming of the Messiah.[35] In contrast, Jens Tismar suggests
that the jackals represent those Jews who, at the time of Kafka's writing,
were hiring Arab labor to help colonize Palestine and thus importing the
allegedly parasitical existence of the *galuth* (Diaspora) into the Promised
Land (314–15). In the eyes of these critics, the jackals thus come to sym-
bolize a wide variety of concepts associated with Judaism, encompassing
the sacred and the secular, the ancient and the modern.

Yet readings that seek a single, unified, extra-diegetic referent for
the jackals are inevitably confounded by the inherent contradictions in
these creatures. How, for example, can one reconcile Rubinstein's Messianic reading with the jackals' physical harassment of their supposed savior? How can Tismar's reference to the Zionist exploitation of Arab labor
account for the jackals' abject and hateful attitude towards their Arab
neighbors? Above all, how does one explain the fact that the jackals exhibit
all the power of reason in their eloquent address to the Westerner, only
to be revealed as brutish beasts when the Arab leader produces the camel
carcass? My contention here is that the jackals can only be understood in
relation to their European interlocutor. Here I would concur with Sander
L. Gilman, who claims that "the jackals represent the Western fantasy of
the Jews as always haunting the edges of 'culture.'"[36] By presenting the
jackals as simultaneously murderous rebels and venal slaves, persuasive
orators and dumb beasts, the text signals that these fantastic creatures
do not represent the Jews *per se*, but rather embody a variety of anti-
Semitic notions, with all their attendant contradictions. In this respect
they exhibit the ambivalence that Homi Bhabha identifies as intrinsic to
the discourse of the stereotype, a chain of signification that he describes
as "curiously mixed and split, polymorphous and perverse, an articulation
of multiple belief."[37] Moreover, the text distinguishes between the jackals
and the Jews themselves by investing the animals with characteristics that
represent an inversion of Jewish reality: their matriarchal religion (*DL*,
270) and their consumption of carrion as opposed to *treff* meat (*DL*, 271
and 273). These details suggest a looking glass world in which certain features have been reversed, as in a mirror. In this context the jackals' ability
to transfix the narrator, despite their inherent illogicality, symbolizes the
hold of such stereotypical notions on the European imagination.

Nowhere is the contradictory nature of the stereotype more apparent than in the jackals' behavior towards their putative Messiah. When they seize the tails of his shirt and coat in their mouths, they perform an assertive variation on the theme of touching the hem of the savior's garment. Although the chief jackal deems this gesture "eine Ehrenbezeugung" or "a token of their esteem" (*DL*, 272), the implicit threat therein is not lost on the narrator. Finally, the jackals' spokesdog addresses the narrator as "du edles Herz und süßes Eingeweide" (*DL*, 273; you noble heart and sweet innards). This epithet suggests that the jackals wish eventually to feast upon and savor their savior, a plan that travesties the Christian Eucharist. In this way the European can simultaneously indulge two contradictory Christian fantasies regarding the Jews. In a play on the dual meaning of the German "Christ" as both "Christ" and "Christian," he casts himself as the Messiah foretold in Jewish prophecy. Conversely, he indulges in the anti-Semitic fantasy of the blood libel, which alleges that Jews ritually slaughter and consume Christians. This slur points not to Jewish ritual but to the ambiguous cannibalistic imagery of the Christian rite of communion. Thus Kafka's text deftly suggests both the inherent contradictions in Christian prejudices against Judaism and the origins of these notions in the practices of the Christian Church.

However, the fact that the jackals' weapon of choice is a rusty pair of sewing scissors (*DL*, 274) indicates that they pose a threat to neither their European Messiah nor their Arab nemesis. For the jackals, blessed with language but no opposable thumbs, are unable to use this instrument for the murderous scheme they envisage, and if it were to be used for its actual purpose, (to cut thread) it would be of supreme irrelevance to them. Critics have sought to explain this motif in terms of Jewish ritual: Sander L. Gilman perceives in the sewing scissors a conflation of the traditional *shehita* method of slaughter (the cutting of the animal's throat) and the allegations, propagated by anti-Semites, of ritual murder,[38] while William C. Rubenstein considers the motif a reference to the rite of circumcision.[39] One might also propose a biographical reading, since the scissors evoke the realm of Hermann Kafka, the purveyor of ladies' accessories. The overdetermined quality of this symbol prevents the development of a simple one-on-one correlation with an extra-diegetic reality. Rather, we should consider the motif of the scissors in terms of its function within the diegesis. At once associated with the cutting of thread and the conjoining of cloth, this tool embodies the profoundly ambivalent relationship between the jackals and their Arab masters. On the one hand, the scissors clearly represent the division between the two groups. On the other, the caravan leader claims that as long as there are Arabs this pair of rusty scissors will accompany them through the desert until the end of their days (*DL*, 274). Paradoxically, the weapon intended to annihilate the Arabs thus becomes, in the eyes of those same Arabs, an indication of the continued existence. Moreover, the dual functions of the scissors for the jackals and the Arabs, as an instrument of genocide and as a guarantee of survival respectively, ensure the proximity of the two groups. Kafka's use of the term "Nähschere" (*DL*, 274; sewing scissors) highlights this ambivalence between proximity and separation, since the prefix "Näh" (sewing) is semantically, etymologically, and homonymically related to the word "Nähe" (nearness or closeness.)

Notions of distance and proximity first appear in the passage describing the arrival of the jackals: "'. . . das Klagegeheul eines Schakals in der Ferne . . . Und was so weit gewesen war, war plötzlich nah. Ein Gewimmel von Schakalen um mich her" (*DL*, 270; a jackal howled in the distance . . . And what had once been so far away was all at once quite near, *CS*, 407). Here the telegraphic style of the first and last phrases conveys the suddenness with which the jackals appear and encircle the speaker. However, it is the second sentence that is most worthy of note. With its symmetry, internal rhymes, and iambic rhythm this sentence parodies the grand German poetic tradition, which from Goethe to Hofmannsthal repeatedly posits a mystical union between the individual and the cosmos in which distance and difference are annihilated. Consider, for example, how Goethe's poem "Selige Sehnsucht" (Divine Longing), which itself forms part of the intercultural project of the *West-östlicher Divan*, describes the transcendence of distance in pursuit of spiritual transformation:

> Keine Ferne macht dich schwierig,
> Kommst geflogen und gebannt,
> Und zuletzt, des Lichts begierig,
> Bist du Schmetterling verbrannt.[40]

> [From no weight of distance tiring
> You're in spellbound flight held fast,
> And you are, the light desiring,
> Moth, in fire consumed at last.][41]

Or consider how Hofmannsthal's magician in "Ein Traum von Großer Magie" (A Dream of Great Magic)[42] recalls this Romantic vision by overcoming distance and difference so that "Ihm war nichts nah und fern" (Nothing was near or far to him).[43] By ironically invoking this tradition of transcendence at the point at the point of the jackals' arrival, Kafka suggests the complicity of the German literary and cultural discourse in reinforcing stereotypical conceptions of difference.

Moreover, Kafka's allusion to German literary tradition also responds to developments in Austro-German/Jewish relations in the Habsburg Empire. As Pieter M. Judson explains, ostensibly liberal organizations in the Dual Monarchy were committed to an inclusive vision of German national identity that encompassed both the Jew and the anti-Semite,[44] with the result that "by 1900 antisemitism had somehow become nor-

malized in Austrian *Bürger* culture" (70). In this context Kafka's association of the jackals with the German poetic tradition beloved of the liberal
Bildungsbürger or educated middle-class suggests a response to the contemporary co-opting of anti-Semitic sentiment in Austrian politics.

However, the text does not present the ability to stereotype as the sole
preserve of the European. As the caravan leader explains, the jackals select
the narrator as their latest Messianic candidate, not because of any individual qualities he may possess, but simply because he is a European (*DL*,
274). By having the Arab address the Westerner as "Herr," meaning both
"Lord" and "Mister," Kafka plays on the confusion between the sacred and
mundane that afflicts not only the jackals' but also the European's own
understanding of the West and the so-called "White Man's Burden." The
revelation that the narrator is only the latest in a long line of potential sav-
iors definitively undermines any pretense of objectivity on his part. For
his arrival does not merely influence but rather initiates the whole course
of events. Far from being a neutral observer, the European traveler visiting the desert unwittingly acts as the protagonist in this endlessly repeated
drama. The iterability and fixed locale of this scenario again recall Bhabha's
notion of the stereotype "as a form of knowledge and identification that
vacillates between what is always 'in place,' already known, and something
that must be anxiously repeated" (66). Moreover, this repetition endows
the text with a metaleptic function. By metalepsis I mean "any intrusion by
the extradiegetic narrator or narratee into the diegetic universe . . . or the
inverse" as defined by Gérard Genette.[45] For despite Kafka's subversion of
the narrator, every narratee or reader inevitably identifies with the speaker's
situation and repeats the attempt to mediate between the jackals and Arabs
in order to provide the text with a stable meaning.

One aspect of this text, however, militates against the allocation of
fixed identities. The triangulation in this story between the jackals, the
Arabs, and the narrator prevents the establishment of clear subject-object
relations, since every connection is impinged upon by a third party or
the other Other, as it were. Consider, for example, how the jackals influence the speaker's perception of his Arab companions by communicating
their disgust for their masters. In so doing, the jackals must first over-
come the revulsion that they themselves provoke in the narrator, who
clenches his teeth in order to withstand the stench emanating from the
animals' open maws (*DL*, 271). Second, they must convince him of the
counter-intuitive claim that the Arabs are irredeemably filthy because they
consume freshly slaughtered meat instead of carrion. Nevertheless, the
jackals' efforts meet with some success. When they contemplate the mere
sight of the Arabs, the pack hide their heads and their paws and convey
such a profound sense of revulsion that the narrator would have preferred
to have fled from their circle with a high leap (*DL*, 272). Thus the jackals
communicate to the narrator a disgust that should be incomprehensible

to him, since it reverses human notions of what is fit for consumption. Indeed, the narrator's reaction to the jackals' disgust suggests his unconscious recognition that he, as a living being like the Arabs, is also an abomination in the eyes of the jackals, and that he should remove himself from their sight. Moreover, the Western speaker describes the caravan leader creeping up to them against the wind (*DL*, 274). The implication that the Arab would have to remain downwind of both the jackals and the narrator suggests that the animals' vision of the Arab contagion has itself contaminated the perspective of the narrator, who previously perceived the Arab as "hoch und weiß" (*DL*, 270; tall [or high] and white). Thus Kafka's text conveys the virulence of racist rhetoric.

However, Kafka deconstructs the discourse of difference employed by the jackals by undermining the premises on which it is founded. Consider, for example, the chief spokesdog's claim that the jackals find the Arabs so abhorrent that they will not even murder them for fear of sullying themselves: "'Wir werden sie doch nicht töten. Soviel Wasser hätte der Nil nicht, um uns rein zu waschen. Wir laufen doch schon vor dem bloßen Anblick ihres lebenden Leibes weg, in reinere Luft, in die Wüste, die deshalb unsere Heimat ist" (*D*, 272; We're not proposing to kill them. All the water in the Nile couldn't cleanse us of that. Why, the mere sight of their living flesh makes us turn tail and flee into cleaner air, into the desert, which for that very reason is our home, *CS*, 409). Here Kafka parodies racist rhetoric by having the jackals, the absurd embodiment of anti-Semitic clichés, employ precisely that notion of racial contagion used against the Jews. The chief jackal's claim that they have had to run away in order to find their homeland supports this reading. Through the peculiar mixture of conventional logic and irrational contradiction that Gerhard Neumann terms "das gleitende Paradox" (the sliding paradox),[46] Kafka expresses the situation of Jewish minorities in turn-of-the century Europe who unexpectedly found their homeland in countries in which they had merely sought refuge. Further, the notion that one must go out and seek one's *Heimat* subverts the nationalist principle that "Blut und Boden" ("blood and soil") are indivisible.

Indeed, later in the text, Kafka has his jackals undermine the basic dichotomy on which racism is predicated. Railing against the alleged filthiness of the Arabs, the head jackal declares "'Schmutz ist ihr Weiß; Schmutz ist ihr Schwarz; ein Grauen ist ihr Bart; speien muß man beim Anblick ihrer Augenwinkel; und heben sie den Arm, tut sich in der Achselhöhle eine Hölle auf'" (*DL*, 283; Filth is their white; filth is their black; their beards are a horror; the very sight of their eye sockets makes one want to spit; and when they lift an arm, the murk of hell yawns in their armpit, *CS*, 410). While seeking to create an absolute opposition between the supposedly pestilential Arabs and pristine Europeans, Kafka's jackal subverts the basic dichotomy between black and white that underlies racist beliefs. The appearance of the word "*Grau*en" or "horror" ("grau" meaning "gray") immediately after "black" and white" challenges this concept of an absolute opposition still further. Finally, Kafka's play on "Achsel*höhle*" (armpit) and "Hölle" (hell) suggests that the jackals' image of the Arab is a product of rhetoric rather than reality. In this way, Kafka uses the jackals' racist invective to highlight the rhetorical excesses and logical aporia of the discourse.

However, while the jackals and the European narrator both employ racist tropes, the Arabs put metaphorical language to a different use. The caravan leader describes the jackals to the narrator thus: "'Es sind unsere Hunde; schöner als die Eurigen'" (*DL*, 274; They are our dogs; finer dogs than any of yours, *CS*, 410). How can he possibly consider these carrion-consuming, conspiratorial, and craven creatures superior to European dogs? The answer lies in the metaphorical associations of the word "Hund" (dog).[47] For if we read the term as signifying all that is cur-like and contemptible, then the jackals are indeed preeminent canines. Through the Arabs' unusual interpretation of the word "Hund," which ascribes the figurative baseness associated with dogs to actual canines (the jackals), Kafka suggests the arbitrary and flexible nature of the animal metaphors that abound in racist and anti-Semitic discourse. In this way, the genuine alterity of the Arabs' notions of difference and hierarchy in dogs reveal that the supposedly essential differences between Europeans and Arabs cited by the jackals and given credence by the narrator are nothing more than culturally constructed conceits.

Unlike the narrators/protagonists of "Beschreibung eines Kampfes" and "Schakale und Araber," who are unprepared for their quasi-ethnological encounters, the visitor to Kafka's penal colony in "In der Strafkolonie" is described as a "Forschungsreisende" (traveling researcher) on an expressly anthropological mission to examine judicial procedures in every country (*DL*, 229). In this text, as in "Beschreibung eines Kampfes" and "Schakale und Araber," Kafka subjects his Western protagonist to the radical decentering described by Derrida as he finds himself uprooted from his customary sphere and besieged by disturbing alien cultural practices.

Despite the text's complexity, critics tend to subsume it under a single category, offering allegorical readings based on such fields as religion, law, or aesthetics. In so doing they focus exclusively on a single salient theme in a dense, contradictory, discursive network. It is perhaps more productive to consider how these categories interact within the interpretive frameworks suggested by the text itself. In this regard, the field of anthropology, so conspicuously neglected by its alleged practitioner, the Traveler,[48] might offer a new perspective. Let us consider the Old Commandant's regime as the judicial equivalent of the cargo cult. Just as the illiterate, indigenous populations of remote areas performed the rituals of writing in the hope that cargo might magically appear, so the followers of the Old Commandant on Kafka's fictional island inscribe the sentence on

the body of the convict in the belief that justice will be done in a supernatural fashion.

Although Papua New Guinea, the island on which many of the cargo
cults appeared, was under German jurisdiction from 1885 to 1914, I do
not intend to argue that these cults represent an extra-diegetic referent for
Kafka's text. Rather I mean to use the anthropological concept as an analogy to illustrate what happens when a practical process rooted in social reality, such as the passing of a sentence on a convicted criminal, becomes the
object of cultic veneration. Kafka's story thus depicts a Western society that
has gone "native," in that it has reverted to ritualistic practices and a belief
in magic. By showing that this regression has occurred within one generation, Kafka's text suggests the tenuousness of Western civilization.

This emphasis on the regressive and ritualistic tendencies of the colonial regime represents one way of undermining the traditional opposition
between the "civilized" colonizer and the "primitive" native. Another
is to contemplate the historical function of actual penal colonies. Walter
Müller-Seidel's *Die Deportation des Menschen* (1986) paved the way for
subsequent postcolonial readings by asserting the relevance of the historical institution of the penal colony for Kafka's story.[49] However, many
of the later postcolonial interpretations lose the focus of Müller-Seidel's
study and instead subsume the text under the general rubric of colonialism. Such an approach ignores the fact that the penal colony arose far
more out of a concern with the punishment of European convicts than
with the colonization of overseas territories. Indeed, the debate over the
penal colonies in Germany and Austria centered on the health and welfare of the *Volk*, which, it was claimed, could only be preserved through
the permanent removal overseas of degenerate elements. Consider, for
example, how Hans Groß, an ardent advocate of penal colonies and one
of Kafka's law professors,[50] presents the threat posed by degeneracy in an
article entitled "Deportation und Degeneration":

> Unserer Zeit droht viel weniger die Gefahr von gewissen schweren
> Verbrechern, die vielleicht kerngesund sind, — die möge man entspre-
> chend einsperren; viel mehr haben wir zu befürchten von den echten
> Degenerierten, die Verbrechen oder auch nur fortgesetzt Übertre-
> tungen begehen, die unsere Kultur herangezüchtet hat und die man
> dem ausliefern soll, dessen Entziehung an ihrer Existenz schuld ist,
> der Natur. Das können wir tun, wenn wir endlich die Courage zum
> Versuche haben: Deportation für die straffälligen Degenerierten.[51]

> [In our era we are far less threatened by the danger posed by certain
> serious criminals who are perhaps essentially healthy — these may be
> locked up appropriately. Rather we have much more to fear from the
> genuine degenerates who commit crimes or perhaps only commit
> misdemeanors repeatedly, whom our culture has bred, and whom we

must now hand over to that authority whose removal is responsible
for their existence: Nature. We can do this when we finally have the
courage to attempt deportation for the degenerate offenders.]

As Müller-Seidel points out, Groß emphasizes degeneracy as the primary
criterion for deportation, rather than criminality (58). Under Groß's
scheme a serious felon can be safely incarcerated at home, while a mere
habitual offender should be dispatched to a penal colony forthwith if
degenerate tendencies are detected. Here Groß's deployment of the opposition between culture and nature reveals the basic assumptions behind the
establishment of penal colonies. The removal of "nature," that is, the principle of natural selection, has allowed European culture to breed degenerate specimens. Therefore, the transportation of said degenerates to a state
of unalloyed "nature," that is, an overseas penal colony, will rectify this situation. By leaving the term "nature" so nebulous, Groß can simultaneously
denounce the degeneration of the *Volk* and tacitly reinforce the notion that
culture, however debased, is the sole preserve of the West. Thus, as this
excerpt indicates, the penal colony represented a peculiarly insular colonial
institution that combined a paranoid obsession with eugenics at home with
a racist disregard for indigenous populations abroad.

It is the insularity of both the historical penal colony and Kafka's fictitious depiction that eludes those postcolonial critics who cast various
figures and institutions as the colonized "Other." The most idiosyncratic
example of this tendency comes from David Pan. Despite beginning from
the premise that the conflict is intra-European, "between a European primitive and European civilized perspective on law and culture,"[52] Pan goes
on to describe the text as "the tragedy of primitive culture," as represented
by the Old Commandant's regime, which succumbs to the "predations of
a universalist rationalization," embodied by the Traveler (40). By placing
the Old Commandant's colonial regime in the position of a threatened
indigenous culture, Pan only succeeds in reinscribing precisely that binary
opposition between barbarism and civilization that the text interrogates.
The same can be said of those critics who cast the Prisoner as simply and
solely the colonized native.[53] However, while Rolf Goebel proceeds from
the same assumption,[54] he then admits that "It is not even clear, after all,
if the Prisoner really *is* a native in the literal sense of the word — an indigenous inhabitant of the island whose subject position was formed before the
arrival of the . . . colonists" (201). This confusion stems from the mixed
signals that the text sends with regard to both the convict's ethnicity and
his position on the island. As Elizabeth Boa points out, the reference to his
"wulstig" (thick) lips (*DL*, 211) can be construed as a "racist marker suggesting African features,"[55] but this hint hardly accords with the ostensible
setting of the tropical Far East, as suggested by the teahouse (*DL*, 246).
Indeed, taken in conjunction with the initial description of the Prisoner as

"ein stumpfsinniger, breitmäuliger Mensch mit verwahrlostem Haar und Gesicht" (*DL*, 203; a vacant-looking, wide-mouthed person with unkempt hair and face), those bulbous lips might indicate a physiognomy associated with degeneracy, a condition for which, according to Groß and his fellow advocates for penal colonies, deportation was the only cure. However, we see that the convict is initially described as a soldier in the colonial army (*DL*, 203) and that he is even able to strike up a rapport with his fellow enlisted man, the guard. Thus the text places the figure of the convict in all the subject positions available in the context of the penal colony: the colonized native, the degenerate deportee, and the lowly soldier. Equally, his actions and reactions run the gamut of those associated with the position of subaltern, whether as a degenerate deportee or "primitive" native. His responses range from his violent rebellion against his superior to his abject submission as a prisoner described as "hündisch ergeben" (*DL*, 203; so like a submissive dog, *CS*, 140), from his childlike clownish capering on being released (*DL*, 239) to his vengeful glee on realizing it is now the Officer who will submit to the machine (*DL*, 241). Yet despite the multiple roles played by the prisoner, the fact remains that the only convict we encounter in this penal colony is a soldier of the colonizing power facing summary execution on an unproven charge. From the very beginning Kafka's text suggests that the insularity of this system will lead to its self-annihilation long before the officer's suicide or the destruction of his machine.

In order to interrogate not only the island's judicial system but also the attitudes of the Western Traveler who comes to inspect it, this text repeatedly turns the anthropological gaze inward. By focusing on the presumptions of sovereignty, rationality, and even humanity displayed by the Traveler in his ethnological encounter with the island, we can see how this story challenges some of the foundational assumptions behind the West's self-conception.

Like "Schakale und Araber," "In der Strafkolonie" undermines the protagonist's pretensions to objectivity by placing him in a situation in which his very presence impinges upon the phenomenon under observation. Indeed, both the Traveler and the Officer suspect an ulterior motive in the New Commandant's invitation to witness the execution (*DL*, 223 and 225 respectively): that the Commandant will exploit the Traveler's probable outrage in order to push for the abolition of the practice. The predetermined function of this act of observation thus militates against impartial analysis. Conversely, the Officer makes strenuous efforts to enlist the Traveler's support for the Old Commandant's juridical system. Here the visitor's physical situation reflects his lack of independence. For a start, the Officer directs the Traveler's movements with regard to the machine, obliging him to come closer to observe particular aspects of the apparatus, forcibly ushering him to his seat (*DL*, 213) and even holding him back when the Prisoner ventures too far forward (*DL*, 216).

Moreover, the Officer's solicitation of the Traveler's support comes to resemble a sexual overture: he takes the visitor by the hand and makes him feel the cotton "bed" (*DL*, 208), walks arm in arm with him (*DL*, 212), and finally embraces him with his head on the Traveler's shoulder (*DL*, 226). The Officer's homoerotic attraction toward his interlocutor not only suggests the unpredictable effects of the latter's presence on the objects of his study, but also underlines the impossibility of detached and impartial observation. Indeed, while the Traveler subscribes to the notion of unobtrusive observation, that is, of traveling "only as an observer, with no intention at all of altering other people's methods of administering justice" (*DL*, 222; *CS*, 151), the conclusion of the text demonstrates that such surveillance inevitably obtrudes upon its object: the Traveler's ultimate rejection of the Officer's overtures and his method of execution leads to the latter's suicide and to the collapse of his machine. Thus the Traveler, whose stated aim is to witness the execution, does not merely disrupt, but rather destroys, the entire judicial system under observation.

Of course the annihilation of an abhorrent practice, however anthropologically intriguing it may be, is to be welcomed. Why then should we not consider the Traveler's intervention a timely reassertion of truly enlightened Western values in the face of barbarism and wanton cruelty?[56] Here I would like to depart from the tendency of some critics to duplicate the adversarial tenor of the text and side wholly with either the Traveler or the Officer in their readings. David Pan, for example, takes the opposing view of the conflict and declares unequivocally that "the officer is the hero."[57] It is not surprising that critics such as Pan throw their support behind one antagonist in the conflict between the Officer and the Traveler. For as Axel Hecker trenchantly observes, the critics themselves can be divided into "officers" and "travelers." The former offer narrow and specific interpretations of the text that attempt to read the text in allegorical terms.[58] The latter seek a more balanced view, weighing the evidence in a more judicious fashion, but, according to Hecker, fail to provide a comprehensive and definitive statement of the text's meaning (117). At the risk of showing my hand and siding with my fellow travelers, I take the view that the adversarial structure of the text invites a critical evaluation of both the Officer and the Traveler. For if the text unflinchingly depicts the horrors perpetrated by the Old Commandant's colonial regime, it also portrays the Western visitor's response to these atrocities as wholly inadequate. Indeed, a closer inspection of the work reveals that the Traveler fails to uphold the Enlightenment principles of impartiality, humanitarianism, logic, and egalitarianism, and instead succumbs to equivocation, indifference, superstition, and excessive deference to authority.

While the text presents the Traveler's goal of impartiality as unattainable, it also casts doubt on the morality of his objective. Although dissatisfied with the judicial process (or lack of it), he tells himself that he is in a penal colony, where "extraordinary measures were needed and . . . military discipline must be enforced to the last" (*DL*, 214; *CS*, 146). Here the categories that the Traveler invokes to justify his inaction are irrelevant. Certainly, one can imagine that the context of a penal colony and a military outpost might result in a somewhat abbreviated judicial process. However, these circumstances cannot begin to justify the fact that the Officer refuses even to inform the accused of the charges against him before passing the automatic verdict of guilty. Nor is there anything "necessary" about a prolonged period of torture in which the law allegedly transgressed by the convict is inscribed upon his body until he eventually succumbs to his wounds. Thus the Traveler represents a peculiarly bloodless brand of cultural relativism[59] that seems willing to accept any atrocity in the name of difference and to invoke spurious grounds for its own inaction.

A subsequent passage in the text confirms the equivocation behind the Traveler's supposedly principled neutrality:

> Der Reisende überlegte: Es ist immer bedenklich, in fremde Verhältnisse einzugreifen. Er war weder Bürger der Strafkolonie, noch Bürger des Staates, dem sie angehörte. Wenn er diese Exekution verurteilen oder gar hintertreiben wollte, konnte man ihm sagen: Du bist ein Fremder, sei still. Darauf hätte er nichts erwidern, sondern nur hinzufügen können, daß er sich in diesem Falle selbst nicht begreife, denn er reise nur mit der Absicht zu sehen und keineswegs etwa, um fremde Gerichtsverfassungen zu ändern. Nun lagen aber hier die Dinge allerdings sehr verführerisch. Die Ungerechtigkeit des Verfahrens und die Unmenschlichkeit der Exekution war zweifellos. Niemand konnte irgendeine Eigennützigkeit des Reisenden annehmen, denn der Verurteilte war ihm fremd, kein Landsmann und ein gar nicht zum Mitleid auffordernder Mensch. (*DL*, 222)

> [The explorer thought to himself: It's always a ticklish matter to intervene decisively in other people's affairs. He was neither a member of the penal colony nor a citizen of the state to which it belonged. Were he to denounce this execution or actually try to stop it, they would say to him: You are a foreigner, mind your own business. He could make no answer to that, unless he were to add that he was amazed at himself in this connection, for he traveled only as an observer, with no intention at all of altering other people's methods of administering justice. Yet here he found himself strongly tempted. The injustice of the procedure and the inhumanity of the execution were undeniable, No one could suppose that he had a selfish interest in the matter, for the condemned man was a complete stranger, not a fellow countryman or even at all sympathetic to him. (*CS*, 151–52)]

Here the Traveler suggests his consternation by repeatedly invoking the term "fremd" (foreign or strange) in order to separate himself from the execution, the trial, and the Prisoner respectively. While his initial misgivings about intervening in foreign affairs appear justified, his reference to his citizenship in the second sentence seems utterly misplaced. After all, the Officer's description of the juridical procedure has already revealed that the notion of citizenship, with all its attendant rights, has absolutely no bearing on the island. Moreover, later in the same paragraph he contradicts his own claim that a foreigner has no right to object to the process by observing that the courtesy with which he has been received and his invitation to the execution even seem to suggest that his judgment on this trial was being sought (*DL*, 222). Far from silencing foreign criticism, the New Commandant's regime has expressly invited an outsider to comment on the judicial process in order to further its reforms. Through the Traveler's subsequent deliberations the text reveals that his preoccupation with his foreign status does not represent a professional precept but rather a personal pretext for his own inaction.

For a researcher apparently engaged in comparative ethnology, the Traveler harbors an extremely rigid notion of alterity, or "otherness." He even experiences the desire to relinquish his neutrality and intervene in the island's affairs as a moment of self-alienation, admitting "daß er sich in diesem Falle selbst nicht begreife" (*DL*, 222; that he was amazed at himself in this connection, *CS* 151; or, more literally: that he did not understand himself in this case.) His inability to understand his own impulse suggests a highly circumscribed self-conception. Moreover, this passage indicates the paradox arising from the Traveler's insistence on neutrality: he can contemplate intervention only when the conditions confirm his fundamental impartiality, that is, when the injustice of the procedure and the inhumanity of the execution are beyond doubt, and when the convict is revealed to be neither a personal acquaintance, nor a compatriot, nor a remotely sympathetic individual (*DL*, 222). Here the extended modifier "ein gar nicht zum Mitleid auffordernder Mensch" (*DL*, 222; literally: a human being who inspired no compassion whatsoever) emphasizes the word "Mensch" (human being) and thus undermines the Traveler's caveats by suggesting the torture of a fellow human being might in itself warrant immediate intervention. Yet while he readily concedes the injustice of the process and the inhumanity of the execution, the researcher considers the need to intercede a temptation that must be resisted in pursuit of the higher ideal of neutrality. Ironically, it is only when the Officer impinges on his impartiality and solicits his support directly that the Traveler reveals his opposition to the process. Until that moment he seems grimly determined to sacrifice the hapless prisoner on the altar of "scientific" objectivity. Through the character's equivocations and rationalizations Kafka indicates the degeneration of the fundamental precepts of the Enlightenment. The categorical imperative to protect one's fellow man from barbarism is now perceived as a siren temptation to abandon the ideal of an utterly dispassionate impartiality that is untempered by humanitarian concerns.

The Traveler's desire to distance himself from the proceedings contrasts starkly with his interest in the execution machine itself. Indeed, during the Officer's detailed description of the apparatus, the Traveler starts to reveal attitudes that resemble those of his interlocutor. Having referred to the cotton wadding ("Watte") on which the victim is placed, the Officer then considers the felt stump used as a gag and dispassionately explains that it is designed to prevent the convict from screaming or biting his tongue, and that the condemned man is obliged to take it in his mouth or his neck will be broken by the strap (*DL*, 208). To which the Traveler blandly responds, "'Das ist Watte?'" (*DL*, 208; Is that cotton wool? *CS*, 143). Such moments reveal the intensely dark and perverse humor within the text. Fascinated by the technical specifications of the apparatus, the Traveler glibly ignores the horrifying torment inflicted by the machine. Indeed, a few lines later we are informed that "Der Reisende war schon ein wenig für den Apparat gewonnen" (*DL*, 208; literally: the Traveler had already been won over to the machine a little). Thus the man on an anthropological mission to observe cultural differences privileges the allure of technology over the welfare of his fellow human beings.

However, the description of the sunlit torture device that follows literally casts an ironic light on the Traveler's incipient admiration for the contraption. As Mark Anderson explains, in the harsh glare of the "schattenlosen Tal" in which the story takes place "light is an obstacle to perception."[60] The Traveler has to shade his eyes from the sun in order to survey the machine, which consists of a Bed and Designer, joined by brass rods "die in der Sonne fast Strahlen warfen" (*DL*, 208; that almost flashed out rays in the sunlight, *CS*, 143). Although the auratic appearance of the device presages the Officer's subsequent claim that it enlightens its victims as to their sins (*DL*, 219), the caveat "fast" (almost) questions the possibility of such illumination. Nevertheless, by presenting the scene through the eyes of the Traveler, the text hints symbolically at his susceptibility to the quasi-religious vision of the machine offered by the Officer.

Indeed, in the course of the narrative the Traveler unconsciously adopts many of the Officer's attitudes towards the machine, his rationalist interest in technology giving way to an occult fetishization. For example, when the machine malfunctions during the Officer's suicide, impaling him instantly rather than gradually inscribing his skin, the Traveler observes, "das war ja keine Folter mehr, wie sie der Offizier erreichen wollte, das war unmittelbarer Mord" (*DL*, 245; this was no exquisite torture such as the officer desired, this was plain murder, *CS*, 165). His response indicates the impact of the Officer's views on his value system. Rather than perceiving the instantaneous execution as the more humane option, the visitor now subscribes to the Officer's notion that prolonged torture is preferable. More importantly, when he removes the Officer's corpse from the needles he searches the face in vain for a sign of the promised salvation (*DL*, 245). This final action suggests that the Officer has made a belated convert of the Traveler after all.

Although the Traveler shares much of the Officer's ethos, it is not surprising that he should reject the Officer's overtures and ultimately side with the authority of the New Commandant. Throughout the text the Traveler seems preoccupied with maintaining the status quo of hierarchical power relations. Thus it is the Traveler, not the Officer, who initially notices to his horror that the Prisoner has ventured too far forward and motions to drive him back, because the Traveler believes that what the Prisoner is doing constitutes a punishable offence (*DL*, 216). Such punctiliousness seems grotesquely misplaced, given the agonizing torment that the Prisoner is about to endure. More importantly, when the Officer finally demands the Traveler's verdict, the latter, described with some irony as "ehrlich" (honest) and "ohne Furcht" (without fear), nevertheless hesitates to voice his opinion in front of the Soldier and Prisoner, lest he set the lower orders a bad example (*DL*, 235). Indeed, despite his rejection of the Old Commandant's penal system, the Traveler's deference to authority extends even to the *ancien régime*. He is therefore disconcerted when the lowly harbor workers in the teahouse treat the Old Commandant's prophetic and admonitory gravestone with derision and encourage the Traveler to share their scorn (*DL*, 248). He pretends to ignore their subversive, conspiratorial smiles and dispenses coins among them, not so much as an act of charity, but rather as an attempt to reimpose some semblance of social order. This concern with maintaining hierarchy comes to the fore in his final action, when he brandishes a knotted rope to deter the Prisoner and Soldier from jumping on board his boat to escape the island (*DL*, 248). This blatant intervention indicates that despite his profound misgivings about the colony's system of justice, he still wishes to uphold its basic functions as a military barrack and prison. Moreover, the Traveler's somewhat histrionic response to the Soldier and Prisoner suggests that he regards their particular presence as a threat. This reaction can best be understood in light of the rapprochement that takes place between the convict and the guard. Even before the Prisoner is released, they peaceably share a meal of rice porridge (*DL*, 230 and 235). After his liberation, the convict amuses the Soldier by capering in a shirt and pants split down the back (*DL*, 239). The levity of the underlings' understanding finds its analogue in the mirthless solidarity of the two "Herren," the Traveler and the Officer. Their adherence to the same code of honor becomes apparent when we learn that the researcher considers the Officer's plan to commit suicide "vollständig richtig" (completely correct) and that he would have acted in the same way in that situation (*DL*, 241). For the Traveler, the laxity that leads a guard to befriend a convict represents a contagion that must be quarantined on the remote island. Moreover, the instrument for restoring order, the knotted rope, recalls the hangman's noose. Through this symbol the text suggests an analogy between the supposedly civilized Western judicial code and the atrocities perpetrated on the island, with both systems eschewing any notion of justice in favor of the arbitrary assertion of hierarchical power.

The fact that the final scene indicates an equivalence between the Western penal system and that of the penal colony should come as no surprise. After all, the horrific abuses carried out on the island arise not from an alien, indigenous culture, but from the European colonial power that has subjugated the territory. Indeed, aside from the Traveler, all the figures and customs connected with the main plot of the abortive execution and the Officer's suicide represent this colonizing force. As we have seen, even the Prisoner is a former colonial soldier who has been sentenced to death for dereliction of duty and insubordination (*DL*, 203).

However, Kafka takes care to avoid specifying the identity of this imperium. For while the Traveler and the Officer converse in French, it is clear from the bemused responses of the Soldier and the Prisoner that the colony does not identify itself with France. To confuse matters further, the ceremonial dagger, which the Officer unceremoniously breaks and discards before submitting himself to the machine (*DL*, 240), suggests the military uniform of Austria-Hungary, an empire devoid of overseas colonies. By obscuring the identity of the colonizing power, Kafka suggests that the peculiar horrors found in this penal colony are representative of Western imperialism in general. Thus when the Officer describes how the New Commandant will introduce the Traveler as "'ein großer Forscher des Abendlandes'" (*DL* 229; a great Western researcher), an ambiguity arises as to whether he is a scholar from, or of, the West. Through the figure of the Traveler, a European anthropologist studying a European colony, the text turns the Western anthropological gaze upon itself to excoriate the barbarism of the supposedly enlightened Occident.

With the demise of the Old Commandant and the rise of his successor, one might expect the end of the barbaric *ancien régime*. However, for the Officer, the self-contained nature of the Old Commandant's system will ensure its survival long after the death of its founder: "Wir, seine Freunde, wußten schon bei seinem Tod, daß die Einrichtung der Kolonie so in sich eingeschlossen ist, daß sein Nachfolger, und habe er tausend neue Pläne im Kopf, wenigstens während vieler Jahre nichts von dem Alten wird ändern können" (*DL*, 206; We who were his friends knew even before he died that the organization of the whole penal colony was so perfect that his successor, even with a thousand new schemes in his head, would find it impossible to alter anything, at least for many years to come, *CS*, 141). As a fanatical devotee of the former leader, the Officer is unable to see how his continued allegiance to the old system and his schemes to thwart the New Commandant's reforms constitute an act of insubordination far more serious than that committed by the convict. But he is not alone in his admiration for the Old Commandant's gifts: the Traveler cannot conceal his wonder at the man's versatility, exclaiming "Hat er denn alles in sich vereinigt? War er Soldat, Richter, Konstrukteur, Chemiker, Zeichner?" (*DL*, 210; Did he combine everything in himself, then? Was he soldier, judge, mechanic, chemist, and draughtsman? *CS*, 144). Contrary to John Donne's dictum, one man does indeed appear to have been an island in this case. Nevertheless, the Traveler's enthusiasm for an autocratic founder of a totalitarian judicial and ideological system again calls into question his credentials as a critical and objective thinker. After all, while the various roles described above are not necessarily mutually exclusive, in the field of justice no one person can fulfill the roles of judge, jury, and executioner, as the Officer claims to do. The task of the critic is therefore to engage in the critical analysis omitted by the Traveler and to point out the inherent contradictions within the Old Commandant's system.

The former régime embraces a number of positions in its penal code that are either inconsistent or absolutely antithetical. Among these are the summary executions practiced on the island, which negate one of the primary purposes of the historical penal colony: to provide an alternative to capital punishment.[61] Further, the prolonged torture enacted by the complex, electrically powered apparatus flies in the face of the historic desire to perform executions more swiftly and therefore more humanely through mechanization, whether through the guillotine or the electric chair. Finally, the Officer's rapturous description of the enlightenment supposedly experienced by the victim during the execution seeks to bridge the irreconcilable divide between capital punishment and rehabilitation:

> "Verstand geht dem Blödesten auf. Um die Augen beginnt es. Von hier aus verbreitete es sich. Ein Anblick, der einen verführen könnte, sich mit unter die Egge zu legen . . . der Mann fängt bloß an, die Schrift zu entziffern, er spitzt den Mund, als horche er. Sie haben gesehen, es ist nicht leicht, die Schrift mit den Augen zu entziffern; unser Mann entziffert sie aber mit seinen Wunden. Es ist allerdings viel Arbeit; er braucht sechs Stunden zu ihrer Vollendung. Dann aber spießt ihn die Egge vollständig auf und wirft ihn in die Grube, . . . Dann ist das Gericht zu Ende, und wir . . . scharren ihn ein." (*DL*, 219–20)

> ["Enlightenment comes to the most dull-witted. It begins around the eyes. From there it radiates. A moment that might tempt one to get under the Harrow oneself . . . the man begins to [decipher] the inscription, he purses his mouth as if he were listening. You have seen how difficult it is to decipher the script with one's eyes; but our man deciphers it with his wounds. To be sure, this is a hard

task; he needs six hours to accomplish it. By that time the Harrow has pierced him quite through and casts him into the pit . . . Then the judgment has been fulfilled, and we . . . bury him." (CS, 150, slightly amended)]

Here the need to attain "Verstand," that is, to understand one's crime rationally, and the arduousness of this task evoke the eighteenth- and nineteenth-century discourses of rehabilitation, which focused on both the moral education of the prisoner's soul and the physical edification of his body through hard labor. However, the penal colony's system of reform results in a mangled corpse rather than a rehabilitated criminal. Thus Kafka's text collapses the historical schema suggested by Michel Foucault in *Discipline and Punish*,[62] whereby the locus of punishment shifts from the body to the soul, into a single, paradoxical act that combines an execution with an education. Moreover, the Officer's claim that one is tempted by the sight of the convict's enlightenment to join him under the harrow attests to the power of the Old Commandant's epistemo-juridical system to transcend its own logical incoherence and engender absolute conviction in its followers.

Indeed, since the condemned man is in no position to benefit from his hard-won knowledge, the edifying effects of the execution must be sought among the witnesses. Thus the Officer's nostalgic account of past executions switches the focus from the victims of the executions to the crowds that used to attend these public spectacles:

"Es war unmöglich, allen die Bitte aus der Nähe zuschaun zu dürfen zu gewähren. Der Kommandant in seiner Einsicht ordnete an, daß vor allem die Kinder berücksichtigt werden sollten; ich allerdings durfte kraft meines Berufes immer dabei stehen; oft hockte ich dort, zwei kleine Kinder rechts und links in meinen Armen. Wie nahmen wir alle den Ausdruck der Verklärung von dem gemarterten Gesicht, wie hielten wir unsere Wangen in den Schein dieser endlich erreichten und schon vergehenden Gerechtigkeit!" (DL, 226)

["It was impossible to grant all the requests to be allowed to watch it from nearby. The commandant in his wisdom ordained that the children should have the preference; I, of course, because of my office had the privilege of always being at hand; often enough I would be squatting there with a small child in each arm. How we all absorbed the look of transfiguration on the face of the sufferer, how we bathed our cheeks in the radiance of that justice, achieved at last and fading so quickly!" (CS, 154)]

Here the condemned man is transformed from the reader of his wounds to a text for others to decipher.[63] However, the Officer's emphasis on the visual reception of the prisoner's "transfiguration" ("Verklärung") casts doubt upon the truth claims in his account. On a practical level, the Commandant's order to show special attention to the children and give these most impressionable members of the community the closest vantage points suggests that this spectacle was intended as a means of indoctrination. Moreover, as Richard Gray explains, the Officer undercuts his own narrative by describing the Prisoner's expression as a "Schein," a term that not only denotes a "glow," but also a mere "semblance" (231). This term thus undermines the Officer's claim to discern an essential transformation within the prisoner based on purely visual information. Finally, by suggesting that justice must be seen to be done in order to be done at all, the Officer inadvertently calls into question the "trial" at hand, for which the Traveler is the sole spectator. For in the absence of the ideological community that claimed to perceive the fleeting manifestation of "justice" in the execution, the ritual ceases to have any meaning.

In invoking the edification of both the audience and the victim of the execution, the Officer imbues the process with such religious significance that the convicted criminal emerges as something of a martyred saint. The ecclesiastical rhetoric is most apparent in the term "Verklärung" (transfiguration), but is also to found in the participial adjective "gemartert" (tortured). (The noun from which the verb derives, "Marter," or "torment," is etymologically linked to the noun "Märtyrium," martyrdom.) In addition, the "Schein" allegedly emanating from the prisoner bathes its audience in a beatific radiance. However, in his use of religious terminology, the Officer, the true believer, inadvertently reveals the *modus operandi* of the ideology to which he subscribes. For in an attempt to reconcile the ennoblement and murder of the convicted man, the system of belief appropriates, or more aptly, colonizes, the realm of religion. Of course, the implicit theological claim in the Officer's speech is nonsensical: no faith would advise torturing individuals to death in order to bask in the reflected glory of their martyrdom. But as we have seen in our examination of the former régime's contradictory positions, logical coherence is not a priority in this totalitarian system. Its objective is rather the occupation of ideological territory, and it is willing to indulge in internal contradictions, mystification, and outright obscurantism in order to assimilate and subordinate every aspect of thought and action on the island.

My perception that there is a tendency toward obfuscation in the Old Commandant's system contrasts starkly with Richard Gray's view that the regime embodies a "totalizing ideology of transparency" (226). For Gray, the direct inscription of the prisoner's crimes into his flesh results in the "perfect, for all intents and purposes *immediate* semiotic transmission of the signified" (225; his italics). In support of this argument, he then cites the glass harrow, which allows the spectators to view the inscription directly and "thus concretizes the drive for transparency associated with the machine as a semiotic apparatus" (226). However, the glass harrow also concretizes the legal notion of transparency: the Old Commandant travesties this principle by rendering the apparatus transparent while constructing a judicial system that remains opaque to the accused. Moreover, the understanding that the victim allegedly derives from the execution does not represent an "immediate semiotic transmission" but rather the protracted, arduous labor of decipherment that the Officer considers essential to the process. The condemned man's hermeneutic difficulties arise from the Old Commandant's arcane designs for the inscriptions, which leave even the well-educated Traveler completely baffled:

> Der Reisende hätte gern etwas Anerkennendes gesagt, aber er sah nur labyrinthartige, vielfach kreuzende Linien, die so dicht das Papier bedeckten, daß man nur mit Mühe die weißen Zwischenräume erkannte. "Lesen Sie," sagte der Offizier. "Ich kann nicht," sagte der Reisende. "Es ist sehr kunstvoll," sagte er ausweichend, "aber ich kann es nicht entziffern." (*DL*, 217)

> [The explorer would have liked to say something appreciative, but all he could see was a labyrinth of lines crossing and recrossing each other which covered the paper so thickly that it was difficult to discern the blank spaces between them "Read it," said the Officer. "I can't," said the explorer. "Yet it's clear enough," said the officer. "It's very ingenious," said the explorer evasively, "but I can't make it out." (*CS*, 148–49)]

It is difficult to discern an ideology of transparency in the obscurantism of the Officer's designs, to which, as Gray states, the Traveler responds with "alienation and total comprehension" (224). The Traveler's evasive reply that the manuscript is very "kunstvoll" (literally: artistic) inadvertently reveals the degree to which the regime has co-opted the field of aesthetics, as evinced by the "theatrical" spectacle of the execution, with its adherence to the Aristotelian unities. However, it is in their indecipherability, rather than their artistry, that these manuscripts serve as symbolic blueprints for the Commandant's ideology as a whole. For just as the elaborate designs efface the white page and with it the basic semiotic distinction between ink and paper, so the ideological system annihilates any trace of alterity, including the crucial internal distinctions between, for example, the judiciary, the arts, and organized religion, in its pursuit of a monolithic hegemony.

This inability to tolerate alterity ultimately leads to the demise of the system. Although the New Commandant's incremental reforms have marginalized its practices and driven away its followers, the deathblow comes from the foreign Traveler. Confronted with his rejection, the Officer applies the precepts of the system to himself, submitting to the harrow and the apt inscription "Sei gerecht!" (*DL*, 238; Be just, *CS*, 161).[64] The

Officer thus adds the role of executed convict to those of judge, jury, and executioner. However, feedback tends to produce distortion: the "justice" invoked by the inscription denies the Officer his longed-for redemption (*DL*, 245) and dictates that the machine, as the embodiment of the Old Commandant's regime, should self-destruct (*DL*, 243–44). Thus the system, faced with the external perspective that resists assimilation, turns upon and consumes itself.

In this regard the reforms advanced by the New Commandant would seem to herald a welcome return to civilization. The invitation extended to the Traveler brings about the demise of the repellant system of executions; the insular cargo cult of justice practiced by his predecessor is replaced by genuine cargo as the island joins the global shipping network; the once mighty Old Commandant now lies in a neglected grave under a table in a teahouse, a fate that plays on the expression "unter den Tisch fallen" (to go by the board.) However, the modus operandi of the new regime is disconcertingly familiar: instead of public executions, the colonists are now obliged to witness meetings of the higher administrative officials (*DL*, 232). Further, the burden of this process of modernization seems to fall disproportionately on the harbor workers whom the Traveler encounters in the teahouse: "Alle waren ohne Rock, ihre Hemden waren zerrissen, es war armes, gedemütigtes Volk" (*DL*, 247; All were without jackets, their shirts were torn, they were a poor humiliated people). Here the term "Volk" (people) indicates that these workers represent a distinct ethnic group, and raises the possibility that they are the remnants of the island's indigenous population. In this regard Kafka's relegation of this group to the epilogue of the text represents an ironic performative of the marginalization that these people have already suffered at the hands of their European oppressors. By showing the material suffering of these workers, the text indicates that the atavistic brutality of the Old Commandant has been superseded by a modern, bureaucratic indifference toward those who suffer in the name of progress. In a final irony, the regimes of the Old and New Commandant thus occupy the positions traditionally associated with the process of colonization. The Old Commandant's system represents the savagery of a "native" population, while the emerging culture of the New Commandant represents the bureaucratic technology and global ambition of the invading colonizers.

While the new regime still harbors a totalizing ambition to integrate all the population into its modernization, there are some signs on the island of a genuine and resistant alterity. The camaraderie that develops between the Soldier and the Prisoner, for example, undermines the hierarchical order and can serve no rational economic purpose for the new regime. When the downtrodden harbor workers exchange sly smiles on seeing the Old Commandant's gravestone, their lack of deference toward the former ruler suggests that they might also resist his successor. Finally, while the women on the island seem to form a harem around the New Commandant, their indulgence of the Prisoner with sweets suggests that they represent a realm of sensuality, of compassion, even of silliness, that cannot be subsumed by a ruling ideology (*DL*, 223). Ironically, it is the Traveler, the one figure who does escape the island, who shows a marked susceptibility to its ethos. When he wards off the Soldier and Prisoner with the knotted rope, he demonstrates that he is still in thrall to the notions of hierarchy and hegemony that inform the island's ideology.

To conclude, we should perhaps consider the alternative conclusions to "In der Strafkolonie" that Kafka drafted in his diary in August 1917, only to reject them. For it seems that the problem with some of these fragmentary texts is their overemphatic declaration of the themes found in this story. In one passage the Traveler declares, "'Ich will ein Hundsfott sein, wenn ich das zulasse'" (I'll be a mangy cur if I let this come to pass) only to take the words literally and begin running around on all fours (*Ta*, 822). This ending ascribes to language the magical power found in written incantation enacted by the execution in the penal colony. Thus the rationalist Traveler comes not only to believe in but also to enact the incantatory power of language associated with "primitive" modes of thought. In another abortive ending the Traveler seems to ponder what could have gone wrong with the Officer's execution:

> "Wie?" sagte der Reisende plötzlich. War etwas vergessen? Ein entscheidendes Wort? Ein Griff? Eine Handreichung? Wer kann in das Wirrsal eindringen? Verdammte böse tropische Luft, was machst du aus mir? Ich weiß nicht was geschieht. Meine Urteilskraft ist zuhause im Norden geblieben. (*Ta*, 823)

> ["How?" said the Traveler suddenly. "Did they forget something? A crucial word? A handle? A moment when they were supposed to lend a hand? Who can penetrate this confusion? Damn you, evil tropical air, what have you done to me? I don't know what's going on. I've left my powers of judgment at home in the North.]

The Kantian term "Urteilskraft" (powers of judgment)[65] evokes the Western Enlightenment tradition at a point when the protagonist's sovereign rationality is most imperiled by the confusion of events. However, when he blames the deleterious effects of the "tropical air" for his befuddlement and sites the home of reason in his native north, the Traveler indicates the irrational hubris that ironically attaches itself to the Western Enlightenment tradition and inevitably misinforms encounters with the exotic Other. The reference to the north also recalls the protagonist's hailing from "dem hohen Norden" (the far north) in "Schakale und Araber," a notion that the wily jackals seek to exploit. Indeed, in all three texts the protagonists are cast as the representatives of the West who find themselves in ethnological encounters, not with genuine alterity, but rather with the exotic emanations of Occidental fantasy. In "Beschreibung eines Kampfes," the Fat Man emerges as the gargantuan embodiment of Western orientalist clichés; the jackals of "Schakale und Araber" represent an amalgam of anti-Semitic stereotypes; the Officer and the Old Commandant's regime exemplify a dream of absolute colonial control. Yet in each of these works the rational order associated with Western hegemony remains in disarray. Instead of having the supposedly enlightened protagonist impose his logic on these irrational projections, Kafka unmasks the very notion of European rationality as merely another figment of the Western imagination.

Notes

[1] Jacques Derrida, "Structure, Sign, and Play in the Discourse of the Human Sciences," in *Writing and Difference*, trans. Alan Bass (Chicago: U of Chicago P, 1978), 282.

[2] Clifford Geertz, *Available Light: Anthropological Reflections on Philosophical Topics* (Princeton, NJ: Princeton UP, 2000), 39.

[3] Homi Bhabha, *The Location of Culture*, 72.

[4] Cf. Rolf Goebel, *Constructing China: Kafka's Orientalist Discourse*, 36–37.

[5] The nested narratives in "Beschreibung eines Kampfes" contrast with the discrete narrative interpolations of the unfinished novel *Das Schloß* (1922). The fact that Kafka's writing career begins and ends with these two unpublished texts suggests his continued fascination and frustration with the problem of polyphonic narrative.

[6] Walter Sokel, "Kafka's Beginnings: Narcissism, Magic, and the Function of Narration in 'Description of a Struggle,'" in *The Myth of Power and the Self: Essays on Franz Kafka* (Detroit, MI: Wayne State UP), 167. The passage that Sokel cites is from Sigmund Freud, *Totem und Tabu*, 375.

[7] Cf. Judith Ryan, "Kafka before Kafka: The Early Stories," in *A Companion to the Works of Franz Kafka*, ed. James Rolleston (Rochester, NY: Camden House, 2002), 64–65.

[8] Hugo von Hofmannsthal, "Ballade des äußeren Lebens," in *Sämtliche Werke*, vol.1, *Gedichte I*, ed. Eugene Weber (Frankfurt am Main: Suhrkamp, 1994), 15.

[9] Hugo von Hofmannsthal, "Ballad of the Outer Life," trans. Michael Hamburger, in Hofmannsthal, *Poems and Verse Plays*, ed. Michael Hamburger (New York: Pantheon, 1961), 33.

[10] Mark Anderson notes the similarity between the two texts, without inferring that it represents a deliberate parody. See Mark M. Anderson, "The Traffic of Clothes: *Meditation* and *Description of a Struggle*," in *Kafka's Clothes: Ornament and Aestheticism in the Habsburg Fin de Siècle*, 37.

[11] I have again taken the liberty of emending Tania and William Stern's translation to avoid the confusing reference to "Sunday best" instead of simply "clothes" (Kleider).

[12] Hofmannsthal, "Ballad of the Outer Life."

[13] Hofmannsthal, "Ballade des äußeren Lebens."

[14] Hofmannsthal, "Ballad of the Outer Life."

[15] The *Complete Stories* does not contain this passage.

[16] This is by no means the first study to link "Beschreibung eines Kampfes" with Nietsche's essay "Über Wahrheit und Lüge im aussermoralischen Sinne." See, for example, Lukas Trabert, "Erkenntnis- und Sprachproblematik in Franz Kafkas *Beschreibung eines Kampfes* vor dem Hintergrund von Friedrich Nietzsches 'Über Wahrheit und Lüge im aussermoralischen Sinne,'" *Deutsche Vierteljahrsschrift für Literaturwissenschaft und Geistesgeschichte* 61.2 (Jun. 1987): 298–324, and Seiji Hattori, "Funktion und Bedeutung der "Seekrankheit auf festem Lande": Zur poetologischen Struktur von Kafkas *Beschreibung eines Kampfes*," *Studien zur deutschen Literatur und Sprache: Japanische Gesellschaft für Germanistik* 37 (2005): 145.

[17] Friedrich Nietzsche, "Über Wahrheit und Lüge im aussermoralischen Sinne," in *Kritische Studienausgabe*, vol. 1, *Die Geburt der Tragödie, Unzeitgemäße Betrachtungen I–IV, Nachgelassene Schriften, 1870–1873*, ed. Giorgio Colli und Mazzino Montinari (Munich: dtv, 1999), 884 (Nietzsche's italics).

[18] Friedrich Nietzsche, "On Truth and Lying in an Extra-Moral Sense," in *Friedrich Nietzsche on Rhetoric and Language*, ed. and trans. Sander L. Gilman, Carole Blair, and David J. Parent (New York: Oxford UP, 1989), 252.

[19] Perhaps the most startling example of this tendency is Walter Sokel's abstraction of sexuality in his reading of the text. Sokel reads the first narrator's statement, "My acquaintance became very valuable to me as one who gives me worth before people without my having to earn it myself. I looked at my acquaintance with eyes of love" as merely an act of supplication, conveyed through "art 'as a form of prayer'" (Sokel, "Kafka's Beginnings," 169). For a general survey of homoerotic elements in Kafka's texts, see Mark M. Anderson, "Kafka, Homosexuality, and the Aesthetics of 'Male Culture,'" in *Gender and Politics in Austrian Fiction*, ed. Ritchie Robertson and Edward Timms (Edinburgh: Edinburgh UP, 1996), 79–99. For a specific reading of "Beschreibung eines Kampfes" that employs queer theory, see Anjeana Hans, "An Excess of Discourse: "Beschreibung eines Kampfes" and Homosexual Identity," in "Defining Desires: Homosexual Identity and German Discourse, 1900–1933" (PhD diss., Harvard University, 2005), 53–80.

[20] This passage is not included in *The Complete Stories*.

[21] See Helmut Preidel, "Charles IV," in *Encyclopaedia Britannica*, 2004. Encyclopaedia Britannica Premium Service, accessed 12 Mar. 2004, http://www.britannica.com/eb/article?eu=22909.

[22] Other critics have pointed out that both incidents in *Genesis* represent acts of rebellion against paternal authority. Walter Sokel connects Ham's mockery of the naked Noah, "the first rebellion of son against father" with "mankind's self assertion against God" in the building of the Tower of Babel. See Sokel, "Language and Truth in Kafka," *German Quarterly* 52.3 (May 1979): 367. Wolf Kittler takes this argument further by arguing that the "curse of the father" is brought down on both the Tower of Babel and Ham for violating the "prohibition against seeing the

father as he really is." Kittler, "Brief oder Blick: Die Schreibsituation der frühen Texte von Kafka," in *Der junge Kafka*, ed. Gerhard Kurz (Frankfurt am Main: Surhkamp, 1984), 40–67; here 48. This latter reference is also cited in Seiji Hattori, "Funktion und Bedeutung der "Seekrankheit auf festem Lande," 146.

[23] Hattori provides another alternative reading of Noah's nudity, arguing that it can be interpreted as a momentary return to the paradisiacal state before the Fall. See Hattori, "Funktion und Bedeutung der 'Seekrankheit auf festem Lande,'" 146.

[24] Said, *Orientalism*, 128.

[25] James Whitlark, *Behind the Great Wall: A Post-Jungian Approach to Kafkaesque Literature* (Cranberry, NJ: Associated University Presses, 1991), 100–101.

[26] Max Brod, "Nachwort" to *Franz Kafka, Beschreibung eines Kampfes: Die zwei Fassungen; Parallelausgabe nach den Handschriften*, ed. Max Brod; vol. ed. Ludwig Dietz (Frankfurt am Main: Fischer, 1969), 157. Cited in Goebel, *Constructing China*, 38.

[27] Goebel, *Constructing China*, 38.

[28] Judith Ryan, "Die zwei Fassungen der 'Beschreibung eines Kampfes': Zur Entwicklung von Kafkas Erzähltechnik," *Jahrbuch der Deutschen Schillergesellschaft* 14 (1970): 568.

[29] Ryan, "Die zwei Fassungen," 569–70.

[30] Kittler, "Brief oder Blick," 41.

[31] Walter Sokel, "Das Verhältnis der Erzählperspektive zu Erzählgeschehen und Sinngehalt in 'Vor dem Gesetz,' 'Schakale und Araber' und *Der Prozess*: Ein Beitrag zur Unterscheidung von 'Parabel' und "Geschichte' bei Kafka," *Zeitschrift für Deutsche Philologie* 86 (1967): 284.

[32] Sokel, "Das Verhältnis der Erzählperspektive," 282. Ruth Gross cites Sokel's interpretation in "Hunting Kafka out of Season," in Rolleston, *A Companion to the Works of Franz Kafka*, 257.

[33] The articles by Walter Sokel and Ruth Gross cited above represent two exceptions to this trend. Sokel interprets the jackals and Arabs according to an antithesis found in Nietzsche's *Genealogy of Morals*, with the jackals representing ascetic ideals and the Arabs the contradictory notion of the worldly, elegant life ("das vornehme Leben"). Sokel, "Das Verhältnis der Erzählperspektive zu Ezählgeschehen," 287. Although Gross uses Sokel's article as a springboard she adds a metaliterary twist to her readings of the jackals and Arabs, who she claims represent "modernist authors" and "their readers" respectively (259).

[34] Martin Buber, "Unsere Literaten und die Gemeinschaft," *Der Jude*, Oct. 1916/17, 464. Quoted in Jens Tismar, "Kafkas 'Schakale und Araber' im zionistischen Kontext betrachtet," *Jahrbuch der Deutschen Schillergesellschaft* 19 (1975): 309.

[35] William C. Rubinstein, "Kafka's 'Jackals and Arabs,'" *Monatshefte für Deutschen Unterricht, Deutsche Sprache und Literatur* 59 (1967): 14–17.

[36] Sander L. Gilman, *Franz Kafka, the Jewish Patient* (New York: Routledge, 1995), 158.

37 Homi K. Bhabha, *The Location of Culture*, 82.

38 Gilman, *The Jewish Patient*, 150–52.

39 Rubinstein, "Kafka's Jackals and Arabs," 16.

40 Johann Wolfgang von Goethe, "Selige Sehnsucht," in *Werke: Hamburger Ausgabe*, vol. 2, *Gedichte und Epen II* (Munich: Deutscher Taschenbuch Verlag, 1988), 19, lines 13–16.

41 Johann Wolfgang von Goethe, "Divine Longing," in *Poems of the East and West: Bi-lingual Edition of the Complete Poems*, trans. John Whaley (New York: Peter Lang, 1998), 47.

42 Hugo von Hofmannsthal,"Ein Traum von großer Magie" in *Sämtliche Werke: Kritische Ausgabe, Gedichte I*, ed. Eugene Weber (Frankfurt am Main: Fischer Verlag, 1984), 52–53.

43 Hofmannsthal, "Ein Traum von großer Magie," 53, line 33.

44 Pieter M. Judson, "Rethinking the Liberal Legacy," in *Rethinking Vienna 1900*, ed. Steven Beller (New York: Berghahn Books, 2001), 68.

45 Gérard Genette, *Narrative Discourse: An Essay in Method*, trans. Jane E. Lewin (New York: Cornell UP, 1980), 234–35.

46 Gerhard Neumann, "Umkehrung und Ablenkung: Franz Kafkas 'Gleitendes Paradox,'" *Deutsche Vierteljahrsschrift fur Literaturwissenschaft und Geistesgeschichte* 42 (1968): 703–5.

47 Kafka's most striking use of this term occurs at the end of the novel *Der Proceß*, as K. contemplates the manner of his execution: "'Wie ein Hund!'" Franz Kafka, *Der Proceß*, ed. Malcolm Pasley (Frankfurt am Main: Fischer, 1990), 241.

48 Given that the island is evidently "terra cognita" and under European jurisdiction, I have chosen to render the character's title of "Forschungsreisende" as simply "the Traveler," rather than "the Explorer" favored by some translators. See for example Edwin and Willa Muir's translation, "In the Penal Colony," in *Franz Kafka: The Complete Stories*, ed. Nahum N. Glatzer (New York: Schocken, 1995), 140. Moreover, since the term "Forschungsreisende" occurs only once in the opening sentence and is thereafter replaced by "der Reisende," "the Traveler" reflects Kafka's terminology and usage more accurately.

49 Walter Müller-Seidel, *Die Deportation des Menschen: Kafkas Erzählung "In der Strafkolonie" im europäischen Kontext* (Stuttgart: Metzler, 1986).

50 For details of the scholarly interaction between Groß and Kafka, see Müller-Seidel, *Die Deportation des Menschen*, 50.

51 Hans Groß, "Deportation and Degeneration," *Politisch-Anthropologische Revue: Monatsschrift für das Soziale Leben der Völker* 4 (1905/6): 286. Quoted in Müller-Seidel, *Die Deportation des Menschen*, 58.

52 David Pan, "Kafka as a Populist: Re-Reading 'In the Penal Colony,'" *Telos: A Quarterly Journal of Radical Social Theory* 101 (Fall 1994): 3.

53 For interpretations of the prisoner as a colonized native, see the following: Jie-Oun Lee, "Transformation des Kolonialdiskurses in Franz Kafkas 'In der Strafkolonie,'" *Literatur für Leser* 23.1 (2000): 36; Paul Peters, "Witness to

the Execution: Kafka and Colonialism," *Monatshefte für deutschsprachige Literatur und Kultur* 93.4 (Winter 2001): 409; Karen Piper, "The Language of the Machine: A Postcolonial Reading of Kafka," *Journal of the Kafka Society of America* 20.1–2 (Jun.-Dec. 1996): 47; John Zilcosky, *Kafka's Travels: Exoticism, Colonialism, and the Traffic of Writing* (New York: Palgrave Macmillan, 2003), 107.

[54] Rolf Goebel, "Kafka and Postcolonial Critique: *Der Verschollene*, 'In der Strafkolonie,' and 'Beim Bau der chinesischen Mauer,'" in Rolleston, *A Companion to the Works of Franz Kafka*, 199.

[55] Elizabeth Boa, *Gender, Class and Race in the Letters and the Fictions* (Oxford: Clarendon, 1996), 139.

[56] Most recently, Ritchie Robertson has argued for such a positive reading of the Traveler's intervention in a talk entitled "Kafka and Institutions" at the conference "Kafka at 125," held at Duke University and the University of North Carolina, 2–4 April 2009.

[57] Pan, "Kafka as a Populist," 40.

[58] Axel Hecker,"Die Dekonstruktionsmaschine — *In der Strafkolonie*," in *An den Rändern des Lesbaren: Dekonstruktive Lektüren zu Franz Kafka* (Vienna: Passagen, 1998), 115.

[59] Cf. Russell Berman's denunciation of the Traveler as "the prototype of the effete liberal." Russell Berman, *Enlightenment or Empire: Colonial Discourse in German Culture* (Lincoln: U of Nebraska P, 1998), 232.

[60] Mark Anderson, *Kafka's Clothes*, 173.

[61] See Müller-Seidel, *Die Deportation des Menschen*, 26.

[62] Michel Foucault, *Discipline and Punish: The Birth of the Prison*, trans. Alan Sheridan (New York: Vintage Books, 1995).

[63] See Richard Gray, "Disjunctive Signs: Semiotics, Aesthetics, and Failed Mediation in 'In der Strafkolonie,'" in Rolleston, *A Companion to the Works of Franz Kafka*, 213–45, here 229.

[64] This decision represents a departure for the Officer, who had previously shown no such self-awareness in his conduct of the "trial." For example, his decision to ignore the fact that the Soldier is dozing off (*DL*, 216) and his scheme to thwart the New Commandant (*DL*, 227–29) parallel the convict's "crimes" of falling asleep and rebelling against a superior.

[65] For a full discussion of the significance of this term, see Gray, "Disjunctive Signs," 239.

4: The Contingent Continent: Kafka's China in "Beim Bau der chinesischen Mauer" and "Ein altes Blatt"

IN THE PREFACE TO *The Order of Things* Foucault cites an essay by Borges[1] in which "a certain Chinese encyclopaedia" offers the following classification for animals:

> (a) belonging to the Emperor, (b) embalmed, (c) tame, (d) suckling pigs, (e) sirens, (f) fabulous, (g) stray dogs, (h) included in the present classification, (i) frenzied, (j) innumerable, (k) drawn with a very fine camel hair brush, (l) *et cetera*, (m) having just broken the water pitcher, (n) that from a long way off look like flies.[2]

By quoting this passage Foucault suggests the contingent and arbitrary nature of our own systems of taxonomy. For Foucault, China occupies a paradoxical position in the Western imaginary as the site of a pervasive yet perplexing system of order. On the one hand, "in our traditional imagery" Chinese culture is "the most meticulous, the most rigidly ordered, the one . . . most attached to the pure delineation of space; we think of it as a civilization of dikes and dams beneath the eternal face of the sky; we see it spread and frozen over the entire face of a continent surrounded by walls" (xix). However, this realm that is supposedly obsessed with spatial order employs principles of organization that appear unintelligible and chaotic to the Western observer. Referring to the Chinese writing system, which "erects the motionless and still-recognizeable images of things themselves in vertical columns," Foucault argues that the taxonomy proposed above results in "a kind of thought without space," in "words and categories that lack all life and place but are rooted in ceremonial space, overburdened with complex figures, with tangled paths, strange places and secret communications" (xix). He concludes with the claim that "There would appear to be, . . . at the other extremity of the earth . . ., a culture entirely devoted to the ordering of space, but that does not distribute the multiplicity of existing things into any of the categories that make it possible for us to name, speak, and think" (xix). Thus Foucault invokes the staggering alterity of Borges's Chinese encyclopaedia in order to startle the reader out of the assumption that Western epistemological categories are themselves anything more than culturally contingent constructs.

However, there is a slippage in this passage that the sweep and majesty of Foucault's prose cannot quite conceal. (I have quoted this section at length in order to convey the insistent and persuasive quality of his rhetoric.) For although Foucault initially presents his comments on China in the context of the Western imaginary ("In our dreamworld. . . . In our traditional imagery, . . . we think of . . . we see it as . . .") he nevertheless refers in the course of his argument to the *fact* of Chinese pictograms. This detour into the reality of the Chinese alphabet from Borges's fictional encyclopedia, which, as the alphabetization within the excerpt underlines, is of course written in Roman script, appears somewhat specious. After all, could we not just as well argue that the pictorial elements retained in Chinese characters create a system of vital signs, as it were, when compared with the lifeless phonemes of the Western alphabet? Moreover, Foucault fails to acknowledge fully that his depiction of China, which presents a utopian realm of absolute order that nevertheless abounds in arcane and mysterious practices, is itself derived from the Western orientalist discourse. By confusing Borges's fictional encyclopaedia with the reality of the Chinese alphabet, Foucault thus perpetuates received notions concerning China at the very moment that he announces his intent to undertake a probing, self-critical examination of the foundations of Occidental knowledge, "to uncover the deepest strata of Western culture" (24).

My point here is not to take Foucault to task for what is, after all, a single paragraph in a seminal work. Rather I draw attention to the slippage in his argument in order to illustrate the profound difficulty of his undertaking. How are we to employ an image of alterity, here that of China, in order to challenge the fundamental assumptions of Western culture, while remaining cognizant of the fact that that image is itself a discursive formation, a product of those same Occidental preconceptions? In this regard, two stories by Kafka, "Beim Bau der chinesischen Mauer" and "Ein altes Blatt," both written in 1917, seem to show a great awareness of this dilemma, while undertaking a project not unlike Foucault's:[3] that is, the excavation of the foundation of Western epistemology through recourse to that figure of absolute alterity, China. On the one hand, these texts deploy orientalist clichés in a self-aware fashion, subverting the West's supposed knowledge of the Chinese Other in the ironic articulation of its stereotypical assertions. On the other hand, by depicting the Chinese empire as an unfathomable institution that perplexes even its subjects, Kafka undermines the bedrock assumptions that inform national and cultural self-identity in both the East and West. Indeed, as we shall see, the contingent, fragile, and arcane nature of Kafka's Chinese imperium implicitly alludes to the contemporary instability of the Habsburg Empire in 1917, tottering amid the turmoil of the First World War.[4] By suggesting a relationship of analogy in his fictions between China and his own "eastern empire" of Österreich,[5] Kafka thus implicitly challenges the notion of a dichotomy between East and West that is the foundation of the orientalist discourse.

However, Kafka was by no means the first to use the image of China as a metaphor for the Habsburg Empire. As Weiyan Meng points out, the comparison had become something of a tradition for nineteenth-century satirists, who frequently invoked China in order to criticize the decadence, authoritarianism, and political stagnation of Europe's "middle kingdom."[6] Indeed, one of Kafka's favorite authors, Franz Grillparzer, produced one of the earliest sustained allegories on this theme, disguising various Habsburg emperors as oriental despots in order to lampoon their regimes.[7] Moreover, Kafka's Sino-Austrian connection developed from a broad analogy between the two corrupt empires to a more detailed congruence between their institutions and ideologies. In his book *Franz Kafka aus Prag*, Jiri Grusa stresses this political analogy, claiming that Kafka's Chinese metaphors are nothing exotic given the "'Confucian' institutions of the empire," its "Mandarin civil service" and "almost 'Chinese' state religion."[8] Here we need only consider how the word "Mandarin" has entered the English and German lexicons as a term for an elite and inscrutable civil servant in order to grasp how pervasive this image of Chinese bureaucracy is in the West.

I should stress at this stage that I do not intend to examine whether China really epitomized historical stagnation, imperial despotism, and political immaturity, as much of contemporary Europe believed.[9] Instead I will examine the self-critical tendencies in two of Kafka's stories set in China: "Beim Bau der chinesischen Mauer" and "Ein altes Blatt." Both these texts deploy oriental motifs and topoi, not to reinforce Western hegemony, as Edward Said's notion of orientalism would suggest, but rather to allude to the current state of Austria-Hungary. Nor do these works invoke the Sino-Austrian connection merely for satirical effect, but rather to probe received notions of national, ethnic, and historical identity and thus question the fundamental viability of Europe's "middle kingdom."

However, before we consider these two texts, I would like to examine a lesser-known fragment by Kafka that dates from earlier in 1917 and that describes an intercultural encounter between a Western narrator and a Chinese scholar.[10] For this text illustrates Kafka's ability to inflect even the hoariest clichés of the orientalist discourse with moments of self-reflection and self-critique. While lying on his sofa and reading a historical tome, the narrator is interrupted by his maid, who announces an unexpected visitor: "'ein Chineser" (Chinaman,) as she puts it (*NS,* 323). While this exotic guest, who speaks no English yet possesses a calling card, inspires both hilarity and fear in the maid, the narrator declares decisively that this visitor should be shown in. But on glimpsing the narrator's "Riesengestalt" (giant frame) his visitor has second thoughts and dashes into the hallway, only to be caught by the narrator, who carefully pulls his errant guest towards him by his silk belt (*NS*, 324). Now the narrator has a moment to peruse his exotic caller, and we learn that he is obviously an academic, with his small and weak build, horn-rimmed spectacles, and stiff, sparse goatee. He is further described as a "friendly little man," who smiles with "half-closed eyes" (*NS*, 324) Here the reader might understandably experience relief that the text breaks off at this point, since the passage seems to be inextricably entangled, like the unfortunate Chinese scholar, in an orientalist cartoon. Not only are we confronted, as Rolf Goebel points out, with the "stereotypical Western caricature of the weak and ineffective Chinese scholar,"[11] but we also must contend with the racist references to the academic's diminutive physique, obliging smile (especially under the circumstances), and "half-closed eyes." In this context we might readily agree with Goebel's assessment that the text's refusal to allow the Chinese scholar to speak "signifies the considerable difficulty, plaguing its author like so many orientalists before and after him, of allowing for a meaningful cross-cultural dialogue between East and West that transcends racial discrimination and European domination" (22). Moreover, given this description of the Chinese visitor, the narrator with his historical tome certainly appears to be "akin to the typical Saidian orientalist," who is "caught between textuality, the written word of cultural discourse . . ., and the empirical reality of the strange, provocative and puzzling yet irresistibly attractive Orient" (21). Thus Kafka's text seems to show how the failure of intercultural exchange only reinforces stereotypical notions of the oriental Other.

However, such a reading does not take into account how Kafka ironizes his narrator both within the diegesis and at the meta-textual level. Within the realm of the story, the narrator's response to the Chinese visitor betrays a lack of sophistication that undermines his intellectual pretensions when he asks if his Chinese visitor is wearing "Chinesenkleidung" (traditional Chinese clothing; *NS*, 323). This fatuous reaction suggests the limited worldview of a child who expects all foreigners to wear their national costume, as in the picture books. (The fact that the Chinese scholar actually does so indicates that he is perhaps a product of the narrator's reading and imagination, an Other of invention, rather than a representative of genuine alterity.) The narrator confirms the narrowness of his perspective when he asks the maid to check whether the visitor really wants to see him: "'frag ob er mich wirklich besuchen will, der ich unbekannt im Nachbarhaus, wie sehr erst unbekannt in China bin'" (*NS*, 323; ask if he really wants to see me, I who am unknown next door, let alone in China). Moreover, the somewhat unrealistic oratorical flourish "'der ich'" (I who) suggests Kafka's meta-textual subversion of his narrator, whom he presents not as a realistic and therefore persuasive figure, but rather as a self-consciously literary creation. Consider how the speaker introduces himself at the opening of the fragment: "Alt, in großer Leibesfülle, unter leichten Herzbeschwerden lag ich nach dem Mittagessen einen Fuß am Boden auf dem Ruhebett und las ein geschichtliches Werk" (NS, 323; Old, with my great girth and mild heart trouble, I was lying after lunch with one foot on the day bed and was reading a volume of history.) Such a self-description not only violates the notion of verisimilitude (in that first-person narrators rarely introduce themselves with references to their age, weight, and medical conditions), but also transgresses narrative convention. Normally we accept that a first-person narrator is necessarily unreliable in one respect: that is, that his or her single perspective inevitable precludes an objective self-portrait. Here, however, the first-person narrator begins with a description of himself that suggests both the objectivity ("Alt, in großer Leibesfülle") and omniscience ("unter leichten Herzbeschwerden") associated with third-person narrative. By inflecting the narrative with this reflexivity, Kafka does not suggest a greater self-awareness on the part of his narrator, but rather creates an unstable combination of narrative addresses that draw attention to the narrator's doubtful ontological status as a fictional character. The narrator's second reference to his physique confirms this technique: "Aufstehend und meine Riesengestalt reckend, mit der ich jeden Besucher in dem niedrigen Zimmer erschrecken mußte, gieng ich zur Tür" (NS, 323; Standing up and stretching my giant frame, with which I must have scared every visitor in the low room, I went to the door.). Here he breaks with the conventions of realism by making the sudden and unlikely realization that he must have scared all his previous visitors with his gargantuan height and girth and by assimilating the oriental Other's response to his "giant frame" into his own self-description. Thus this fragment playfully subverts the orientalist clichés that pervade his depiction of the Chinese scholar by juxtaposing him with a Western narrator who seems equally implausible and fictitious.

In the context of Kafka's orientalist fictions this fragment recalls the quasi-ethnological encounters, examined in the previous chapter, of "Beschreibung eines Kampfes," "Schakale und Araber," and "In der Strafkolonie." As such, the fragment represents a point in the progressive exotification of Kafka's narrative perspective, from the hermetic reflexivity of "Beschreibung," in which the figure of the Fat Man embodies an amalgam of orientalist stereotypes, to the apparent exoticism of the Chinese narrators in "Beim Bau der chinesischen Mauer" and "Ein altes Blatt." However, we must not confuse Kafka's adoption of Chinese narrative voices in these texts with an unexamined assertion of authority over his subject matter, that is, with the pretense that he can now narrate China from "within." On the contrary, Kafka places his hapless narrators in a literalized orientalist topos, a realm that consists of cliché and conjecture, in order to illustrate the absurdities of the West's vision of China. This self-critical tendency is most apparent in the fact that the native narrators in both texts are, like their Western orientalist counterparts, properly perplexed by the inscrutable policies of the Chinese imperial authorities.

"Beim Bau der chinesischen Mauer" presents itself as a report on the construction of the wall and the people's relationship with their emperor. The text thus recalls the theme of Hofmannsthal's poem "Der Kaiser von China spricht" (The Emperor of China Speaks, 1897), in which the speaker describes both his connection with his subjects and the protective walls surrounding him. However, in many respects Franz Kafka's short story represents the antithesis of Hofmannsthal's poem. Hofmannsthal's Emperor speaks from the center of the realm and personifies the institution of empire, with the scope of his gaze apparently coterminous with his power. In contrast, Kafka's lowly narrator writes from the periphery of the realm in an attempt to fathom its arcane institutions. By placing these two works in dialogue with each other, we can uncover a submerged discourse on Habsburg imperialism and Austrian national identity conveyed through allusive fictions ostensibly set in China.[12] For if in Hofmannsthal's poem the emperor speaks, then in Kafka's story the empire writes back.

Moreover, in "Beim Bau der chinesischen Mauer" Kafka ironizes his narrator's account of the wall's piecemeal method of construction and the people's estranged relationship with their sovereign by having him frequently resort to legend, conjecture, and speculation in his attempt to explain the inconsistencies in both institutions. By employing such an unreliable narratorial voice, the author subtly subverts the unspoken assumptions that inform the concept of national identity in the fields of ethnology, geography, and history.

The piecemeal method of construction employed by the authorities calls into question the apparent purpose of the wall: to protect the Chinese people from the barbaric northern nomads. As the narrator trenchantly remarks, how is it possible for a wall to protect if it is not continuous (*NS*, 338; *CS*, 235)?[13] Even the ostensibly definitive declaration with which the text begins — "Die chinesische Mauer ist an ihrer nördlichsten Stelle beendet worden" (*NS*, 337; "The Great Wall of China was finished off at its northernmost corner": *CS*, 235) — gives way to speculation in the light of this fragmentary approach to building. If the builders are merely erecting five-hundred-meter sections of wall to join with another section being built in the opposite direction (*NS*, 337–38; *CS*, 235), then the completion of "the northernmost corner" might only amount to an isolated wall of a thousand meters, with no continuation in sight. Thus the discontinuous method of construction recalls an ambiguity between the geographical and the historical that is already apparent in the first word of the title, "bei," a spatial and temporal preposition that signals both a location by an actual structure and an ongoing process of building.

Caught in Zeno's paradox with regard to the extent of their wall, the Chinese must contend with another conundrum: the northern peoples, against whom the wall is supposedly being built, may enjoy a better overview of the construction than the natives, as a result of their nomadic lifestyle (*NS*, 339; *CS*, 236). Like the creature in Kafka's later story "Der Bau" (The Burrow, 1923), the Chinese cannot survey the exterior of their defenses, partly because of the danger of stepping beyond the protective enclosure, and partly because the extent of their fortifications is beyond the purview of any individual (*NS*, 338–39; *CS*, 235–36).

In describing the speed with which the nomads migrate, the narrator likens them to "Heuschrecken" (*NS*, 339; locusts, *CS*, 236), a term that invokes their bestial status and vast numbers, while implicitly comparing them to the Biblical plague. Such xenophobia plays an important role in the imperial building project, for the Chinese regard the northern peoples as nothing less than a satanic horde:

> Wir lesen von ihnen in den Büchern der Alten, die Grausamkeiten, die sie ihrer Natur gemäß begehn, machen uns aufseufzen in unserer friedlichen Laube, auf den wahrheitsgetreuen Bildern der Künstler sehen wir diese Gesichter der Verdammnis, die aufgerissenen Mäuler, die mit hochgespitzten Zähnen besteckten Kiefer, die verkniffenen Augen, die schon nach dem Raub zu schielen scheinen, den das Maul zermalmen und zerreißen wird. Sind die Kinder böse, halten wir ihnen diese Bilder hin und schon fliegen sie weinend an unseren Hals. (*NS*, 347)

> [We read of them in books of the ancients; the cruelties they commit in accordance with their nature make us sigh in our leafy arbors. The faithful representations of the artist show us these faces of the damned, their gaping mouths, their jaws furnished with great pointed teeth, their half-shut eyes that already seem to be seeking out the victim that their jaws will rend and devour. When our children are unruly we show them these pictures, and at once they fly weeping into our arms. (*CS*, 241)]

However, this passage subtly subverts the ostensible opposition between the civilized Chinese and the barbaric northerners. First, it emphasizes the mediated, textual nature of the Chinese populace's information concerning the northern peoples. As the narrator admits, no one in the south has ever encountered these tribes and therefore no one can verify whether they commit atrocities according to their innate nature, or even indeed whether the horrifying book illustrations are really "wahrheitsgetreu" (faithful). Further, the pleasant location in which the Chinese choose to peruse these grotesque images undermines their apparent import. Leafy arbors, redolent of poetry and *belles lettres*, and the readers' sighs suggest the aesthetic pleasure, the frisson of sublimated fear, that the Chinese derive from surveying "the faces of the damned." Moreover, the locals' use of these images as bogeymen to discipline unruly children indicates that these visions are merely phantoms of their own making. Finally, the image of the monstrous northerners has a clear extra-diegetic referent in the "yellow peril," a racist conception that arose in the West at the turn of the nineteenth century, which saw East Asians as marauding invaders. This notion is most apparent in the reference to the northerners' "half-shut eyes," a marker of racial difference that constantly figures in stereotypical representations of East Asians. By depicting the Chinese themselves as proponents of the "yellow peril" myth, the text thus parodies racist discourse.

Elsewhere the text further deconstructs the apparently absolute dichotomy between the nomads and the natives. First we learn that gruesome atrocities are not confined to the barbaric north. In contrast to the unspecified crimes of the nomads, the text offers specific details of one Chinese empress, who thousands of years ago drank her husband's blood "in langen Zügen" (NS, 353; in long draughts, CS, 245). Indeed, Kafka seems to have considered drawing an even clearer parallel between the emperor's inner circle and the northern barbarians. In the extant text the author describes "die glänzende und doch dunkle Menge des Hofstaats" (NS, 350; the brilliant and yet [darkly] ambiguous throng of nobles and courtiers, CS, 243) as "immer bemüht mit vergifteten Pfeilen den Kaiser von seiner Wagschale abzuschießen" (NS, 350; perpetually labor[ing] to unseat the ruler from his place with poisoned arrows, CS, 243), while in a deleted passage that appears in the English translation at the end of "The News of the Building of the Chinese Wall: A Fragment," he presents ""die ungläubigen Völker . . . unter ihnen . . . Dämonen"[14] (infidel tribes, among them demons" who engage in the same activity of shooting arrows at the emperor (CS, 249). More importantly, Kafka's story blurs the fundamental distinction between the sedentary Chinese and the migratory northerners by describing how the construction of the wall obliges young building supervisors to adopt a nomadic lifestyle (NS, 341–42; CS, 237–38). Thus the text subverts the distinction between civilization and barbarism by demonstrating that the Chinese exhibit the tendencies, such as bloodthirstiness and nomadism, that they attribute to the reviled northern peoples. In this way the story suggests that the Chinese people's ignorance of the textualized nomads is matched only by their lack of self-knowledge.

Indeed, if the Chinese people's knowledge of the Other is mediated, then so is their self-identity. Here the Chinese children's reaction to the pictures of the northerners is instructive. They fling themselves weeping into their parents' arms (NS, 347; CS, 241). This is precisely the reaction of the narrator and his fellow nursery-school pupils when their teacher, instructing them in the officially sanctioned science of architecture, knocks down their first attempts to build a wall (*NS*, 340; *CS*, 236).[15] The repetition of this gesture shows how the Chinese leadership unifies the nation by combining the external threat of the northern tribes with the internal goal of constructing the wall. Indeed, as the narrator investigates the origins of the project, it becomes clear that the leadership's primary objective is the inculcation of national pride. He comes across an early study of the structure, which maintains that the Great Wall was the foundation for a new Tower of Babel. Significantly, this book contains only "nebulous plans" for the final, unimaginable structure, but detailed proposals on how to harness the people's energies for this new work (*NS*, 344; *CS*, 239). Writing in 1917, Kafka was doubtless aware of the carnage on the battlefields of Europe wrought by the mobilization of nationalist energies. Nevertheless, he chooses to emphasize the sense of purpose that the individual derives from playing a small part in a grand scheme:

> Wir — ich rede wohl hier im Namen vieler — haben eigentlich erst im Nachbuchstabieren der Anordnungen der obersten Führerschaft uns selbst kennengelernt und gefunden, daß ohne die Führerschaft weder unsere Schulweisheit noch unser Menschenverstand, auch nur für das kleine Amt, das wir innerhalb des großen Ganzen hatten, ausgereicht hätte. (*NS*, 344–45)

> [We — and here I speak in the name of many people — did not really know ourselves until we had carefully scrutinized the decrees of the high command, when we discovered that without the high command neither our book learning nor our human understanding would have sufficed for the humble tasks which we performed in the great whole. (*CS*, 239)]

Here the naive narrator demonstrates the extent of his indoctrination by casting the leadership as munificent benefactors whose directions enable lowly subjects like himself to develop their identity. He does not pause to consider that this very sense of self arises from the leadership's propagandizing efforts, that is, their declaration, fifty years before the start of construction, that the craft of wall-building be considered the most important science and that all other subjects be recognized only in as far as they pertain to this preeminent discipline (*NS*, 339–40; *CS*, 236). Through the occluded viewpoint of his narrator, Kafka thus explores not only the techniques of official indoctrination but also its seductive effects on an insecure population that longs for nothing more than the role of a very small cog in an unimaginably large machine.

My reading of the construction of the wall as an attempt to inculcate national pride is based upon the priorities revealed by the early study of the structure, with its nebulous plans for the new Tower of Babel and its detailed proposals for mobilizing the people's energy (*NS*, 344; *CS*, 239). Of course, many critics have preferred to interpret the structure metaphorically. For example, both Clement Greenberg and Ritchie Robertson view the wall as the Torah and the Chinese as the Jews.[16] Conversely, Wolf Kittler employs language rather than religion as his point of reference, interpreting the Wall as a meta-linguistic construct (*TB*, 11–15). However, the reference to the Tower of Babel, an Old Testament motif that deals explicitly with the origin of language, undermines both the Judaic or meta-linguistic allegorical readings of the Wall, since allegory relies on the pristine separation of sign from signified. Instead Kafka's insertion of a Talmudic tale into a narrative set in China ironizes both the Western misappropriation of other cultural legacies and the fundamental notion of ethnic and national difference.

Kafka's appropriation of the Tower of Babel motif builds upon the irony inherent in the original text. In this story of a collective Fall (*TB*, 11), humans build the tower with the intent of making a name for themselves, "lest [they] be scattered abroad upon the face of the whole earth" (Gen. 11:4). Inevitably, this structure incurs the wrath of God, who "confound[s] their language" and "scatter[s] them abroad upon the face of all the earth" (Gen. 11:7 and 11:9). Kafka seems to have found the double bind at the heart of this narrative attractive, for he returns to the theme in the 1920 story, published under the title "Das Stadtwappen" (The City's Coat of Arms) in which the city of Babel sports a crest depicting the fist of God that will one day destroy it.[17] In "Beim Bau der chinesischen Mauer," the ultimate division of humanity is already inscribed in the new Babel project, which aims at merely national unity rather than the incorporation of the whole globe. Yet while the Biblical narrative explains the origin of different languages and cultures, its appearance in a text set in China undermines that very notion of difference by suggesting that this Judaic legend is common to both East and West.

Moreover, the Chinese narrator's reference to Babel represents an ironic reversal of the Western orientalist's decontextualization and appropriation of Asian religious motifs. In this regard the scholar cited by the narrator provides a salutary lesson in the unpredictable effects of cultural syncretism. On the one hand, this academic literalizes and concretizes the myth by claiming that he has examined the actual site of the original tower and found the flaw in its foundation that caused it to collapse. On the other hand, the scholar's hypothesis that the Great Wall is the only sure foundation for a new Tower of Babel must, according to the narrator, represent an abstraction, "could obviously be meant only in a spiritual sense" (*NS*, 344; *CS*, 239), since the wall only forms a quarter or semi-circle. In this way Kafka's Tower of Babel motif satirizes both the literalist and figurative tendencies of Biblical exegesis. More importantly, the fact that the scholar regards the fall of the first tower as an incentive to build better, rather than as an interdiction against challenging God's supremacy, indicates the degree of distortion that inevitably accompanies such cultural misappropriation.

Kafka's deployment of the Tower of Babel motif in this text contrasts with his earlier use of the symbol in "Beschreibung eines Kampfes" (1904–8). In the earlier story, the comparison between the swaying Supplicant and the tower suggests that the Judeo-Christian tradition has lost its auratic authority and become merely an inventory of common images (*NS*, 89; *CS*, 33). In the Chinese story the motif is subjected to an equally blasphemous misappropriation, but here Kafka exploits its thematic content in order to offer an ironic, self-reflexive, and self-critical commentary on the pitfalls of exploiting a foreign cultural legacy.

If Kafka's depiction of Chinese occidentalism is subtly reminiscent of the West's attitudes toward Asian cultures, then his account of Chinese patriotism evokes in a much starker fashion the nationalism of contemporary Europe. This self-reflective tendency is particularly apparent in the following speech, in which the narrator exults in the patriotic pride experienced by the young building supervisors as they travel about the country to great fanfare:

> Wie ewig hoffende Kinder nahmen sie von der Heimat Abschied, die Lust wieder am Volkswerk zu arbeiten wurde unbezwinglich, sie reisten früher von zuhause fort als es nötig gewesen wäre, das halbe Dorf begleitete sie lange Strecken weit, auf allen Wegen Grüße, Wimpel und Fahnen, niemals hatten sie gesehn, wie groß und reich und schön und liebenswert ihr Land war, jeder Landsmann war ein Bruder, für den man eine Schutzmauer baute und der mit allem was er hatte und war sein Leben lang dafür dankte, Einheit! Einheit! Brust an Brust, ein Reigen des Volkes, Blut, nicht mehr eingesperrt im kärglichen Kreislauf des Körpers, sondern süß rollend und doch wiederkehrend durch das unendliche China. (*NS*, 342)

> [Like eternally hopeful children they then said farewell to their homes; the desire once more to labor on the wall of the nation became irresistible. They set off earlier than they needed; half the village accompanied them for long distances. Groups of people with banners and streamers waving were on all the roads; never before had they seen how great and rich and beautiful and worthy of love their country was. Every fellow countryman was a brother for whom one was building a wall of protection, and who would return life-long thanks for it with all that he had and did. Unity! Unity! Shoulder to shoulder, a ring of brothers, a current of blood no longer confined within the narrow circulation of one body, but sweetly rolling and yet ever returning throughout the endless leagues of China. (*CS*, 238)]

Here the scene of jubilation that bids farewell to the building supervisors recalls the jingoistic displays with which European volunteers were dispatched to the front in the First World War. While J. M. Rignall discerns "an ironic distance between narrator and builders" in the term "ewig hoffende Kinder,"[18] it seems the ironic distance is located rather between the author and a narrator who seeks to convey the boundless optimism of the young builders but inadvertently suggests their irredeemable naiveté. In this regard the narrator's neologism "Volkswerk" (people's project) also indicates his uncritical attitude toward the leadership. First, the term ignores the fact that the construction project was imposed from on high rather than spontaneously arising from the populace. Further, it presupposes the existence of a Chinese "Volk" or people and thus elides his earlier suggestion that the Chinese are laboring, not to build a concrete edifice, but rather to create an intangible sense of national identity. In fact, the term "Volkswerk" can be read not only as project for or by the people, but also as one whose purpose is to create the Chinese nation in the first place. In this regard, the narrator's use of the charged terms "Volk" and "Heimat" (people and homeland), his breathless syntax, which allows no period to check its flow, the pervasive hyperbole, and the alliterative flourish of "kärglichen Kreislauf des Körpers" all convey a powerful emotional empathy with the general patriotic sentiment.

However, Kafka subverts this nationalist rhetoric by employing a narrator whose imagery has disturbing implications. In particular, the racial metaphor of blood engulfs the previous benign images of a nation joined in brotherhood and the roundelay dance, and undermines the implicit notion of the body politic. For when blood is no longer "trapped in the miserable circulation of the body," the organism dies. The grotesque image of blood pulsing through the endless expanse of China evokes the killing fields of the First World War, to which men were dispatched with such patriotic fervor. Thus Kafka subverts the contemporary ethnonationalist discourse in the very act of its articulation by alluding to the carnage wrought by such rhetoric.

"Blut und Boden" (Blood and soil) was of course a nationalist *cri-de-coeur* long before its adoption by the Nazis. However, Kafka complicates the relationship between the Chinese and their land by describing China as simply too enormous to comprehend. On the one hand, the expansiveness of China renders the issue of defense moot, since no invader from the north could ever reach the narrator's southeastern village (*NS*, 347; *CS*, 241). Instead of the population defending their country, it is the land that protects them. On the other hand, the sheer vastness of the country prevents any effective communication between the imperial metropole of Peking and the narrator's remote community. Even though any message from the centre is obsolete long before it reaches the periphery, for

the local people this ancient history has all the force of the latest news
(*NS*, 352–53; *CS*, 244–45). Yet if a government official should stray into
this region, the locals would treat his proclamations as if they had been
issued by a long-dead emperor whose dynasty is now extinct (*NS*, 353;
CS, 245). The narrator's community lives in a state of ahistorical simul-
taneity similar to that which Benedict Anderson attributes to medieval
society in his book *Imagined Communities*. There Anderson describes the
anachronistic art of the Middle Ages that depicts the Nativity with shep-
herds resembling "Burgundian peasants" and the Virgin Mary "figured
as a Tuscan merchant's daughter."[19] Like the artists of the Middle Ages,
Kafka's Chinese have not developed the concept of what Walter Benja-
min terms "homogenous, empty time."[20] According to Anderson, this
change in the Western view of history is vital for the development of a
national consciousness, since it replaces the medieval version of simulta-
neity, based on the eschatological model of prefigurement and fulfillment,
with a secular model in which events take place concurrently within the
same national matrix (24). In contrast, the geographical expanse of Kafka's China warps the population's notion of history to such an extent that
a modern national consciousness cannot develop. Thus Kafka dismantles
the assumption inherent in the phrase "Blut und Boden" or "blood and
soil" — that the ethno-nationalist, historical identity of a people is automatically coterminous with their geographical territory.

However, in "Beim Bau der chinesischen Mauer" Kafka's exploration of the concept of a ground ("Boden or "Grund") goes beyond the
geographical to acquire a philosophical resonance. In this respect the text
recalls Kafka's first story, "Beschreibung eines Kampfes," in which the
characters' unsure footing renders literal the metaphor of their unstable
epistemological and ontological foundation (see chapter 3). Kafka's Chinese narrator expands this trope to encompass his whole nation when he
makes the paradoxical claim that it is the people's nebulous conception of
their emperor that forms the basis of their national identity.

> Eine Tugend ist also diese Auffassung wohl nicht. Umso auffälli-
> ger ist es, daß gerade diese Schwäche eines der wichtigsten Eini-
> gungsmittel unseres Volkes zu sein scheint, ja wenn man sich im
> Ausdruck soweit vorwagen darf, geradezu der Boden auf dem wir
> leben. Hier einen Tadel ausführlich begründen, heißt nicht an
> unserem Gewissen, sondern was viel ärger ist an unsern Beinen rüt-
> teln. Und darum will ich in der Untersuchung vorderhand nicht
> weiter gehn. (*NS*, 356)

> [This attitude then is certainly no virtue. All the more remarkable
> is it that this very weakness should seem to be one of the greatest
> unifying influences among our people; indeed, if one may dare to
> use the expression, the very ground on which we live. To set about

establishing a fundamental defect here would mean undermining not only our consciences, but, what is far worse, our feet. And for that reason I shall not proceed any further at this stage with my enquiry into these questions. (*CS*, 247–48)]

Here the narrator again fails to rein in his metaphorical discourse. The figure of the ground, which he introduces with an apology ("wenn man sich im Ausdruck soweit vorwagen darf"; if one may dare to use the expression), becomes literalized in the verb "begründen" and most especially in the zeugma that yokes together the metaphorical and literal connotations of the verb "rütteln" (to shake, here translated as "to undermine") to describe how it is not only the Chinese people's conscience, but also their legs, that are shaken. Thus his concrete interpretation of the trope of "the ground beneath our feet"[21] leads the narrator to desist in his digging for explanations, for fear that his excavation might undermine the Chinese people's bedrock assumptions. This act of self-censorship, which arises not from external intimidation but from the narrator's inherent timidity, ultimately confirms his inability to report objectively on his own people's national and imperial institutions and ideologies.

This notion that the people's relationship with their emperor is at once too deep-seated and too delicate to bear scrutiny has a clear extra-diegetic referent in the Habsburg myth, the concept of a supra-national allegiance to the monarchy that represented the official ethos of Austria-Hungary. In his book *Der Habsburgische Mythos in der österreichischen Literatur* (The Habsburg Myth in Austrian Literature), Claudio Magris describes the concept as "the ideological foundation of the Danube Monarchy," an "intellectual and propagandistic support in the struggle against the modern awakening of nationalist energies" and "a weapon in the Habsburg struggle against history."[22] Kafka's narrator offers a literally nebulous image for this ahistorical, supra-national ideal, when he claims that the people are unable to envisage the teeming multitudes of the imperial capital and that it is easier for the to believe that "Peking und sein Kaiser wären eines, etwa eine Wolke, ruhig unter der Sonne sich wandelnd im Laufe der Zeiten" (*NS*, 354; Peking and its Emperor are one, a cloud say, peacefully voyaging beneath the sun in the course of the ages, *CS*, 247). In positing a cloud-like amalgam of the emperor and his metropolis that floats above the earth and through the ages, Kafka's narrator sums up the appeal of the hazy Habsburg myth in its transcendence of both geography and history.

However, the narrator's decision to end his investigation reflects not only the delicacy of the people's relationship with their emperor but also his view that humanity is basically capricious and destructive: "Das menschliche Wesen, leichtfertig in seinem Grunde, von der Natur des auffliegenden Staubes, verträgt keine Fesselung, fesselt es sich selbst, wird es bald wahnsinng an den Fesseln zu rütteln anfangen und Mauer Kette und sich selbst in allen Himmelsrichtungen zerreißen" (*NS*, 344; Human nature, essentially changeable, unstable as the dust [thrown into the air], can endure no restraint; if it binds itself it soon begins to tear madly at its bonds, until it rends everything asunder, the wall, the bonds, and its very self, *CS*, 239). This sententious pronouncement, which recalls Ecclesiastes 3:20 ("all are of the dust, and all turn to dust again"), is something of a non-sequitur, since it follows the narrator's rather mild observation that in the past the wild ideas and confusion surrounding the Wall arose from so many people focusing on the same project (*NS*, 344; *CS*, 239). The context for this remark suggests that the narrator is mistaken in ascribing humanity's tendency to resist the restraints of structure to a fundamental thoughtlessness ("leichtfertig"). On the contrary, as the etymological origin of the verb "to analyze" (German "analysieren") in the verb "to undo" indicates, the tendency to want to loosen the bonds of order is a function of the rational mind. Thus the narrator applies this pessimistic view of human nature to himself when he terminates his enquiry into the people's conception of their monarch lest the delicate ground of national identity be undermined by the ravages of reason.

Elsewhere in the text, however, the narrator suggests that the destabilization that he fears may simply be part of the human condition. When he describes how his teacher knocked down their first attempts to build a wall, he refers to himself and his fellow pupils as small children who were hardly sure of their feet (*NS*, 340; *CS*, 236). The repetition of this motif in the narrator's refusal to undermine the footing of the Chinese people by investigating their notion of the emperor suggests that the narrator and his nation are trapped in a state of arrested political development. Moreover, in linking the analyses of the Wall and the emperor, the image of quaking legs indicates that neither institution offers a stable ground for the construction of a national identity.

But this is not quite the whole story. In the most famous passage of the text, the legend describing a message from a dying emperor that never reaches its addressee, Kafka offers a more nuanced vision of the relationship between reason and the individual national consciousness. Significantly, Kafka published this passage separately under the title "Eine kaiserliche Botschaft" (An Imperial Message), thus removing any references to China. This is appropriate, given that the passage offers, with astonishing concision, a brief history of Western thought.[23] In its play of light and darkness, the opening sentence invokes the foundational moment of Western philosophy, Plato's cave: "Der Kaiser, so heißt es, hat gerade Dir, dem jämmerlichen Untertanen, dem winzig vor der kaiserlichen Sonne in die fernste Ferne geflüchteten Schatten, gerade Dir hat der Kaiser von seinem Sterbebett aus eine Botschaft gesendet" (*NS*, 351; The Emperor, so it runs, has sent a message to you, the humble subject, the insignificant shadow cowering in the remotest distance before the imperial sun; the Emperor from his death bed has sent a message to you alone, CS, 244). Although the text strenuously emphasizes the dichotomy between the "imperial sun" and the darkness of "the humble subject's" existence, it is the dying emperor who will soon enter the realm that Classical mythology associated with the shades. Nevertheless, following the heliotropic impulse that Derrida discerns in the history of Western philosophy, "the movement by which the sun turns into metaphor; . . . or . . . that which turns philosophical metaphor toward the sun,"[24] this "imperial sun" is then transformed into a sign, the crest emblazoned on the messenger's chest. Yet the enlightenment promised by the symbol of the sun never arrives. Although the messenger is powerful and indefatigable, he is trapped in the endless palaces at the core of the realm (NS, 352; CS 244), which evoke the suffocating and omnipresent bureaucracy of the Habsburg Empire. Through this image of the infinitely delayed emissary, who bears the bifurcated image of the imperial and empirical sun, Kafka conveys one of the central paradoxes of Austrian and European history: the conflict between the institution of empire and the ideal of Enlightenment.

Indeed, even the *Bildungsbürger*, the past standard-bearers of the rationalist tradition, now represent an obstacle to the transmission of its message. In one of the many hypothetical scenarios that the legend raises only to dismiss, the messenger might emerge from the palatial labyrinth only to find "die Residenzstadt vor ihm, die Mitte der Welt, hochgeschüttet voll ihres Bodensatzes" (NS, 352; the imperial capital . . . before him, the center of the world, crammed to bursting with its own sediment, CS, 244). Here the residential town in the middle of the world suggests the realm of the middle class, while the accumulated sediment or "Bodensatz" recalls Schopenhauer's notion of the "Satz vom Grund" or "Principle of Sufficient Reason," an allusion that suggests the incompatibility between the Austrian philosopher's metaphysics and the rationalist tradition. Thus in a highly wrought allegory, Kafka presents an indictment of the bourgeoisie similar to that offered by Musil's realistic depiction of the protagonist's family in *Die Verwirrungen des Zöglings Törleß*: both authors perceive in the contemporary *Bildungsbürger* a manifest failure to fulfill the ideals of the Enlightenment to which they owe their existence.

However, we must not lose sight of the fact that this network of allusions to the history of Western thought appears in a legend that purports to explain the Chinese people's relationship with their emperor. By inserting these extra-diegetic references into "Beim Bau der chinesischen Mauer," Kafka subverts one of the fundamental assumptions of Western orientalism: the notion that while the East represents the realm of myth and mystification, the West exemplifies reason and objectivity. For here it is the Western philosophical tradition that has become the

stuff of legend, a Romantic notion that can only be intuited, not rationally understood, by the light of the moon rather than that sun: "Du
aber sitzt an Deinem Fenster und erträumst sie Dir wenn der Abend
kommt" (*NS*, 352; But you sit at your window when evening falls and
dream it to yourself, *CS*, 244).

Although the legend withholds the precise content of the missive, it
seems reasonable to assume that it must be connected to the emperor's
death, which presumably occurs shortly after the messenger's departure.[25]
In this regard the text alludes to the extra-diegetic reality of the faltering
Habsburg dynasty, invoking not only Franz Josef's death the previous
year but also the rumors about the monarch that circulated before his
actual demise. As Dorothy Gies McGuigan explains, in his declining years
the emperor became the subject of what today might be described as
"conspiracy theories": "For years there had been rumors abroad that the
Austrian Emperor was really dead, and that there existed in Vienna a kind
of college that trained men to play his part in public."[26] The fact that
Franz Josef seems to have passed into legend before his death has wider
ramifications, given that his long reign had become synonymous with the
institution of empire itself. In this historical context the claims of Kafka's
narrator regarding the immortality of the imperial system acquire considerable poignancy: "Das Kaisertum ist unsterblich, aber der einzelne Kaiser fällt und stürzt ab, selbst ganze Dynastien sinken endlich nieder und
veratmen durch ein einziges Röcheln" (*NS*, 350; The Empire is immor-
tal, but the Emperor himself totters and falls from his throne, yes, whole
dynasties sink in the end and breathe their last in one death rattle, *CS*,
243). For as the term "Habsburg Empire" suggests, it was precisely this
distinction between dynasty and empire that the Dual Monarchy lacked.
By positing an endless Chinese empire, Kafka thus questions by inference
the survival of his native Austria-Hungary.

However, as the conclusion of the passage describing the imperial
message suggests, even the lowly imperial subject is able to intuit the content of the missive, to conceive his or her relation to the imperium. In this
respect the term "kaiserliche Botschaft" (imperial message) suggests not
only the missive's origin with the emperor but also its content as a reflection on the nature of imperial identity. Thus in this passage Kafka reverses
the trajectory of Hofmannsthal's poem "Der Kaiser von China spricht":
here national identity does not radiate from the center outward or from
the top down, but flows upward and inward from the lowly periphery to
the illustrious core of the realm. While the second-person address, which
encompasses the reader, emphasizes the emancipatory nature of the conclusion, the setting of the sun in the final line suggests that this "imagined
community" is the product of Romantic fantasy rather than enlightened
reason. In this way Kafka both heralds and critiques the rise of the modern, individuated, national consciousness.

Despite their oriental garb, Hofmannsthal and Kafka's texts offer valuable insights into the collapse of the Habsburg Empire and its foundational myth of supranational dynastic allegiance. For if the ethnonationalism of Hofmannsthal's Emperor excludes the various minorities of the realm, then, as Kafka's lowly subject demonstrates, one is free to imagine one's own version of national identity. Thus for their Habsburg audience these ostensibly exotic "Chinese" texts offer some disconcerting home truths.

Perhaps the most disquieting aspect of "Beim Bau der chinesischen Mauer" lies in the fundamental dissonance between the two objects of the narrator's scrutiny: the nationalist project of the wall and the people's relationship with their emperor. As Wolf Kittler observes, the text breaks off before it can establish a clear relationship or hierarchy between the committee behind the wall and the office of the emperor (*TB*, 71). Indeed, Kafka's fragmentary text ends on the verge of self-contradiction: while the narrator is at pains to stress that the committee and its decision to build the wall have existed since time immemorial (*NS*, 348; *CS*, 242), he is nevertheless about to attribute the decision to a single event, an incursion by nomads into the imperial capital, when the text ends abruptly (*NS*, 357; *CS*, 249). In this regard the incomplete and incoherent nature of the text offers an ironic perfomative of the confusion regarding cause and effect that must necessarily attend the narrator's attempt to provide a historical analysis of the supposedly eternal institutions of the wall and the emperor.

Although the narrator cannot specifically address the relationship between the committee that instituted the wall and the emperor, Kafka's imagery nevertheless suggests points of comparison between the two themes. Earlier we saw how the recapitulation of the image of quaking legs connects the narrator's childhood indoctrination in wall-building with his decision to end his enquiry into the office of emperor, and thus suggests that neither institution provides sufficient rational grounds for the construction of a national identity. Conversely, the notion of waiting by a window at dusk for inspiration links the lowly subject in the "imperial message" passage and the illustrious wall-building committee:

In der Stube der Führerschaft — wo sie war und wer dort saß, weiß und wußte niemand, in dieser Stube kreisten wohl alle menschlichen Gedanken und Wünsche und in Gegenkreisen alle menschlichen Ziele und Erfüllungen, durch das Fenster aber fiel der Abglanz der göttlichen Welten auf die Pläne zeichnenden Hände der Führerschaft. (*NS*, 345)

[In the office of the command — where it was and who sat there no one I have asked knew then or knows now — in that office one may be certain that all human thoughts and desires revolved in a circle, and all human aims and fulfillments in a counter-circle. And through

the window the reflected splendors of divine worlds fell on the hands
of the leaders as they traced their plans. (*CS*, 239–40)]

Here Kafka undermines his narrator's mystification of the leadership and
their deliberations by having him concede that his depiction is completely
speculative, since none of the people the narrator quizzed on the matter
had any notion where it took place or who took part. Further, the narrator overburdens to the point of absurdity the caveat "wohl" (probably),
which normally accompanies a reasonable surmise, by using it to introduce
an outlandish and grandiose image in which all the thoughts and desires
of humanity whirl about the room in one direction and all their goals and
fulfillments in the other. Although this concept attributes a quasi-divine
omniscience to the leadership, the narrator stops short of deifying the
committee. Instead, he insists on the mediated nature of their inspiration
through the image of the reflected light of divine worlds that is cast upon
their hand as they draw their plans. In short, like the wretched subject of
the legend, the committee sits by a window and hopes for a visit from an
unspecified muse. By recapitulating this figure in the legend of the imperial message, Kafka suggests that at both ends of the political hierarchy
national identity arises not from the rational mind, but rather from the
speculative imagination.

The narrator's attempt to elevate the committee to a quasi-divine status is one example of the unstable frames of reference that he employs in
his account of the wall-building project and the office of the emperor.
To understand the fundamental instability of the narrator's epistemology, it is useful to refer to Max Weber's taxonomy of legitimate authority.
For Weber, power can be divided into three pure types: rational, which is
based in law and in the recognition of authority; traditional, which derives
from a quotidian belief in the sanctity of immemorial custom; and char-
ismatic, which arises from an unusual faith in the sanctity, heroism, or
otherwise exemplary character of a particular individual.[27] While Weber
concedes that history does not produce absolutely pure forms of these
types of authority (124), the narrator combines these different categories
with astonishing alacrity. On the one hand, the wall-building committee,
which should enjoy a rational legitimacy in light of its project for national
defense, becomes both a traditional authority, as evinced by the narrator's claim that leadership "has existed from all eternity and the decision
to build the wall likewise" (*NS*, 348; *CS*, 242), and a quasi-charismatic
body, as demonstrated by the narrator's description of their deliberations.
On the other hand, the emperor, who should wield an unparalleled char-
ismatic authority, finds that his power derives from tradition, from the
customs surrounding his office, rather than from his person. Moreover,
when the imperial bureaucracy aspires to a rational authority, dispatch-
ing an official to the narrator's backwater home village, it is thwarted by

the traditional beliefs that have accrued to the people's notion of imperial authority. Trapped in their time warp, the local villagers smile qui-
etly as an imperial official talks about an emperor whom they consider
long since dead as if he were alive, and then blithely ignore these current
imperial edicts to continue obeying their chosen monarch, who has long
since turned to dust (*NS*, 353–54; *CS*, 245). Thus the narrator is unable
to establish a secure source of authority for either the committee or the
emperor, let alone a hierarchy between the two.

Indeed, the fact that the narrator associates both institutions with
the same modes of legitimacy underscores the uncomfortable fact at the
heart of the text: that there is no means of reconciling the project to construct the wall with the authority of the emperor. In its fragmentary and
inconclusive state, "Beim Bau der chinesischen Mauer" thus encapsulates
the intractable conflict at the root of the Habsburg Empire's demise: the
clash between the nationalist aspirations of the Dual Monarchy's various
ethnic groups, as symbolized by the wall, and the institution of empire
itself. In this regard Kafka offers a rationale for his own textual practice in
the narrator's assessment of his discipline, which he terms "the comparative history of peoples": "es gibt bestimmte Fragen denen man nur mit
diesem Mittel gewissermaßen an den Nerv herankommt" (*NS*, 348; there
are certain questions that one can probe to the marrow, as it were, only
by this method, *CS*, 242). By creating an allusive China that invites comparison with his homeland, Kafka is thus able to penetrate to the core of
the Habsburg Empire's nebulous self-identity.

If "Beim Bau der chinesischen Mauer" hints at the rifts within the
empire, then its companion piece, "Ein altes Blatt," confronts the complete collapse of the political order. For in this text barbaric nomads have
inexplicably invaded the center of the Chinese capital. However, while
the opening line, which tentatively suggests that the national system of
defense has been much neglected (*DL*, 263; *CS*, 415), alludes to the
contemporary disaster of the First World War, the text also invokes the
ancient origins of Austria in the dissolution of the Roman Empire and the
invasion of the barbarian tribes. In this respect "Ein altes Blatt" reveals a
similar *modus operandi* to "Beim Bau der chinesischen Mauer." Through
their Chinese settings both texts defamiliarize and deterritorialize their
allusions to the Dual Monarchy, creating hybrid environments that not
only implicitly undermine the fundamental orientalist notion of an East/
West dichotomy but also explicitly interrogate the nature of national and
cultural identity.

In Kafka's own manuscript the text of "Ein altes Blatt" is followed
by a fragment that appears to refer to the latter work (*NS*, 361). These
four sentences cast an ironic light not only on the preceding narrative
but also on the whole enterprise of orientalist scholarship by presenting
the attempt to apprehend a foreign culture as a practical impossibility.

The fragment begins with a characteristically self-defeating gesture by presenting a rendering of an old Chinese manuscript while simultaneously problematizing the whole notion of translation: "Diese (vielleicht allzusehr europäisierende) Übersetzung" (NS, 361; this translation [which perhaps Europeanizes its subject all too greatly]). Through the participial adjective "europäisierend" Kafka invokes the notion that translation inevitably distorts the original work by dislocating it from its cultural context. However, the adverbial collocation "vielleicht allzusehr" (perhaps all too greatly) confounds the issue of Europeanization by undermining the criterion that is apparent in the evaluation "allzusehr" with the indeterminacy of the qualifying "vielleicht." Moreover, the incompleteness of these lines, which introduce a text that never appears, offers an ironic performative in relation to the manuscript they describe: a fragment for which one can never hope to find a continuation (NS, 361). Finally, these barely decipherable pages are revealed to be "allzu beschädigt . . ., als daß ihnen etwas bestimmtes entnommen werden könnte" (NS, 361; all too damaged . . . for anything definite to be gathered from them). Thus the text almost completely withdraws its initial offer of meaningful communication. Through this fragment Kafka subverts the central premise of Western orientalist scholarship:. that the East can be thoroughly understood through the diligent study of its ancient texts.[28]

If we consider this fragment as a projected introduction to the preceding text, "Ein altes Blatt," then the process of contextualization endows it with greater significance. For example, there is an evident irony in the fact that the text was donated by "ein Freund der Aktion" or "a friend of the military campaign" (NS, 361), since it deals with the paralysis of both the speaker and his nation in the face of an invasion by barbaric nomads. In the final line of "Ein altes Blatt" the narrator, a cobbler, ascribes the situation to some sort of misunderstanding (DL, 267; CS, 417). He and his fellow shopkeepers do not feel equal to the task with which they have evidently been entrusted: defending their country (DL, 267; CS, 417). Indeed, the very existence of the manuscript stands as a testimony to the narrator's inaction. What purpose does it serve to commit his thoughts to paper at such a time of crisis? To whom are his observations addressed? The subsequent fragment offers a further ironic reflection on the futility of the shoemaker's writing, since the ultimate recipients of the text, Western orientalists, are unable to decipher its meaning with any confidence.

These manifold failures of communication are doubly ironic, given that the narrator cites the apparent absence of language among the invaders as one of the most important differences between the natives and the nomads. These invaders represent the ontological antithesis of the northern barbarians depicted in "Beim Bau der chinesischen Mauer."[29] The latter are described as an utterly remote group, who for the southern Chinese exist only as children's bogeymen and monsters in ancient tomes, that is, as purely linguistic and textual creations (*NS,* 347). In contrast, the nomads in "Ein altes Blatt" represent an all too real extralinguistic threat, which has somehow infiltrated the heart of the nation.

For the shoemaker the apparent absence of language among the nomads relegates them to the level of beasts: "Unter einander verständigen sie sich ähnlich wie die Dohlen" (*DL,* 264; They communicate with each other much as jackdaws do, *CS,* 416). However, Kafka deconstructs this binary opposition between the verbal human and non-linguistic animal through both the narrative itself and an extradiegetic reference. In the course of his narration the shoemaker describes the citizens' increasingly desperate attempts to communicate with the invaders via non-verbal gestures, which come to resemble the nomads' grimaces.[30] According to the narrator, one may gesture at the nomads until one's jaw and wrists are dislocated, and still they will not have understood and will never understand. Conversely, the nomads grimace until one can see just the whites of their eyes and their mouths begin to froth and yet "they do not mean anything by [it], not even a threat; they do it because it is their nature to do it" (*DL,* 265; *CS,* 416). In the eyes of the shoemaker the nomads' repulsive facial contortions cannot possibly represent a similar, indeed mirroring, attempt at communication, but are merely undertaken because that is their nature. Here the narrator reveals his admittedly understandable bias against the barbarian invaders. For while he concedes that he is unable to speak with these nomads, he nevertheless assumes knowledge of their motivation, ascribing their gestures not to a desire to communicate, but to an inherent nature that defies logical analysis (*DL,* 264; *CS,* 416). By attributing this sentiment to a Chinese narrator, Kafka satirizes the essentialist notions of difference found in the contemporary ethnological discourse. Outside the diegesis, the fact that "Dohle" or "jackdaw" can be rendered as *kavka* in Czech has not escaped critics' notice.[31] In associating his name, which imitates the bird's call, with the non-linguistic, carnivorous barbarians, Kafka, the vegetarian dandy who famously declared that he consisted of nothing but literature,[32] signs his work with a bilingual pun that deconstructs the opposition between human language and animal noises. By linking his own name with the uncivilized and animalistic nomads, he parodies the notions of the bestial and sub-human found in the racist theorization of ethnic difference at the time.

It is not surprising that the nomads have been the focus of most critical responses to "Ein altes Blatt." They have been variously interpreted in psychoanalytical terms, as an invasion of the Lacanian Real, for example (*TB,* 94), or in a historico-political context, as a metaphor for the violent and irrational forces released at times of social upheaval.[33] In this respect we must consider Kafka's decontextualisation of his work, in both his alteration of the title from "Ein altes Blatt *aus China*" ("An Old Manuscript *from China*") and in his decision to publish the text without its companion piece "Beim Bau der chinesischen Mauer" in the collection entitled *Ein Landarzt*. As a result of this decontextualization, Kafka's reader associates terms such as "empire" and "emperor" with the contemporary reality of Austria-Hungary. However, given the nomads' primitive methods of warfare (bows and arrows and horseback riding), one is reminded of the origins of the imperial project (and indeed of Austria itself) in ancient Rome. One of the most fascinating aspects of this text is that the invaders recall no figures in Occidental history more than the Germanic barbarians, as described in the writings of the preeminent emperor, Julius Caesar, and the ethnographer and historian Tacitus.[34] (It is safe to assume that Kafka's humanist education at the *Altstädter Deutsches Gymnasium* in Prague would have made him aware, for reasons of both patriotism and pedagogy, of these Latin accounts of the ancient Germanic tribes.) In his war commentaries Caesar describes them as "fierce and violent savages" (26) who lead a nomadic life and enjoy a highly carnivorous diet (126). Indeed, in battle with the Germans the Gauls are said to find it impossible "even to stand up to the fierce, keen look in their eyes," a moment recalled by the natives' automatic deference before the invaders in Kafka's text: "Whatever they need, they take. You cannot call it taking by force. They grab at something and you simply stand aside and leave them to it" (*NS*, 265; *CS*, 416). In addition, Tacitus details the Germans' reverence for their horses as a source of prophecy (68), and also describes the Germans' predilection for a wordless chant called a *barritus* that was intended to intimidate their enemies in battle (64). In his depiction of the nomadic invaders Kafka exaggerates to the point of absurdity the barbaric traits found in the Roman descriptions of the Germanic tribes. While the latter were merely carnivorous, Kafka's nomads rend a live ox with their teeth (*NS*, 266; *CS*, 417); while the ancient Teutons held their horses in high esteem, the barbarians in "Ein altes Blatt" are happy to share a bone with their carnivorous steeds (*NS*, 265; *CS*, 417); and finally, while the Germanic peoples intimidated their enemies with guttural cries, the invaders in the fictional text are apparently devoid of language (*NS*, 264; *CS*, 416). Indeed, Kafka's narrator hints darkly that the invading hordes may be tempted by the ultimate barbarism of cannibalism, even if the local citizens maintain the supply of meat (*NS*, 265; *CS*, 417). Thus Kafka's nomads epitomize all the tendencies associated with the abject primitive or ignoble savage in the European imagination. However, by alluding to the Roman image of the Germanic savage, Kafka not only deconstructs any hierarchization between civilization and barbarism but also hints at the combination of contradictory forces that gave rise to his own Austrian culture.

Kafka's dualistic depiction of civilized order and barbaric chaos evokes the Nietzschean conception of the Apollonian and Dionysian. "Ein altes Blatt" invokes the latter concept in the nomads' brutal rending of a live ox, which recalls a similar atrocity perpetrated by the Maenads in Euripides' *Bacchae*.[35] This Bacchic association is reinforced by the description of the nomads after their unusual repast: they lie around the remains of the ox "like drunkards around a wine cask" (*NS*, 266; *CS*, 417). It is fascinating to note, however, that it is this horrific spectacle of the ox being torn apart that draws the emperor to the window (*NS*, 266; *CS*, 417) in a way that the Apollonian order and hushed reverence of the square before the nomads' arrival was never able to do (*TB*, 90 and 92). While his bowed head may indicate his abject defeat, it may also betoken his reverence for this bloody offering (*TB*, 90 and 92). Thus Kafka makes the counter-intuitive suggestion that the irrational, Dionysian desires for ritual and sacrifice cannot be repressed without endangering the social order. While Thomas Mann's protagonist Hans Castorp dreams of the coexistence of Apollonian and Bacchic forces in *Der Zauberberg*,[36] Kafka depicts the practical difficulties of coping with an eruption of Dionysian energy on one's doorstep as part of a waking reality. In the context of a story originally set in China, Kafka's invocation of the orgiastic impulse at the root of Western culture again subverts the traditional orientalist dichotomy of the irrational East and Apollonian West.

However, we must remember that Kafka is alluding not only to Classical archetypes and ancient history in this narrative, but also to contemporary events. In this regard the opening sentence — "Es ist, als wäre viel vernachlässigt worden in der Verteidigung unseres Vaterlandes" (*NS*, 263; It looks as if much had been neglected in our country's system of defense, *CS*, 415) — acquires a greater poignancy in the face of the disaster of the First World War. The fact that the narrator couches his criticism of the authorities' abject failure in the subjunctive voice suggests that he is unable to comprehend fully that the immemorial order has been shattered and that the page on which he so diligently works will soon be turned. With breathtaking concision Kafka thus collapses the ancient origins and ultimate dissolution of the Austro-Hungarian Empire into a single brief narrative.

In conclusion, the dense network of allusions to the Dual Monarchy found in these texts show how Kafka develops the Austria-China analogy from a vehicle for political satire to a medium for profound political and cultural introspection. However, this self-critical tendency is not confined to Kafka's invocation of the domestic political sphere. In both "Beim Bau der chinesichen Mauer" and "Ein altes Blatt" Kafka uses the baffling alterity of the nomads to reflect ironically on the impossibility of intercultural exchange and thus implicitly question both the project of orientalism and his own fictional depiction of China. The complex and multivalent reflexivity of Kafka's texts demands a thoroughgoing reevaluation of the notion of orientalism advanced by Edward Said, that is, that the discourse invariably acts as the ideological cohort to Western imperialism. Instead Kafka's texts suggest a pluralistic and heterogeneous set of discourses that can encompass not only negative depictions of the West but also a self-critical examination of their own epistemological and ideological premises. Nevertheless, we must not confuse the self-critique found in these works with a desire on Kafka's part to posit in China's alterity an alternative to Western civilization. Rather he acknowledges the limitations of intercultural communication by deploying, in a self-conscious and ironic fashion, the inventory of orientalist stereotypes surrounding China in order to veil his critique of his own "eastern empire."

Notes

¹ Jorge Luis Borges, "The Analytical Language of John Wilkins," in *Other Inquisitions, 1937–1952,* trans. Ruth L. C. Simms (New York: Washington Square, 1966), 106–10.

² Michel Foucault, *The Order of Things: An Archaeology of the Human Sciences* (New York: Vintage Books, 1994), xv; Borges, "The Analytical Language of John Wilkins," 108. Seiji Hattori also cites this passage in connection with "Beim Bau der chinesischen Mauer" (211), but he does not consider the implicit orientalism in Foucault's analysis of this quotation. See Seiji Hattori, "Kafkas China-Motiv und das 'heterotopische' Denken," in *Akten des Germanistenkongresses Paris 2005: "Germanistik im Konflikt der Kulturen," Jahrbuch für Internationale Germanistik* 9 (2007): 207–12.

³ In a brief aside in his article "The Bureaucrat as Nomad: The Search for Community in Kafka's *Beim Bau der chinesischen Mauer*" Richard Heinemann also links Kafka's text to Foucault's archeology of Western epistemological categories. Richard Heinemann. "The Bureaucrat as Nomad: The Search for Community in Kafka's *Beim Bau der chinesischen Mauer,*" *Journal of the Kafka Society of America* 18.1 (Jun. 1994): 24, and 27, n. 17). However, although Heinemann notes that "Foucault's description of this imaginary [the Western vision of China] seems directly lifted from the pages of Kafka," he does not take into consideration that both Foucault and Kafka draw their images from the tradition of orientalist stereotypes surrounding China.

⁴ This study of Kafka's Chinese stories is not the first to draw the analogy between Kafka's fictionalized China and the contemporary condition of Austria-Hungary. See, for example, Yeon-Soo Kim, "Kafkas literarisches Spiel mit dem europäischen Orientalismus — Analyse zu China-Bildern in der Erzählung *Beim Bau der chinesischen Mauer,*" paper presented at the conference *Intercultural Kafka*, organized by the German Kafka Society and the Gießen Graduate Center for Cultural Studies, Castle Rauischholzhausen, near Marburg, 20–23 July 2009, 13. However, while Kim also perceives in Kafka's orientalist fiction the opportunity for critical self-reflection with regard to Kafka's native "eastern empire" (1 and 20–21), she does not link this tendency to the practice of orientalism itself. My thanks to the

author for generously providing this paper before the publication of the conference proceedings.

[5] Cf. Kim, "Kafkas literarisches Spiel," 13.

[6] Weiyan Meng, *Kafka und China*, 17–18.

[7] Grillparzer, "Nachrichten aus Cochinchina" in *Sämtliche Werke*, vol. 3, *Ausgewählte Briefe, Gespräche, Berichte* (Munich: Carl Hanser, 1964), 93–95. Note that the setting, Cochinchina (a Chinese vassal state belonging to Vietnam), was originally China itself, and that the term "Chinese" remains unchanged on page 95. Grillparzer seems unsure whether to represent Austria as a despotic empire or merely as a satellite of one.

[8] Grusa, *Franz Kafka aus Prag*, 10; quoted in Meng, *Kafka und China*, 17–18.

[9] Rolf Goebel argues for the influence of Herder's *Ideen zur Philosophie der Geschichte der Menschheit* (1787) on this conception of China among Kafka and his contemporaries. See Rolf Goebel, "Opening Up Kafka's Context: Herder's Orientalist Poetics," in *Constructing China: Kafka's Orientalist Discourse*, 15–31.

[10] The text in question begins "Alt, in großer Leibesfülle, unter leichten Herzbeschwerden, lag ich . . ." (*NS*, 323–24).

[11] Rolf Goebel, "Kafka's Orientalist Rhetoric: China, the Middle East, India," *Journal of the Kafka Society of America* 15.1/2 (1991): 21.

[12] This makes it all the more remarkable that so few critics have sought to compare these two works. To my knowledge, Heinz Politzer's article "Zwei kaiserliche Botschaften: Zu den Texten von Hofmannsthal und Kafka," *Modern Austrian Literature* 11.3/4 (1978): 105–22 offers the only attempt to do so.

[13] All the translations for "Beim Bau der chinesischen Mauer" are taken from "The Great Wall of China," trans. Willa Muir and Edwin Muir, in *CS*, 235–48.

[14] Franz Kafka, *Nachgelassene Schriften und Fragmente I: Apparatband*, ed. Malcolm Pasley (Frankfurt am Main: S. Fischer Verlag, 1993), 303.

[15] Gerhard Oberlin describes the teacher's pedagogical method as "the simulation of a barbarian attack," and argues that such an approach is designed to produce dependence rather than independence among the children, to create "subjects, instead of citizens" (125). Gerhard Oberlin, "Die Grenzen der Zivilisation: Franz Kafkas Erzählungen *Beim Bau der chinesischen Mauer* und *Ein altes Blatt*," *Orbis Litterarum* 61.2 (2006): 114–32.

[16] See Clement Greenberg, "At the Building of the Great Chinese Wall," in *Franz Kafka Today*, ed. Angel Flores and Homer Swander (Madison: U of Wisconsin P, 1958), 77–78, and Ritchie Robertson, *Kafka: Judaism, Politics, and Literature* (Oxford: Oxford UP, 1985), 174.

[17] Franz Kafka, *Nachgelassene Schriften und Fragmente II: In der Fassung der Handschriften*, ed. Jost Schillemeit, (Frankfurt am Main: S. Fischer Verlag, 1992), 318–19, and 323; here 323.

[18] J. M. Rignall, "History and Consciousness in *Beim Bau der chinesischen Mauer*," in *Paths and Labyrinths: Nine Papers from a Kafka Symposium*, ed. J. P. Stern and J. J. White (London: Institute of Germanic Studies, U of London, 1985), 119.

[19] Benedict Anderson, *Imagined Communities: Reflections on the Origin and Spread of Nationalism*, rev. ed. (New York: Verso, 1992), 22.

[20] Anderson, *Imagined Communities*, 24.

[21] The ubiquity of this metaphor becomes apparent when we consider that Foucault employs the same figure in *The Order of Things* to affirm that his epistemological archaeology coincides with a general upheaval in Western thought: "In attempting to uncover the deepest strata of Western culture, I am restoring to our silent and apparently immobile soil its rifts, its instability, its flaws; and it is the same ground that is once more stirring beneath our feet" (xxiv).

[22] Claudio Magris, *Der habsburgische Mythos in der österreichischen Literatur* (Salzburg: Otto Müller Verlag, 1966), 12.

[23] I am indebted to Judith Ryan for this suggestion.

[24] Jacques Derrida, "White Mythology: Metaphor in the Text of Philosophy," *New Literary History* 6.1 (Autumn 1974): 51.

[25] Cf. Heinz Politzer's assertion that if the story has any point at all, then it is the news of the emperor's death. Heinz Politzer, *Franz Kafka, der Künstler* (Frankfurt am Main: Fischer, 1965), 138. Quoted in *TB*, 50.

[26] Dororothy Gies-McGuigan, *The Habsburgs* (Garden City, NY: Doubleday, 1966), 387.

[27] Max Weber, *Wirtschaft und Gesellschaft: Grundriss der verstehenden Soziologie*, Studienausgabe (Tübingen: J. C. B. Mohr [Paul Siebeck], 1972), 124.

[28] Edward Said notes the orientalists' preference for the ancient over the modern: "Proper knowledge of the Orient proceeded from a thorough study of classical texts and only after that to an application of those texts to the modern Orient" (*Orientalism*, 79).

[29] Cf. Goebel, *Constructing China*, 92.

[30] Cf. Goebel, *Constructing China*, 97.

[31] See Goebel, *Constructing China* 98; *TB*, 108; and Clayton Koelb, *Kafka's Rhetoric: The Passion of Reading* (Ithaca, NY: Cornell UP, 1989), 25.

[32] In a letter to his prospective father-in-law, Carl Bauer, that Kafka composed in his diary but never sent off, he writes: "Since I am nothing more than literature and can and want to be nothing else, my job will never be able to seize me completely, but it may well be able to ruin me utterly" (*Ta*, 579).

[33] Robertson, *Kafka*, 185.

[34] Julius Caesar, *War Commentaries*, trans. Rex Warner (New York: Mentor Books, 1960); Tacitus, *Tacitus' Agricola, Germany, and Dialogue on Orators*, rev. ed., trans. Herbert W. Benario (Norman: U of Oklahoma P).

[35] Cf. Robertson, *Kafka*, 185.

[36] Thomas Mann, *Der Zauberberg* (Frankfurt am Main: Fischer, 1991), 668–74.

Conclusion

THE SELF-CRITICAL TENDENCY found in the orientalist fictions of Hofmannsthal, Musil, and Kafka poses a significant challenge to the conventional notion of orientalism as formulated by Edward Said. For these texts manifest two basic modes of self-critique, both of which refute central premises of the Saidian conception of the discourse. First, in implying an analogous relationship between Occident and Orient these works subvert the fundamental orientalist notions of an East/West dichotomy and of European superiority. Second, in those texts with Eastern settings or figures, the use of orientalist tropes and topoi to allude to the "eastern empire" of Austria Hungary suggests a meta-textual subversion of the discourse itself. Thus, even as they exploit the orientalist inventory of images and received notions for suggestive meanings, these works challenge the basic conception of orientalism as a hegemonic discourse.

The question arises as to whether the self-critique undertaken by these Habsburg fictions constitutes an Austrian *Sonderweg*[1] within the broader context of European orientalism. As we have seen, the liminal situation of the Dual Monarchy, its ethnic diversity, and its lack of overseas colonies all contributed to an orientalist discourse marked by self-reflection and self-critique. Yet the elucidation of these tendencies in canonical works of Austrian orientalist fiction encourages the recognition of other mutinous voices in other traditions of orientalist and colonialist literature. For example, let us consider Kafka's deconstruction of the opposition between civilization and barbarism in his Chinese stories, "Beim Bau der chinesischen Mauer" and "Ein altes Blatt." In a similar fashion, Theodor Fontane undermines the opposition between the civilized self and the barbaric Other in *Effi Briest* when he has his heroine learn to her shock that the two great sacrificial stones at the Herthasee were not erected by an alien Slavic tribe but by the Germanic tribes from which all the modern-day Germans are descended.[2] Moreover, it seems to me that the schema that I developed in chapter 2 to examine orientalist and exoticist discourses in Musil's *Die Verwirrungen des Zöglings Törleß* may also be applied to Fontane's novel. Musil presents the territory of Moravia as a paracolonial space in which the Austro-German elite rules over the local Czechs. Similarly, Fontane depicts Kessin as a region in which imperial Prussia presides over the indigenous Polish majority. While Musil depicts India as the repository of the Beinebergs' mystical fantasies, Fontane turns to China and the figure of the Chinese ghost as both the object and sublimation of his heroine's erotic imagination. In this way, Fontane's novel resembles Musil's in its self-critical examination of the exoticist fantasies that accompany encounters with alterity, whether proximate (Moravia, Kessin) or remote (India, China).

And yet this last motif of the Chinese ghost points to an important distinction between the German and Austrian varieties of orientalist fiction. For as Crampas craftily explains to Effi in his pursuit of her, Innstetten uses the story of the Chinese ghost as a pedagogical device to occupy and subdue his young, energetic wife during the long nights when he is away (282–83). The uncanny or unhomely (*unheimlich*) figure of the Chinese ghost is thereby domesticated, one might even say colonized, to become an instrument of patriarchal Prussian authority. This motif thus suggests the influence of the German colonial concession of Kiao-Chau in China, which only became a colony in 1898 but was the focus of imperial and commercial interest from 1860 onward. Fontane's sequestration of the Chinese ghost to the domestic sphere stands in contrast to Hofmannsthal and Kafka's ambivalent and free-floating deployment of Chinese motifs and topoi that invoke both the native and the exotic, the Self and the Other.

Austria-Hungary's lack of overseas colonies, its proximity to its various eastern "subject" peoples, and its liminal position vis-à-vis the Orient result in an orientalist fiction that presents a paradoxical vision of the East as both extremely close and utterly remote. On the one hand, the absence of overseas territories means that the Eastern, colonial possessions of the other European imperial powers figure as unattainable, distant objects of fantasy. On the other, as objects of fantasy, orientalist and colonialist scenarios are employed by Habsburg authors to represent not only their near neighbors and fellow subjects to the East but also themselves, as representatives of the "eastern empire" of Österreich.

This peculiarly Austrian vision of the East as the site of both fantastic projection and self-critical introspection continues beyond the lifespan of the Dual Monarchy itself. For example, in the first novel of his *Schlafwandler* trilogy, *Pasenow oder die Romantik* (1930),[3] Hermann Broch depicts the East as a literal site of projection and introspection when his hero, Joachim, visits a slideshow or *Kaiserpanorama* on India with his fiancée, Elisabeth. Here Broch combines the global and the intimate in a moment of wistful yearning. On visiting the slideshow shortly before their wedding, both Joachim and Elisabeth imagine that they see their mutual friend Eduard von Bertrand on the screen in the guise of a colonial explorer in India. For both characters Bertrand represents lost amorous possibilities: in Joachim's eyes he is indelibly associated with Ruzena, his former Czech lover, while Elisabeth receives a declaration of undying love from Bertrand at the same moment that he expresses a desire to travel the world and never see her again (112). The observation that although Joachim and Elisabeth never speak of it, the word India has a magical resonance for them both (169) suggests not only their enthrallment to the exoticism represented by Bertrand, but also their mutual alienation from each other in a fantasy that they each harbor individually and yet cannot discuss together. This moment recalls an earlier conversation, when Joachim ascribes to Bertrand's personality a similar quality of self-alienation: "'Er ist nie ganz er selbst'" (He is never fully himself) and Elisabeth replies "'Sie meinen, dass er alles aus großer Entfernung sieht, gewissermaßen mit den Augen eines Fremden?'" (You mean that he sees things from a great distance. Through the eyes of a stranger, as it were? 122; 108–9). The figure of Bertrand thus intimates that the imperialist impulse does not reflect the magisterial authority promised in the term *Kaiserpanorama* (emperor's panorama) but rather signals alienation from both the world and the self. Although the Austrian Broch refracts this vision of the self through his Prussian protagonist Joachim, the intense introspection that attends this encounter with the exotic represents a legacy of Habsburg orientalist fiction.

Yet Broch's scene in the *Kaiserpanorama* points to the future as well as the past, to the contemporary era of globalization. For the young couple's visit to the slideshow invokes what John Tomlinson describes as the salient feature of the globalization process: "*complex connectivity* . . . the rapidly developing and ever-densening network of interconnections and interdependences that characterize modern social life."[4] This complex skein of global networks is apparent in the medium and message of the *Kaiserpanorama*, that is, its technological transmission of distant Indian vistas and its ideological transmission of colonialist, orientalist, and commercialist worldviews.

Although the *Kaiserpanorama* represents a relatively primitive technological medium, it nevertheless provides the compression of space-time that many theorists associate with globalization.[5] In the contemporary world the reduction of geographical distance and travel time occurs physically, through air travel, and virtually, through the transmission of electronic media.[6] In this nineteenth-century version of virtual reality, European travelers' arduous journeys are reproduced for the curious and more sedentary viewer. (Thus even before Joachim and Elisabeth mentally project Bertrand into these scenes, these Western figures provide crucial points of identification.) As such, however, the *Kaiserpanorama* offers what John Tomlinson describes as "the paradigmatic experience of global modernity for most people — . . . that of staying in one place but experiencing the 'dis-placement' that global modernity *brings to them*" (9). Indeed, the rather rudimentary mechanism of the slideshow offers a visual correlation to this notion of displacement by providing a bewildering succession of geographically disparate images. Furthermore, these mediated images induce a very modern sense of alienation in the members of the audience, who are described as avoiding conversations with each other (*PR*, 166). Of course, the fact that Joachim and Elisabeth sit side by side and apparently experience the same imaginary vision of Bertrand without sharing this fantasy exacerbates the alienation inherent in this televisual medium. Here my use of the adverb "apparently" stems from Broch's unusual use of the second person to describe the experience of the *Kaiserpanorama*. (Only retrospectively does the author explain that it is Joachim and Elisabeth who have visited the show; *PR*, 169.) Broch's second-person address simultaneously involves the reader in the action and distances her from events in which she is evidently only vicariously participating. In this way the author finds a literary equivalent for the televisual medium that, according to one media theorist, offers both "dispassionate proximity" and "intimate detachment."[7]

The content of the panoramic images attests to the significance of the colonialist and orientalist discourses. The audience is treated to slideshow scenes of colonial governance in the "Regierungsgebäude in Kalkutta" (Government Building in Calcutta), of imperialist munificence in "Partie aus dem Königspark in Kalkutta" (Excursion from the King's Park, Calcutta), and of international commerce in "Hafenpartie in Bombay" (Harbor Excursion in Bombay"; 167). While these pictures provide evidence of the fact of colonial domination, the next three in the sequence suggest the ideological and imaginative impulses behind the imperialist project. The slide of the "native mother in Ceylon" indicates an ostensibly scientific orientalist and ethnographic interest in remote and indigenous peoples. Yet the description of the woman reveals the nexus of the exotic and erotic in the European imagination: "sie lächelt mit weißen Zähnen zwischen roten Lippen und erwartet vielleicht den weißen Sahib, der aus dem Abendlande gekommen ist, weil er die Europäerinnen verschmäht hat" (168; she is smiling with white teeth between red lips and is perhaps waiting for the white Sahib, who has come from the West because he has spurned European women). The figure of the white sahib refers specifically to Bertrand and his abandonment of Elisabeth in favor of globetrotting adventure after his declaration of love, but also more generally invokes the Western male fantasy of the alluring and available oriental woman. Finally, the last two pictures, which depict a temple building in Delhi and an elephant-hunting expedition, draw on the long-established European association of the East with both mystical religiosity and rip-roaring adventure. In this way the *Kaiserpanorama* invokes the tropes of the colonial experience: the white man's burden of administering the native population, the commercial exploitation of their territory, the allure of exotic females, the spirituality associated with their religions, and the excitement of the safari. Nevertheless, the German audience must remain spectators at the show, excluded by not only their physical distance but also by their nation's belated entrance on the world stage as a colonial power.

Joachim and Elisabeth succeed in forging a personal connection to these images by imaginatively inserting Bertrand into the scenes. Bertrand himself, as a cotton importer, and, in the subsequent novel of the trilogy, a shipping magnate, has a personal stake in the expansion of world trade. And yet even this sophisticated captain of international industry appears to be astounded by the spectacle of incipient globalization, surveying the ships in Bombay Harbor in awe:

> Gestützt auf einen Spazierstock, bewegt er sich nicht, weil er gebannt von der starren Takelage der Schiffe, von ihren Schloten und Kranen, gebannt von den Stößen der Baumwollballen am Kai, gebannt zu ihnen hinüberschaut und man kann sein beschattetes Gesicht nicht erkennen. (*PR*, 167)

> [Propped up on a walking stick, he does not move, because he is spellbound by the the taut rigging of the ships, by their funnels and cranes, spellbound by the bundles of cotton bales on the quay, and gazes at them spellbound, and his face is in shadow and cannot be recognized.]

Here the detail of the bales of cotton explicitly connects the scene to Bertrand and the multinational manufacturing process. However, in the manner of a figure in a landscape by Caspar David Friedrich, the man who comes to represent Bertrand has a concealed face and thereby intensifies the awestruck gaze of the viewer before the sublime spectacle of global trade by providing a figure with which the viewer can identify.

Thus far the overlapping networks that connect Joachim and Elisabeth to the Indian scenes bring to mind Roland Robertson's definition of the concept of global unicity.[8] Robertson identifies four major components in the phenomenon of global unicity: individual "selves," "national societies," the "world system of societies," and the overarching collectivity of "humankind."[9] Three of these components are reflected in this scene: Joachim and Elisabeth have an individual and intimate connection to the wider world through Bertrand; the nationalist implications of colonial ambition are evident in the name of the apparatus, the *Kaiserpanorama*; the scenes of colonial administration and commerce indicate a "world system of societies," albeit in an exploitative and imperialist form. What is missing is of course the sense of a global, collective human identity. On the contrary, Bertrand repeatedly invokes apocalyptic visions of racial warfare, in which he espouses a Spenglerian cultural pessimism regarding the decadence and inevitable fall of Western civilization. In *Die Schlafwandler*, Joachim recalls these tirades as he imagines Bertrand entering a temple in Delhi: "Dort mag der Unchristliche lernen, daß selbst untergeordnete Rassen Gott zu dienen verstehen. Aber hat er nicht selber gesagt, daß es dem Mohren obliege, die Herrschaft Christi wieder aufzurichten?" (168;

there the bad Christian may learn that even subject races know how to serve God. But did he not once say himself that it would devolve to the black races to set up the Kingdom of Christ again? 149) Here the paradigmatic conflict of the Crusades is reversed: instead of the Christians forcibly converting the Moors at the point of the sword, it is the Africans who will, in Bertrand's eyes, have to invade Europe to restore Christianity and set a black Pope on the throne of Saint Peter amid the smoking ruins of Rome (*PR*, 33; *Sl*, 29). This global punishment fantasy recalls the visions of racial warfare that Törleß experiences when he sees night fall, in Musil's novel (see chapter 2). Here the casual use of the term "subject races" and the unexamined assumption that Indian temple-goers also worship a single deity demonstrate an ethnocentric attitude on the part of the spectator that ultimately reinforces the binary opposition between the European self and non-European Other. In this way the shared racial ideology and cultural pessimism of these figures countermands the notion of collective humanity that theorists discern in contemporary globalization.

The appearance of Bertrand in Joachim and Elisabeth's imaginations suggests not only the ideological but also the personal impediments to an open and accepting encounter with alterity. Like a much more sinister version of the heroic, pith-helmeted explorer in Woody Allen's film *The Purple Rose of Cairo*, the figure of Bertrand detaches himself from the screen to address his audience personally (*PR*, 167; *Sl*, 169). His admonition that he can never again be "crossed out" of their lives, however far away he may be, has important ramifications for Joachim and Elisabeth's future happiness, as he represents for both of them the loss of other amorous possibilities. But for our purposes Bertrand's emergence in the *Kaiserpanorama* signals that the personal preoccupations of the percipient, his or her desires, fears, and projections, will always obtrude upon the contemplation of the Other.

I have lingered over this scene in Broch's novel because it indicates a link between the orientalist texts from the late Habsburg era discussed in this study and our own era of globalization. On the one hand, Broch's choice of Indian vistas suggests that some of the broader ideological preconceptions of the colonialist and orientalist discourses remain fundamentally unchallenged. On the other hand, the insertion of Bertrand into these scenes suggests the author's interest in conveying the internal thought processes that attend the Western indvidual's encounter with alterity and thereby providing the opportunity to criticize the Occidental conceptions of the self and the Other from within. This same dynamic between broader, received notions of the oriental Other and a subversive interest in the individual experience of alterity is at play in the texts by Hofmannsthal, Musil, and Kafka analyzed in this study.

While many of the works by Hofmannsthal, Musil, and Kafka implicitly challenge the logic of orientalist stereotypes by deploying them to

allude to the West in general and Austria in particular, they do not explicitly address the content of these received notions. Rather, they expose the
protagonist's conception of the self and alterity to internal critique. For
example, although Hofmannsthal's "Märchen der 672. Nacht" alludes
to Vienna, and his poem "Der Kaiser von China spricht" invokes the
Emperor Franz Josef, these self-critical references do not overturn the orientalist clichés of a mysterious and threatening Arabia and an autocratic
and totalitarian China. Yet Hofmannsthal's depiction of the merchant's
son and the Chinese emperor's internal struggles to comprehend alterity
do subvert these characters' solipsistic worldviews. Moreover, by connecting these figures to the European discourses of aestheticism, orientalism,
and ethnocentrism, these texts suggest a wider critique of the egocentric tendencies in Western culture. Musil's depiction in *Die Verwirrungen
des Zöglings Törleß* of the local Czech women, and in particular of the
prostitute Božena, seem to draw on stereotypical notions of the primitive, sensual, and depraved Other. But his depictions of the febrile and
masochistic fantasies that Törleß experiences in his encounters with these
women undermine any ideas of ethnic or cultural superiority. Neither the
Fat Man in Kafka's "Beschreibung eines Kampfes" nor the jackals in his
"Schakale und Araber" enjoy the opportunity to reflect on their status
as amalgams of orientalist and anti-Semitic stereotypes respectively. But
the response of their interlocutors, both Western narrators, demonstrates
the hold of these *idées reçues* on the Western mind. While the demise of
the Old Commandant's judicial system in Kafka's penal colony can be
interpreted as the restoration of Western values to this errant outpost, the
insights Kafka provides into the Traveler's thought process undermine his
pretensions to represent occidental rationality. Finally, the Chinese narrators in Kafka's "Beim Bau der chinesischen Mauer" and "Ein altes Blatt"
remain unaware that their nation conforms to Western notions of China
as both absurdly centralized and autocratic and terminally decadent and
enfeebled. However, their internal struggles to comprehend the strange-
ness of their own imperial societies resonate far beyond the borders of
their fictional nation to strike a chord with Kafka's Habsburg readership.
This self-reflective and self-critical exploration of cultural attitudes does
not merely reverse the power dynamic between the European self and
non-European Other. Such a maneuver would in any case only reinforce
the notion of a binary division between East and West. Instead, these texts
depict the self's inner struggle to comprehend the Other and thereby
oblige the reader to confront the destabilizing and unsettling effects of an
encounter with alterity.

The way in which these texts simultaneously resort to and subvert
orientalist stereotypes leaves the ontological status of the East in question
and thus suggests the ultimate unknowability of the oriental Other. It is
perhaps in this irresolvable ambiguity that these works offer a salutary

experience for the contemporary reader. In recent years we have on the one hand seen the re-emergence of fundamental, not to say fundamentalist, dichotomies that frequently take the form of the so-called clash of civilizations, the orientalist opposition between East and West. On the other hand, we in developed countries enjoy such an access to the rest of the word through international travel and electronic media that we seem to be on the verge of a new era of global cosmopolitanism. In such an environment, the complex interplay between self and other depicted and performed by Habsburg orientalist fiction not only subverts the concept of an oriental/occidental dichotomy but also offers a timely reminder that the Western window on the world can serve as a mirror.

Notes

[1] I have borrowed this term from German historiography, where it denotes the "special path" or unique course of German history.

[2] Theodor Fontane, *Effi Briest, Sämtliche Werke VII*, ed. Edgar Gross (Munich: Nymphenburger Verlagshandlung, 1959), 413.

[3] Hermann Broch, *Pasenow oder die Romantik. Die Schlafwandler: Eine Romantrilogie*, vol.1, ed. Paul Michael Lützeler (Frankfurt am Main: Suhrkamp Verlag, 1979), 9–181.

[4] John Tomlinson, *Globalization and Culture* (Chicago: U of Chicago P, 1999), 2.

[5] See for example, David Harvey, *The Condition of Post-Modernity* (Oxford: Blackwell, 1989), 11. Cited in Tomlinson, *Globalization and Culture*, 3. More recently James Beckford has also described the compression of space-time as a defining feature of globalization. See Beckford, *Social Theory and Religion* (Cambridge: Cambridge UP, 2003), 119. Cited in Bryan S. Turner, "Theories of Globalization: Issues and Origins," in *The Routledge International Handbook of Globalization Studies*, ed. Bryan S. Turner (New York: Routledge, 2010), 3–23.

[6] See Tomlinson, *Globalization and Culture*, 3.

[7] C. Gallaz. Cited in Tomlinson, *Globalization and Culture*, 176.

[8] Robertson employs the term "unicity" as a more neutral alternative to the rather idealistic term "global unity." See Roland Robertson, *Social Theory and Global Culture* (London: Sage, 1992), 6.

[9] Robertson, *Social Theory and Global Culture*, 27.

Works Cited

Adorno, Theodor, and Max Horkheimer. *Dialektik der Aufklärung*. Frankfurt am Main: S. Fischer Verlag, 1969.

Agnew, Hugh LeCaine. *The Czechs and the Lands of the Bohemian Crown*. Stanford, CA: Hoover Institution Press, Stanford University, 2004.

Alewyn, Richard. *Hofmannsthals Wandlung*. Frankfurt am Main: Klostermann, 1949.

Amossy, Ruth. "Stereotypes and Representation in Fiction." Translated by Therese Heidingsfeld. *Poetics Today* 5.4 (1984): 689–700.

Anderson, Benedict. *Imagined Communities: Reflections on the Origin and Spread of Nationalism*. Rev. ed. New York: Verso, 1992.

Anderson, Mark M. "Kafka, Homosexuality, and the Aesthetics of 'Male Culture.'" In *Gender and Politics in Austrian Fiction*, edited by Ritchie Robertson and Edward Timms (Edinburgh: Edinburgh UP, 1996), 79–99.

———. *Kafka's Clothes: Ornament and Aestheticism in the Habsburg Fin de Siècle*. Oxford: Clarendon; New York: Oxford UP, 1992.

———. "The Traffic of Clothes: *Meditation* and *Description of a Struggle*." In *Kafka's Clothes*, 19–49.

Babinger, Franz. "Orient und deutsche Literatur." *Deutsche Philologie im Aufriss* (1957): 321–44.

Barker, Andrew W. "The Triumph of Life in Hofmannsthal's 'Das Märchen der 672. Nacht.'" *Modern Language Review* 74 (1979): 341–48.

Beasley-Murray, Tim. "German-Language Culture and the Slav Stranger Within." *Central Europe* 4.2 (Nov. 2006): 131–45.

Beckford, James. *Social Theory and Religion*. Cambridge: Cambridge UP, 2003.

Berman, Nina. "K.u.k. Colonialism: Hofmannsthal in North Africa." *New German Critique* 75 (Fall 1998): 3–27.

———. "Orientalism, Imperialism, and Nationalism: Karl May's *Orientzyklus*." In Friedrichsmeyer, Lennox, and Zantop, *The Imperialist Imagination: German Colonialism and its Legacy*, 51–68.

———. *Orientalismus, Kolonialismus und Moderne: Zum Bild des Orients in der deutschsprachigen Literatur um 1900*. Stuttgart: M & P, Verlag für Wissenschaft und Forschung, 1996.

Berman, Russell. *Enlightenment or Empire: Colonial Discourse in German Culture*. Lincoln: U of Nebraska P, 1998.

———. "German Colonialism: Another *Sonderweg?*" *European Studies Journal* 16.2 (Fall 1999): 25–36.

Bhabha, Homi K. *The Location of Culture*. London: Routledge, 1994.

Boa, Elizabeth. *Gender, Class and Race in the Letters and the Fictions.* Oxford: Clarendon, 1996.

Böhlke, Effi. "Rußlandbilder aus dem 18. und 19. Jahrhundert, entworfen in der deutschen und französischen politisch-philosophischen Literatur." *Osteuropa: Zeitschrift für Gegenwartsfragen des Ostens* 52.5 (May 2002): 576–97.

Borges, Jorge Luis. "The Analytical Language of John Wilkins." In *Other Inquisitions, 1937–1952.* Translated by Ruth L. C. Simms, 106–10. New York: Washington Square, 1966.

Broch, Hermann. *Hofmannsthal und seine Zeit.* Edited by Paul Michael Lützeler. Frankfurt am Main: Suhrkamp, 2001.

———. *Pasenow oder die Romantik. Die Schlafwandler: Eine Romantrilogie.* Vol.1. Edited by Paul Michael Lützeler, 9–181. Frankfurt am Main: Suhrkamp Verlag, 1979. In English, *The Sleepwalkers: A Trilogy.* Translated by Willa Muir and Edwin Muir. New York: Pantheon, 1964.

Brod, Max. "Nachwort." In *Franz Kafka, Beschreibung eines Kampfes: Die zwei Fassungen; Parallelausgabe nach den Handschriften,* ed. Max Brod; vol. ed. Ludwig Dietz, 157. Frankfurt am Main: Fischer, 1969.

Buber, Martin. "Unsere Literaten und die Gemeinschaft." *Der Jude,* October 1916/17, 457–64.

Caesar, Julius. *War Commentaries.* Translated by Rex Warner. New York: Mentor Books, 1960.

Cohn, Dorrit. "'Als Traum erzählt': The Case for a Freudian Reading of Hofmannsthal's 'Märchen der 672. Nacht.'" *Deutsche Vierteljahrsschrift für Literaturwissenschaft und Geistesgeschichte* 54 (1980): 284–305.

Corngold, Stanley. "Patterns of Justification in *Young Törless.*" In *Neverending Stories: Toward a Critical Narratology,* edited by Ann Fehn, Ingeborg Hoesterey, and Maria Tatar, 138–59. Princeton, NJ, Princeton UP, 1992.

Csáky, Moritz, Johannes Feichtinger, and Ursula Prutsch, eds. *Habsburg Postcolonial: Machtstrukturen und kollektives Gedächtnis.* Innsbruck: Studien Verlag, 2003.

———. "'Was man Nation und Rasse heißt, sind Ergebnisse und keine Ursachen': Zur Konstruktion kollektiver Identitäten in Zentraleuropa." In Müller-Funk, Plener, and Ruthner, *Kakanien revisited: Das Eigene und das Fremde (in) der österreichisch-ungarischen Monarchie,* 33–49.

Derrida, Jacques. "Structure, Sign, and Play in the Discourse of the Human Sciences." In *Writing and Difference,* translated by Alan Bass, 278–93. Chicago: U of Chicago P, 1978.

———. "White Mythology: Metaphor in the Text of Philosophy." *New Literary History* 6.1 (Autumn 1974): 5–74.

Dunker, Axel. *Kontrapünktische Lektüren: Koloniale Strukturen in der deutschsprachigen Literatur des 19. Jahrhunderts.* Munich: Wilhem Fink, 2008.

Escher, Georg. "Prager *Femmes Fatales* — Stadt, Geschlecht, Identität." *Kakanien Revisited*. 6 Jun. 2004. http://www.kakanien.ac.at/beitr/fall-studieGEscher1.pdf (accessed 29 May 2007).

Feichtinger, Johannes. "Habsburg (Post-)Colonial: Anmerkungen zur inneren Kolonisierung im Zentraleuropa." In Csáky, Feichtinger, and Prutsch, *Habsburg Postcolonial*, 13–31.

Fontane, Theodor. *Effi Briest*. In *Sämtliche Werke*, vol. 7: *Frau Jenny Treibel, Effi Briest*, edited by Edgar Gross, 169–427. Munich: Nymphenburger Verlagshandlung, 1959.

Foucault, Michel. *Discipline and Punish: The Birth of the Prison*. Translated by Alan Sheridan. 1978. Reprint, New York: Vintage Books, 1995.

———. *The Order of Things: An Archaeology of the Human Sciences*. New York: Vintage Books, 1994.

Foulston, Lynn, and Stuart Abbott. *Hindu Goddesses: Beliefs and Practices*. Portland, OR: Sussex Academic, 2009.

Freud, Sigmund. *Totem und Tabu*. Vol. 9 of *Gesammelte Werke: Chronologisch geordnet*, edited by Anna Freud, Edward Bibring, and Ernst Kris. Frankfurt am Main; S. Fischer Verlag, 1973.

Friedrichsmeyer, Sara, Sara Lennox, and Susanne Zantop, eds. *The Imperialist Imagination: German Colonialism and Its Legacy*. Ann Arbor: U of Michigan P, 1998.

Frye, Lawrence O. "'Das Märchen der 672. Nacht' von Hofmannsthal: Todesgang als Kunstmärchen und Kunstkritik." *Zeitschrift für Deutsche Philologie* 108.4 (1989): 530–51.

Fuchs-Sumiyoshi, Andrea. *Orientalismus in der deutschen Literatur: Untersuchungen zu Werken des 19. und 20. Jahrhunderts, von Goethes "West-östlichem Divan" bis Thomas Manns "Joseph" Tetralogie*. Hildesheim: Olms, 1984.

Geertz, Clifford. *Available Light: Anthropological Reflections on Philosophical Topics*. Princeton, NJ: Princeton UP, 2000.

Genette, Gérard. *Narrative Discourse: An Essay in Method*. Translated by Jane E. Lewin. New York: Cornell UP, 1980.

Genno, Charles N. "The Nexus between Mathematics and Reality and Phantasy in Musil's Works." *Neophilologus* 70.2 (Apr. 1986): 270–78.

Gies-McGuigan, Dorothy. *The Habsburgs*. Garden City, NY: Doubleday, 1966.

Gilman, Sander L. *Franz Kafka, the Jewish Patient*. New York: Routledge, 1995.

Glajar, Valentina. *The German Legacy in East Central Europe as Recorded in Recent German-Language Literature*. Rochester, NY: Camden House, 2004.

Goebel, Rolf. *Constructing China: Kafka's Orientalist Discourse*. Columbia, SC: Camden House, 1997.

———. "Kafka and Postcolonial Critique: *Der Verschollene*, 'In der Strafkolonie,' and 'Beim Bau der chinesischen Mauer.'" In Rolleston, *A Companion to the Works of Franz Kafka*, 187–212.

————. "Kafka and the East: The Case for Cultural Construction." *Symposium: A Quarterly Journal in Modern Literatures* 55.4 (Winter 2002): 190–98.

————. "Kafka's Orientalist Rhetoric: China, the Middle East, India." *Journal of the Kafka Society of America* 15.1–2 (1991): 21–28.

————. "Opening Up Kafka's Context: Herder's Orientalist Poetics." In *Constructing China: Kafka's Orientalist Discourse*, 15–31.

Goethe, Johann Wolfgang von. "Selige Sehnsucht." In *Werke: Hamburger Ausgabe*, vol. 2, *Gedichte und Epen II*, 18–19. Munich: Deutscher Taschenbuch Verlag, 1988. In English, "Divine Longing." In *Poems of the East and West: West-Eastern Divan- West-Oestlicher Divan; Bi-lingual Edition of the Complete Poems*, translated by John Whaley, 47. New York: Peter Lang, 1998.

Gray, Richard. "Disjunctive Signs: Semiotics, Aesthetics and Failed Mediation in 'In der Strafkolonie.'" In Rolleston, *A Companion to the Works of Franz Kafka*, 213–45.

Greenberg. Clement. "At the Building of the Great Chinese Wall." In *Franz Kafka Today*, edited by Angel Flores and Homer Swander, 77–81. Madison: U of Wisconsin P, 1958.

Grillparzer, Franz. "Nachrichten aus Cochinchina." In *Sämtliche Werke*, vol. 3, *Ausgewählte Briefe, Gespräche, Berichte*, 93–95.

————. *Sämtliche Werke*. Vol. 3: *Ausgewählte Briefe, Gespräche, Berichte*. Munich: Carl Hanser, 1964.

Groß, Hans. "Deportation und Degeneration." *Politisch-Anthropologische Revue: Monatsschrift für das soziale Leben der Völker* 4 (1905/6): 281–316.

Gross, Ruth. "Hunting Kafka out of Season." In Rolleston, *A Companion to the Works of Franz Kafka*, 247–79.

Grusa, Jiri. *Franz Kafka aus Prag*. Frankfurt am Main: Fischer Verlag, 1983.

Haag, Ingrid "Kryptogramme der Liebesangst: Zu Hofmannsthals *Märchen der 672. Nacht* und zu seinem *Andreas*-Fragment," *Cahiers d'Études Germaniques* 50 (2006): 127–43.

Hecker, Axel. "Die Dekonstruktionsmaschine — In der Strafkolonie." In *An den Rändern des Lesbaren: Dekonstruktive Lektüren zu Franz Kafka*. Vienna: Passagen, 1998, 79–119.

Hans, Anjeana. "An Excess of Discourse: 'Beschreibung eines Kampfes' and Homosexual Identity." In "Defining Desires: Homosexual Identity and German Discourse 1900–1933" (PhD diss., Harvard University, 2005), 53–80.

Hárs, Endre, Wolfgang Müller-Funk, Ursula Reber, and Clemens Ruthner, eds. *Zentren, Peripherien und kollektive Identitäten in Österreich-Ungarn*. Tübingen: A. Franke Verlag, 2006.

Hattori, Seiji. "Funktion und Bedeutung der 'Seekrankheit auf festem Lande': Zur poetologischen Struktur von Kafkas *Beschreibung eines Kampfes*." *Studien zur deutschen Literatur und Sprache: Japanische Gesellschaft für Germanistik* 37 (2005): 143–62.

————. "Kafkas China-Motiv und das 'heterotopische' Denken." In *Akten des Germanistenkongresses Paris 2005: "Germanistik im Konflikt der Kuturen,"* *Jahrbuch für Internationale Germanistik* 9 (2007): 207–12.

Hechter, Michael. *Internal Colonialism: The Celtic Fringe in British National Development, 1536–1966.* Berkeley: U of California P, 1975.

Heinemann, Richard. "The Bureaucrat as Nomad: The Search for Community in Kafka's *Beim Bau der chinesischen Mauer.*" *Journal of the Kafka Society of America* 18.1 (June 1994): 21–29.

Hofmannsthal, Hugo von. "Ballade des äußeren Lebens." In *Sämtliche Werke*, vol. 1, *Gedichte I*, edited by Eugene Weber, 15. Frankfurt am Main: Suhrkamp, 1994. In English, "Ballad of the Outer Life." Translated by Michael Hamburger. In *Hofmannsthal, Poems and Verse Plays*, edited by Michael Hamburger, 33. New York: Pantheon, 1961.

————. "Gabriele D'Annunzio." In *Gesammelte Werke in zehn Einzelbänden*, vol. 8, *Reden und Aufsätze I, 1891–1913*, 174–85. Frankfurt am Main: Fischer Verlag, 1979.

————. "Der Kaiser von China spricht." In *Sämtliche Werke: Kritische Ausgabe*, vol. 1, *Gedichte I*, 72–73.

————. "Das Märchen der 672. Nacht." In *Sämtliche Werke*, vol. 28, *Erzählungen I*, edited by Ellen Ritter, 15–30. Frankfurt am Main: S. Fischer Verlag, 1975. In English, "The Tale of Night Six Hundred and Seventy-Two." Translated by Michael Henry Heim. In *The Whole Difference: Selected Writings of Hugo von Hofmannsthal*, edited by J. D. McClatchy, 39–56. Princeton, NJ: Princeton UP, 2008.

————. *Reden und Aufsätze III: Buch der Freunde; Aufzeichnungen, 1889–1929.* Vol. 10 of *Gesammelte Werke in zehn Einzelbänden*, edited by Bend Schoeller. Frankfurt am Main: S. Fischer Verlag, 1980.

————. *Sämtliche Werke: Kritische Ausgabe*, vol. 1, *Gedichte I*. Edited by Eugene Weber. Frankfurt am Main: Fischer Verlag, 1984.

————. "Ein Traum von großer Magie." In *Sämtliche Werke: Kritische Ausgabe*, vol. 1, *Gedichte I*, 52–53.

Janik, Allan, and Stephen Toulmin. *Wittgenstein's Vienna.* New York: Simon & Schuster, 1973.

Judson, Pieter. "Inventing Germans: Class, Nationality, and Colonial Fantasy at the Margins of the Hapsburg Monarchy." In *Nations, Colonies, and Metropoles*, edited by Daniel A. Segal and Richard Handler. Special issue of *Social Analysis* 33 (1993): 47–67.

————. "Rethinking the Liberal Legacy." In *Rethinking Vienna 1900*, edited by Steven Beller, 58–79. New York: Berghahn Books, 2001.

Kafka, Franz. "Ein altes Blatt." In *Drucke zu Lebzeiten*, 263–67.

————. "Beim Bau der chinesischen Mauer." In *Nachgelassene Schriften und Fragmente I*, 337–57.

————. "Beschreibung eines Kampfes." In *Nachgelassene Schriften und Fragmente I*, 54–120. In English, "Description of a Struggle." Translated by Tania Stern and James Stern. In *Franz Kafka: The Complete Stories*, 9–51.

———. *Drucke zu Lebzeiten*. Edited by Wolf Kittler, Hans-Gerd Koch, and Gerhard Neumann. Frankfurt am Main: S. Fischer Verlag, 1994.

———. *Franz Kafka: The Complete Stories*. Edited by Nahum N. Glatzer. New York: Schocken, 1995.

———. "The Great Wall of China." Translated by Willa and Edwin Muir. In *Franz Kafka: The Complete Stories*, 235–48.

———. "In der Strafkolonie." In *Drucke zu Lebzeiten*, 201–48. In English, "In the Penal Colony." Translated by Edwin Muir and Willa Muir. In *Franz Kafka: The Complete Stories*, 140–67.

———. *Nachgelassene Schriften und Fragmente I: Apparatband*. Edited by Malcolm Pasley. Frankfurt am Main: S. Fischer Verlag, 1993.

———. *Nachgelassene Schriften und Fragmente I*. Edited by Malcolm Pasley. Frankfurt am Main: S. Fischer Verlag, 1993.

———. *Nachgelassene Schriften und Fragmente II: In der Fassung der Handschriften*. Edited by Jost Schillemeit. Frankfurt am Main: S. Fischer Verlag, 1992.

———. *Der Proceß*. Edited by Malcolm Pasley. Frankfurt am Main: S. Fischer Verlag, 1990.

———. "Schakale und Araber." In *Drucke zu Lebzeiten*, 270–75. In English, "Jackals and Arabs." Translated by Willa Muir and Edwin Muir. In *Franz Kafka: The Complete Stories*, 407–11.

———. *Das Schloß*. Edited by Max Brod. 1963. Reprint, Frankfurt am Main: S. Fischer Verlag, 1986.

———. *Tagebücher*. Edited by Hans-Gerd Koch, Michael Müller, and Malcolm Pasley. Frankfurt am Main: S. Fischer Verlag, 1990.

Kant, Immanuel. "Beantwortung der Frage: Was ist Aufklärung?" (1783). In *Was ist Aufklärung? Thesen und Definitionen*, edited by Ehrhard Bahr, 9–17. Stuttgart: Philipp Reclam Jr., 1974.

Kim, Yeon-Soo. "Kafkas literarisches Spiel mit dem europäischen Orientalismus — Analyse zu China-Bildern in der Erzählung *Beim Bau der chinesischen Mauer*." Paper presented at the conference "Intercultural Kafka," organized by the German Kafka Society and the Gießen Graduate Center for Cultural Studies, Castle Rauischholzhausen, near Marburg, Germany, 20–23 July, 2009.

King, Richard. *Orientalism and Religion: Post-Colonial Theory, India and "the Mystic East."* London: Routledge, 1999.

Kipling, Rudyard. "The White Man's Burden." In *Rudyard Kipling*, edited by Daniel Karlin, 479–80; The Oxford Authors. Oxford: Oxford UP, 1999.

Kittler, Wolf. "Brief oder Blick: Die Schreibsituation der frühen Texte von Kafka." In *Der junge Kafka*, 40–67. Frankfurt am Main: Suhrkamp, 1984.

———. *Der Turmbau zu Babel und das Schweigen der Sirenen*. Erlangen: Verlag Palm & Enke, 1985.

Koelb, Clayton. *Kafka's Rhetoric: The Passion of Reading*. Ithaca, NY: Cornell UP, 1989.

Komlosy, Andrea. "Innere Peripherien als Ersatz für Kolonien? Zentrenbildung und Peripherisierung in der Habsburgermonarchie." In *Zentren, Peripherien und kollektive Identitäten*, edited by Endre Hárs, Wolfgang Müller-Funk, Ursula Reber, and Clemens Ruthner, vol. 9 of *Kultur-Herrschaft-Differenz*, 55–78. Tübingen: A. Francke Verlag, 2006.

Kontje, Todd. *German Orientalisms*. Ann Arbor: U of Michigan P, 2004.

———. "Organized Violence/Violating Order: Robert Musil's *Die Verwirrungen des Zöglings Törleß*." *Seminar: A Journal of Germanic Studies* 24.3 (1988): 239–54.

Lee, Jie-Oun. "Transformation des Kolonialdiskurses in Franz Kafkas 'In der Strafkolonie.'" *Literatur für Leser* 23.1 (2000): 34–45.

Lee, Joo-Dong. *Taoistiche Weltanschauung im Werke Franz Kafkas*. Frankfurt am Main: Verlag Peter Lang, 1985.

Lemon, Robert. "Imperial Mystique and Empiricist Mysticism: Exoticism and Inner Colonialism in Musil's *Törleß*." *Modern Austrian Literature* 42.1 (2009): 1–23.

Lowe, Lisa. *Critical Terrains: French and British Orientalisms*. Ithaca, NY: Cornell UP, 1991.

Luft, Robert. "Machtansprüche und kulturelle Muster nichtperipherer Regionen: Die Kernlande Böhmen, Mähren und Schlesien in der späten Habsburger Monarchie." In Csáky, Feichtinger, and Prutsch, *Habsburg Postcolonial: Machtstrukturen und kollektives Gedächtnis*, 165–87.

Mach, Ernst. *Analyse der Empfindungen*. Jena: Verlag von Gustav Fischer, 1885.

Maclean Rogers, Guy. *Alexander: The Ambiguity of Greatness*. New York: Random House, 2004.

Magris, Claudio. *Der habsburgische Mythos in der österreichischen Literatur*. Salzburg: Otto Müller Verlag, 1966.

Mann, Thomas. *Der Zauberberg*. Frankfurt am Main: S. Fischer Verlag, 1991.

Martens, Lorna. *Shadow Lines: Austrian Literature from Freud to Kafka*. Lincoln: U of Nebraska P, 1996.

McBride, Patrizia. *The Void of Ethics: Robert Musil and the Experience of Modernity*. Evanston, IL: Northwestern UP, 2006.

McCort, Dennis. "Kafka and the East: The Case for Spiritual Affinity." *Symposium: A Quarterly Journal in Modern Literatures* 55.4 (Winter 2002): 199–212.

Meng, Weiyan. *Kafka und China*. Munich: Iudicium Verlag, 1986.

Metz, Joseph. "Austrian Inner Colonialism and the Visibility of Difference in Stifter's *Die Narrenburg*." *PMLA* 121.5 (Oct 2006): 1475–92.

Meyer, Imke. "The Insider as Outsider: Representations of the Bourgeoisie in *Fin-de-Siècle* Vienna." *Pacific Coast Philology* 44.1 (2009): 1–16.

Müller-Funk, Wolfgang. "Kakanien Revisited: Über das Verhältnis von Herrschaft und Kultur." In Müller-Funk, Plener, and Ruthner, *Kakanien Revisited: Das Eigene und das Fremde in der österreichischen- ungarischen Monarchie*, 14–33.

Müller-Funk, Wolfgang, Peter Plener, and Clemens Ruthner, eds. *Kakanien Revisited: Das Eigene und das Fremde in der österreichischen-ungarischen Monarchie.* Tübingen: A. Francke Verlag, 2001.

Müller-Seidel, Walter. *Die Deportation des Menschen: Kafkas Erzählung "In der Strafkolonie" im europäischen Kontext.* Stuttgart: Metzler, 1986.

Musil, Robert. *Tagebücher I.* Edited by Adolf Frisé. Reinbek bei Hamburg: Rowohlt, 1983.

———. *Die Verwirrungen des Zöglings Törleß.* In *Prosa und Stücke*, vol. 6 of *Gesammelte Werke in neun Bänden*, edited by Adolf Frisé, 7–140. Hamburg: Rowohlt Taschenbuch Verlag, 1978. In English, Robert Musil, *Young Törless*, translated by Eithner Wilkins and Ernst Kaiser. New York: Noonday, 1958.

Neumann, Gerhard. "Umkehrung und Ablenkung: Franz Kafkas 'Gleitendes Paradox.'" *Deutsche Vierteljahrsschrift fur Literaturwissenschaft und Geistesgeschichte* 42 (1968): 702–44.

Nietzsche, Friedrich. "Über Wahrheit und Lüge im aussermoralischen Sinne." In *Kritische Studienausgabe*, vol. 1, *Die Geburt der Tragödie, Unzeitgemäße Betrachtungen I–IV, Nachgelassene Schriften, 1870–1873*, edited by Giorgio Colli und Mazzino Montinari, 871–90. Munich: dtv, 1999. In English, "On Truth and Lying in an Extra-Moral Sense." In *Friedrich Nietzsche on Rhetoric and Language*, edited and translated by Sander L. Gilman, Carole Blair, and David J. Parent, 246–57. New York: Oxford UP, 1989.

Oberlin, Gerhard. "Die Grenzen der Zivilisation: Franz Kafkas Erzählungen *Beim Bau der chinesischen Mauer* und *Ein altes Blatt.*" *Orbis Litterarum* 61.2 (2006): 114–32.

Pan, David. "Kafka as a Populist: Re-reading 'In the Penal Colony.'" *Telos: A Quarterly Journal of Radical Social Theory* 101 (Fall 1994): 3–40.

Peters, Paul. "Witness to the Execution: Kafka and Colonialism." *Monatshefte für deutschsprachige Literatur und Kultur* 93.4 (Winter 2001): 401–25.

Piper, Karen. "The Language of the Machine: A Postcolonial Reading of Kafka." *Journal of the Kafka Society of America* 20.1–2 (Jun.–Dec. 1996): 42–54.

Polaschegg, Andrea. *Der andere Orientalismus: Regeln deutsch-morgenländischer Imagination im 19. Jahrhundert.* Berlin: Walter de Gruyter, 2005.

Politzer, Heinz. *Franz Kafka, der Künstler.* Frankfurt am Main: Fischer, 1965.

———. "Zwei kaiserliche Botschaften: Zu den Texten von Hofmannsthal und Kafka." *Modern Austrian Literature* 11.3/4 (1978): 105–22.

Pratt, Mary Louise. *Imperial Eyes: Travel Writing and Transculturation.* London: Routledge, 1992.

Preidel, Helmut. "Charles IV." In *Encyclopaedia Britannica*, 2004. Encyclopaedia Britannica Premium Service. http://www.britannica.com/eb/article?eu=22909 (accessed 12 March 2004).

Prutsch, Ursula. "Habsburg Postcolonial." In Csáky, Feichtinger, and Prutsch, *Habsburg Postcolonial: Machtstrukturen und kollektives Gedächtnis*, 33–43.

Pseudo-Callisthenes. *The Romance of Alexander the Great*. Translated by Albert Mugrdich Wolohojian. New York: Columbia UP, 1969.

Rieckmann, Jens. "Von der menschlichen Unzulänglichkeit: Zu Hofmannsthals 'Das Märchen der 672. Nacht.'" *German Quarterly* 54.3 (1981): 298–310.

———. "Zwischen Bewußtsein und Verdrängung: Hofmannsthals jüdisches Erbe." *Deutsche Vierteljahrsschrift für Literaturwissenschaft und Geistesgeschichte* 67.3 (1993): 466–83.

Rignall, J. M. "History and Consciousness in *Beim Bau der chinesischen Mauer*." In *Paths and Labyrinths: Nine Papers from a Kafka Symposium*, edited by J. P. Stern and J. J. White, 111–26. [London]: Institute of Germanic Studies, U of London, 1985.

Robertson, Ritchie. *Kafka: Judaism, Politics, and Literature*. Oxford: Oxford UP, 1985.

———. "'Urheimat Asien': The Re-orientation of German and Austrian Jews, 1900–1925." *German Life and Letters* 49.2 (Apr. 1996): 182–91.

———. "Zum deutschen Slawenbild von Herder bis Musil." In *Das Eigene und das Fremde*, edited by Urs Faes and Béatrice Ziegler, 116–44. Zurich: NZ Verlag, 2000.

Robertson, Roland. *Social Theory and Global Culture*. London: Sage, 1992.

Rolleston, James, ed. *A Companion to the Works of Franz Kafka*. Rochester, NY: Camden House, 2006.

Rubinstein, William C. "Kafka's 'Jackals and Arabs.'" *Monatshefte für Deutschen Unterricht, Deutsche Sprache und Literatur* 59 (1967): 13–18.

Ruthner, Clemens. "Central Europe Goes Postcolonial: New Approaches to the Habsburg Empire around 1900." *Cultural Studies* 16.6 (2002): 877–83.

———. "K.u.k. Kolonialismus als Befund, Begrifflichkeit, und Metapher." In Csáky, Feichtinger, and Prutsch, *Habsburg Postcolonial: Machtstrukturen und kollektives Gedächtnis*, 111–27.

Ryan, Judith. "Kafka before Kafka: The Early Stories." In Rolleston, *A Companion to the Works of Franz Kafka*, 61–83.

———. *The Vanishing Subject: Early Psychology and Literary Modernism*. Chicago: U of Chicago P, 1991.

———. "Die zwei Fassungen der 'Beschreibung eines Kampfes': Zur Entwicklung von Kafkas Erzähltechnik." *Jahrbuch der Deutschen Schillergesellschaft* 14 (1970): 546–72.

Said, Edward. *Culture and Imperialism*. New York: Knopf, 1993.

———. *Orientalism*. 1978. Reprint, London: Penguin Books, 1991.

Sardar, Ziauddin. *Orientalism*. Philadelphia, PA: Open UP, 1999.

Schings, Hans-Jurgen. "Allegorie des Lebens: Zum Formproblem von Hofmannsthals 'Märchen der 672. Nacht.'" *Zeitschrift fur Deutsche Philologie* 86 (1967): 533–61.

Schorske, Carl. *Fin-de-siècle Vienna: Politics and Culture.* New York: Vintage, 1981.

———. "Politics and Patricide in Freud's *Interpretation of Dreams.*" In *Fin-de-siècle Vienna: Politics and Culture,* 181–207.

Schuster, Ingrid. *China und Japan in der deutschen Literatur, 1890–1925.* Bern: Francke Verlag, 1977.

———. *Faszination Ostasien: Zur kulturellen Interaktion Europa-Japan-China; Aufsätze aus drei Jahrzenten.* Frankfurt am Main: Peter Lang, 2007.

Sked, Alan. *The Decline and Fall of the Habsburg Empire, 1815–1918.* 2nd. ed. London: Longman, 2001.

Sluga, Glenda. "Bodies, Souls, and Sovereignty: The Austro-Hungarian Empire and the Legitimacy of Nations." *Ethnicities* 1.2 (2001): 207–32.

Sokel, Walter. "Kafka's Beginnings: Narcissism, Magic, and the Function of Narration in 'Description of a Struggle.'" In *The Myth of Power and the Self: Essays on Franz Kafka,* 166–80. Detroit, MI: Wayne State UP, 2002.

———. "Language and Truth in Kafka." *German Quarterly* 52.3 (May 1979): 364–84.

———. "Das Verhältnis der Erzählperspektive zu Erzählgeschehen und Sinngehalt in 'Vor dem Gesetz,' 'Schakale und Araber' und *Der Prozess.* Ein Beitrag zur Unterscheidung von 'Parabel' und 'Geschichte" bei Kafka." *Zeitschrift fur Deutsche Philologie* 86 (1967): 267–300.

Spector, Scott. *Prague Territories: National Conflict and Cultural Innovation in Franz Kafka's* Fin-de-siècle. Berkeley: U of California P, 2000.

Spengler, Oswald. *Der Untergang des Abendlandes: Umrisse einer Morphologie der Weltgeschichte.* (1923) Munich: C. H. Beck, 1980.

Spies, Otto. *Der Orient in der deutschen Literatur.* Kevelaer, Rhld.: Butzon & Bercker, 1949.

Stern, J. P. "The Education of the Master Race." In *In The Heart of Europe: Essays on Literature and Ideology,* 78–93. Oxford: Blackwell, 1992.

Tacitus. *Tacitus' Agricola, Germany, and Dialogue on Orators.* Rev. ed. Translated by Herbert W. Benario. Norman: U of Oklahoma P, 1991.

Tismar, Jens. "Kafkas 'Schakale und Araber' im zionistischen Kontext betrachtet." *Jahrbuch der Deutschen Schillergesellschaft* 19 (1975): 306–23.

Tomlinson, John. *Globalization and Culture.* Chicago: U of Chicago P, 1999.

Trabert, Lukas. "Erkenntnis- und Sprachproblematik in Franz Kafkas *Beschreibung eines Kampfes* vor dem Hintergrund von Friedrich Nietzsches 'Über Wahrheit und Lüge im aussermoralischen Sinne.'" *Deutsche Vierteljahrsschrift für Literaturwissenschaft und Geistesgeschichte* 61.2 (Jun. 1987): 298–324.

Turner, Bryan S. "Theories of Globalization: Issues and Origins." In *The Routledge International Handbook of Globalization Studies,* edited by Bryan S. Turner, 3–23. New York: Routledge, 2010.

Uhl, Heidemarie. "Zwischen "Habsburgischem Mythos" und (Post-)Kolonialismus: Zentraleuropa als Paradigma für Identititätskonstruktionen in der (Post-)Moderne." In Csáky, Feichtinger, and Prutsch, *Habsburg Postcolonial: Machtstrukturen und kollektives Gedächtnis*, 45–54.

Weber, Max. *Wirtschaft und Gesellschaft: Grundriss der verstehenden Soziologie*. Studienausgabe. Tübingen: J. C. B. Mohr (Paul Siebeck), 1972.

Weininger, Otto. *Geschlecht und Charakter: Eine prinzipielle Untersuchung*. Berlin: Gustav Kiepenheuer; Vienna and Leipzig: Wilhelm Braumüller, 1932.

Whitlark, James. *Behind the Great Wall: A Post-Jungian Approach to Kafkaesque Literature*. Cranberry, NJ: Associated University Presses, 1991.

Wiethölter, Waltraud. "Augen-Blicke: Das Märchen der 672. Nacht." In *Hofmannsthal oder die Geometrie des Subjekts*, 23–46.

———. *Hofmannsthal oder die Geometrie des Subjekts: Psychostrukturelle und ikonographische Studien zum Prosawerk*. Tübingen: Niemeyer Verlag, 1990.

Williams, George M. *Handbook of Hindu Mythology*. Santa Barbara, CA: ABC-CLIO, 2003.

Witte, Bernd. "Dichtung aus dem Geiste des Judentums: Hugo von Hofmannsthals Traum von Asien." *Links* 5 (2005): 61–70.

Zantop, Susanne. *Conquest, Family, and Nation in Precolonial Germany, 1770–1870*. Durham, NC: Duke UP, 1997.

Zilcosky, John. *Kafka's Travels: Exoticism, Colonialism, and the Traffic of Writing*. New York: Palgrave Macmillan, 2003.

Index